Bourdieu

CRITICAL READERS

Blackwell's *Critical Readers* series presents a collection of linked perspectives on continental philosophers, and social and cultural theorists. Edited and introduced by acknowledged experts and written by representatives of different schools and positions, the series embodies debate, dissent, and a committed heterodoxy. From Foucault to Derrida, from Heidegger to Nietzsche, *Critical Readers* address figures whose work requires elucidation by a variety of perspectives. Volumes in the series include both primary and secondary bibliographies.

Bourdieu

A Critical Reader

Edited by
Richard Shusterman

Copyright © Blackwell Publishers Ltd, 1999
Editorial introduction and arrangement copyright © Richard Shusterman, 1999,
with the exception of extracts from Pierre Bourdieu, *Choses dites*, copyright © Les Éditions
de Minuit, Paris; English translation Polity Press, Cambridge, 1990

First published 1999

2 4 6 8 10 9 7 5 3 1

Blackwell Publishers Ltd
108 Cowley Road
Oxford OX4 1JF
UK

Blackwell Publishers Inc.
350 Main Street
Malden, Massachusetts 02148
USA

British Library Cataloguing in Publication Data

A CIP catalogue record for this book is available from the British Library.

Library of Congress Cataloging-in-Publication Data

Bourdieu: a critical reader / edited by Richard Shusterman.
     p.   cm.—(Critical readers)
     Includes bibliographical references and index.
     ISBN 0–631–18817–7 (hc. : alk. paper).—ISBN 0–631–18818–5 (pbk. : alk. paper)
     1. Bourdieu, Pierre.   2. Sociology—Philosophy.   3. Sociology—Methodology.
     I. Shusterman, Richard.   II. Series.
HM24.B6736B67   1999
301'.01—dc21   98–33142
                                                                                                          CIP

Typeset in 10.5pt on 12pt Sabon
by Pure Tech India Ltd, Pondicherry
http//www.puretech.com
Printed in Great Britain by TJ International Ltd, Padstow, Cornwall

This book is printed on acid-free paper

Contents

Contributors

Mitchell Aboulafia, Professor and Chair of Philosophy at the University of Colorado, Denver, is the author of *The Mediating Self: Mead, Sartre, and Self-Determination* and editor of *Philosophy, Social Theory and the Thought of George Herbert Mead*.

James Bohman is Professor of Philosophy at St. Louis University and author of *New Philosophy of Social Science* and *Public Deliberation*.

Pierre Bourdieu, aggregé in Philosophy, is Chair of Sociology at the Collège de France. His wide-ranging and influential work is the focus of this volume.

Jacques Bouveresse is Chair of Philosophy at the Collège de France. His books include *Le mythe de l'intériorité*, *La force de la règle*, and *Wittgenstein Reads Freud*.

Judith Butler, Professor of Rhetoric and Comparative Literature at the University of California, Berkeley, is author of *Gender Trouble*, *Bodies That Matter*, and *Excitable Speech*.

Arthur C. Danto is Emeritus Johnsonian Professor of Philosophy at Columbia University. His works include *The Transfiguration of the Commonplace* and *The Philosophical Disenfranchisement of Art*.

Hubert Dreyfus is Professor of Philosophy at the University of California, Berkeley. His books include *What Computers (Still) Can't Do*, *Being-in-the-World*, and (with Paul Rabinow) *Michel Foucault: Beyond Structuralism and Hermeneutics*.

Charles (Chuck) Dyke is Professor of Philosophy at Temple University, Philadelphia, and author of *Philosophy of Economics* and *The Evolutionary Dynamics of Complex Systems*.

William Earle is Professor of Philosophy at the City University of New York and editor of *The Philosophical Forum.*

Joseph Margolis is Carnell Professor of Philosophy at Temple University, Philadelphia. His most recent books include *Historied Thought, Constructed World* and *What, After All, is a Work of Art?*

Louis Pinto, Director of Research in Philosophy and Sociology at the CNRS, Paris, is author of *Les Philosophes entre le lycée et l'avant-garde* and *Les Neveux de Zarathoustra: La Reception de Nietzsche en France.*

Paul Rabinow, Professor of Anthropology at the University of California, Berkeley, and co-author (with Hubert Dreyfus) of *Michel Foucault: Beyond Structuralism and Hermeneutics*, is the series editor of *Essential Works of Michel Foucault.*

Richard Shusterman is Professor and Chair of Philosophy at Temple University, Philadelphia, and Directeur de Programme at the Collège International de Philosophie, Paris. His books include *Pragmatist Aesthetics* and *Practicing Philosophy.*

Charles Taylor is Professor of Philosophy at McGill University, Montreal. His books include *Hegel, Sources of the Self*, and *Philosophical Arguments.*

Acknowledgements

This book took longer to complete than originally expected. The patience of Stephan Chambers, its commissioning editor, and the understanding of its more punctual contributors are here gratefully acknowledged. J. P. Murphy helped with the translation of the articles of Pierre Bourdieu, Jacques Bouveresse, and Louis Pinto. Anthony Grahame provided valuable copy-editing on both the text and the extensive bibliography presented here. (This bibliography of French and English texts has been slimmed down from the official, comprehensive Bourdieu bibliography, compiled by Yvette Delsaut and Marie-Christine Rivière, and generously made available for selective adaptation in this volume.) Robert Fleeger assisted with proofreading, as did Michael Scoville, who also compiled the index. Marie-Christine Rivière, who has always been extremely helpful in co-ordinating communications with Bourdieu's center in Paris, deserves special thanks.

Introduction: Bourdieu as Philosopher

Richard Shusterman

I

As France's leading living social theorist, Pierre Bourdieu has already had great impact on the social sciences in the English-speaking world, particularly in sociology and anthropology, where his theories have already been the focus of sustained attention.[1] However, much of Bourdieu's work is emphatically directed at distinctively philosophical topics, proposing novel solutions to traditional philosophical questions (of language, action, knowledge, mind, etc.) and engaging in a rich critical dialogue with philosophers past and present. In his most recent books like *Raisons pratiques* and *Méditations pascaliennes*, Bourdieu's focus on philosophy has become increasingly intense and systematic, developing an extended critique of philosophical intellectualism, which, he argues, has also contaminated the social sciences.[2] In elaborating his "critique of scholastic reason" or of the "scholastic point of view" (a term he derives from J. L. Austin), Bourdieu strikingly turns for support to philosophers of what is roughly known as the Anglo-American tradition, in both its analytic and pragmatist forms.

This book hopes to promote a potentially very fruitful dialogue between Bourdieu and philosophers of the English-speaking world by directing philosophical critique back at Bourdieu's own philosophical production. By presenting a critical assessment of his philosophical theories and their import as seen by philosophers from diverse philosophical perspectives, this collection can help us decide whether Bourdieu may profitably be read (*inter alia*) as a philosopher and which dimensions of his thought are most useful for philosophy today. Moreover, the very posing of the question of Bourdieu's philosophical status is useful in raising fruitful questions concerning the current institutional limits of philosophy and how those limits might be overcome to revitalize this discipline through a more robust alliance with the social sciences and the practical social world.

Many would deny that Bourdieu is a philosopher. That denial seems true or false according to whether it is made in terms of the most narrowly literal institutional definition of philosophy or instead in terms of a broadly substantive view of the discipline. I also find the denial true or false according to whether it is made in blame or praise. If being a philosopher means holding an official position as philosopher in an academic institution and confining one's methods and horizons of inquiry to the traditional academic methods and limits of philosophy, then Bourdieu will be refused the rank of philosopher, along with other great thinkers like Marx and Weber. If, however, being a philosopher is a matter of being trained in philosophy and then elaborating significant theories and concepts (e.g. *habitus*, field, *illusio*) concerning established philosophical questions while engaging productively and critically with both traditional and contemporary philosophical discourse and thereby commanding the attention of leading philosophers, then Bourdieu is certainly a philosopher and this volume is proof thereof.

Critique of philosophy's institutional limits and traditional methods should not be confused with disdain for philosophy's tradition and institutional forms. Bourdieu's adoption of the methods of empirical social science do not represent a renunciation of traditional forms of philosophical analysis and argument. It is simply a recognition of their limits and the consequent need to supplement them with other methods of inquiry. Nor should Bourdieu's professional definition as Chair of Sociology at the Collège de France (the most prestigious French academic institution, founded by François I) blind us to the fact that his own university training and early academic career were firmly in philosophy.

A philosophy student at the elite École Normale Supérieure, Bourdieu focused his later graduate work on Leibniz. After passing the *agrégation* (which qualifies one for a university teaching post in France), Bourdieu decided to teach philosophy at the University of Algiers, because of his growing interest in Algeria. Although his teacher (and Foucault's) Georges Canguilhem tried to convince him to continue his philosophical career in France by pursuing research in the phenomenology of affective life, Bourdieu's continuing fascination with Algerian society led to an ever deeper immersion in its sociology and ethnology, and a consequent professional metamorphosis into something more, or other, than a philosopher.

Bourdieu's deep, enduring respect for philosophy and its problems is evident not only in his writings but in the book series he edited for many years with Éditions de Minuit (which published the likes of Adorno, Cassirer, Marcuse, and Searle).[3] By developing his own theories on central philosophical issues while critiquing the views of rival philosophers, Bourdieu tacitly suggests that he is an equal partner in philosophical debate, thus making an implicit claim for philosophical recognition. An acutely insightful analyst of the symbolic stakes and power-strategies of the academic world, Bourdieu must recognize the risks of transgression and retaliatory embarrassment in making a bald self-asserting claim to be a philosopher as well as a sociologist. It is therefore all the more striking that his recent book, *Méditations pascaliennes*, goes so far as to present his whole "project [as a] sort of *negative philosophy*", one which tries "to push the critique (in Kant's sense) of scholarly reason" as far as possible to unearth its deepest unreflective presuppositions (Bourdieu's emphasis, MP 9, 15).

Bourdieu's writings engage most of philosophy's major fields: philosophy of language, philosophy of action, epistemology, philosophy of mind (and body), philosophy of science, political theory, philosophy of education, ethics, and aesthetics. This brief introduction is not the place to attempt a synthetic overview of Bourdieu's still evolving philosophical contributions to these fields. Nor shall I here define and critically assess the major interlocking concepts that Bourdieu systematically deploys in these various fields and that therefore give his theory the sort of systemic integral wholeness that one could expect from a philosophical system. Such key concepts like *habitus*, field, *illusio*, strategy, and symbolic capital are best understood through the kind of detailed analysis, application, and critique that the following new collection of essays seeks to provide. These essays likewise try to situate Bourdieu's theory in the context of different philosophical traditions through which the philosophical import of his work can be better understood and deployed.

II

In "Bourdieu and Anglo-American Philosophy", I begin this work of contextualization by studying his frequent use of some of the central figures of the Anglo-American philosophical tradition in both its analytic and pragmatist forms. Though noting certain strategic motives for Bourdieu's invoking of Austin and Wittgenstein in his struggle to challenge positions in the dominant French philosophical field, my article also shows how their analytic views (and those of pragmatist John Dewey) closely converge with Bourdieu's "social-practice based philosophy", which in fact develops them further. If language is essentially social, deriving its meaning from the complex and context dependent social practices in which it is used, then the analytic project of clarifying meaning must be in terms of those social practices and contexts. But Bourdieu goes much further than either Austin or Wittgenstein in providing the theoretical tools and empirical methods for a systematic analysis of the social forces, structures, and contexts that actually shape linguistic meaning.

Pragmatism's John Dewey likewise insisted on the ultimately social ground of meaning, arguing that social forces incorporate their meanings both in unreflective practical habits that lie beneath discursive thought but also in the most abstract philosophical distinctions like those between theory and practice, ends and means, which Dewey in fact traced to hierarchies in Athenian society. Although Bourdieu shares Dewey's social and genealogical mode of explanation, he provides a far more systematic and fine-grained social analysis through a more rigorous set of empirical methods. Moreover, though sharing Dewey's democratic aims, Bourdieu is much more cautious about using revisionary theory to advance them.

The three subsequent essays in this collection further explore Bourdieu's relationship to analytic philosophy by analyzing his hallmark concept of *habitus* as a tool for explaining and complementing Wittgenstein's famous discussion of rule following. In "Rules, Dispositions, and the *Habitus*", Jacques Bouveresse (France's leading analytic philosopher) usefully traces Bourdieu's idea of *habitus* back to its Leibnizian definition in terms of an agent's disposition to do something regularly but in a spontaneous way. Bouveresse then offers an illuminatingly nuanced account of rules, dispositions, and explanations by studying analytic philosophy's contributions to their analysis, particularly by Wittgenstein (but also noting the work of Quine, Kripke, and Dennett). Though Bourdieu's *habitus* is introduced to overcome the dualism of explaining human behavior by either conscious reasons or brute causes, Bouveresse argues that much of the resistance to the *habitus* derives from the assumption that it must function somehow as an underlying causal mechanism. Since we tend to assume that behavioral explanations must be either in terms of conscious rules or brute causality, and since *habitus* is clearly not the former, one implicitly (but falsely) assumes that it must somehow involve some hidden causal mechanism that Bourdieu's analysis fails to display.

Charles Taylor's "To Follow a Rule" elaborates the usefulness of *habitus* precisely for overcoming our dualistic inability to account for purposeful, intelligent behavior that is not the following of explicit conscious rules. Our traditional mind–body dualism sees human agency simply in terms of a first-person subject who determines its actions by means of conscious will and mental representation of ideas or rules. All other behavioral explanations are therefore reduced to blind, mechanical causality (either physical or social). The *habitus*, Taylor argues, not only provides a middle-ground for purposeful behavior without explicit purposes or rules consciously in mind, but it also offers a better way of understanding personhood. For it includes two crucial aspects that intellectualist first-person accounts of agency neglects: the body and "the other". The *habitus* acts through its *bodily* incorporation of *social relationships* and meanings (i.e. those involving reference to *others*) but without needing to articulate them in terms of explicit rules or reasons.

Joseph Margolis also appreciates the merits of Bourdieu's notions of *habitus* and the logic of practice for freeing us from long dominant dualisms and foundationalisms. But Margolis devotes most of his article to criticizing what he sees as the residual dualism and foundational universalism of these very notions as Bourdieu applies them. He claims that Bourdieu's account of the *habitus*'s "logic of practice" seems to rely invariably on binarism, which Margolis sees as a vestige of the universal structuralist logic that Bourdieu sought to challenge. Margolis also faults Bourdieu for not providing a more specific and direct account of the cognitive processes through which the *habitus* performs its logic of practice. For *habitus* to explain our logic of practice rather than simply act as a handy descriptive name for it, Margolis demands that this notion of *habitus* include some logical account of what he calls "the microprocesses of cognition in the world of practice", two of which he sees as "referential and predicative competence".

The next pair of essays involve a shift of perspective by situating Bourdieu in terms of twentieth-century Continental philosophy. Hubert Dreyfus and Paul Rainbow's article shows how Bourdieu develops the phenomenological tradition that insists on the finitude and embodied situatedness of understanding, a tradition that is traced from Heidegger through Merleau-Ponty to Foucault and Bourdieu. The question, however, is how this ontology of finitude and perspectival situatedness can be reconciled with Bourdieu's claims to the strict scientific status and objectivity of his inquiries.

In "Theory in Practice", Louis Pinto shows how Bourdieu's theory developed through his consistent refusal of a number of dualistic alternatives that dominated the theoretical field of continental philosophy and social science. Pinto's article is very useful for its nuanced account of Bourdieu's positioning in this field, from Sartre and Merleau-Ponty, to Canguilhem, Lévi-Strauss, Cassirer, Durkheim, and Weber. But the article's main task is to reconcile Bourdieu's apparent aim of advancing theory together with his insistent critique of theory's intellectualism and "scholastic point of view". In carefully tracing Bourdieu's handling of the theory/practice relationship, Pinto argues that Bourdieu's theory of practice is motivated by the aim of improving the practice of theory in both social science and philosophy, by opening new spaces for theoretical practice that were previously excluded by the intellectualist presumptions of both phenomenology and varieties of positivism.

Judith Butler's "Performativity's Social Magic" takes up the important political dimension of Bourdieu's work by providing a challenging critique and polemical application of his theories of *habitus*, field, and language, particularly by relating them to strategies of struggle against race and gender oppression. Butler attacks a set of hidden privileging dualisms that she sees in Bourdieu's notion of *habitus* and that she thinks not only weaken his theory but stifle its use for progressive political practice. In his application of Austinian speech-act theory, she detects an effective separation between the linguistic act and the prior (hence also privileged) social conditions required for such action to be successfully performed.

Butler claims that Bourdieu likewise privileges the social field as the dominating objective reality that determines agents' discursive *habitus*, while he fails to recognize sufficiently how change of discursive practice might in turn modify that social field itself. Failure to recognize these socially transformative possibilities of discourse, Butler argues, not only suggests an awkward gap between theory and practice, language and social life (both of which are incorporated in our bodies). It also promotes an unhelpful political quietism about language's power, precluding the possibility that linguistic attempts to revalue or revise certain terms of gender and racist abuse can help achieve a corresponding change of "real" social recognition.

James Bohman's critique of Bourdieu also combines theoretical and political elements. Bohman finds Bourdieu's notion of *habitus* and theory of practice too one-sidedly unreflective and therefore defeatistly deterministic and unable to adequately explain or promote social change. Taking Bourdieu's description of "the logic of practice" (*le sens pratique*) as an account of practical reasoning, Bohman argues that *habitus* is insufficient to capture the latter. Practical reason requires the ideas of regulative norms and conscious rules that the non-reflective, anti-intellectualist notion of *habitus* aims to supplant. By making *habitus*'s essential logic of practice unreflective, Bourdieu denies the ability of practicing agents to critique, reinterpret, and thereby revise their practical logic and behavior, thus compelling them to sustain the social domination incorporated in the *habitus* that allegedly directs their practical action. A truly critical and reflexive view is left only to the sociologist or theorist, who thus assumes the honored role of only possible social liberator.

Bohman further asserts that by confining critical reflexivity to a narrow professional elite, Bourdieu's theory belies the actual presence of diverse forms of non-professional critical and transformative agency. It also tends to discourage the productive exercise of reflective, transformative critique by ordinary practioners, thus diminishing the resources for progressive social change. Bohman claims that this problem is especially embarrassing for what he sees as Bourdieu's aim of providing an emancipatory "constructivist" social theory rather than one that is deterministically descriptive. Bohman suggests that Habermasian critical theory is a more promising form of transformative theory because it appeals to critical reflection and linguistic norms of rational argument that can be realized in the practical reasoning of all social agents, ordinary people as well as professional social theorists.

Pragmatism, which has deeply influenced Habermasian theory of language, communicative action, and the social self, also seems a relevant resource for Bourdieu. One of the four major figures of classic pragmatism, George Herbert Mead not only provides an exemplary combination of the roles of philosopher and sociologist, but also anticipates several of Bourdieu's strategies for evading the dualisms of subject/object, internal/external, voluntarism/determinism, mind/body in understanding the self and its behavior in the social world. Mitchell Aboulafia's essay provides a detailed comparison of Mead's and Bourdieu's social theories, highlighting several striking similarities between the *habitus* and Mead's notions of the "biologic individual", the I/me constellation, and the internalization of the "generalized other". Although appreciative of Bourdieu's general orientation, Aboulafia faults him (in contrast) to Mead for privileging (rather than simply recognizing) the non-reflective, for failing to recognize the continuity of reflective and non-reflective in the logic of practice, and for ignoring how reflexivity enables us to go beyond our personal interests toward a larger self that can be identified with the interests of others. Aboulafia suggests Nietzsche as the source of these Bourdieuean refusals.

William Earle's witty, "Bourdieu Nouveau" provides a fine introduction to Bourdieu's most recent philosophical writings, notably his *Raisons pratiques: sur la théorie de l'action*. Through a nuanced analysis of Bourdieu's idea of field (*champ*), Earle shows how this notion actually involves two different but powerfully related concepts: on the one hand, the global social space of a society, and, on the other hand, a more specific social field in that society (e.g., the field of art, science, politics, fashion, sports, etc.). To clarify Bourdieu's notions of field and *habitus* by demonstrating their explanatory power with respect to a new *explicandum*, Earle usefully applies them to explain certain features of American culture. He even pointedly suggests an explanation why most American philosophers of the dominant analytic and pragmatist persuasions refuse to pay any serious attention to Bourdieu's work, despite its apparent affinities and contributions to central themes of analytic philosophy and pragmatism. While this collection of essays shows there are increasingly more exceptions to such neglect, it also hopes to generate still more philosophical interest and critique of Bourdieu.

The next essay, "Bourdieuean Dynamics: The American Middle-Class Self-Constructs", relates Bourdieu's work to new directions in the philosophy of science. A philosopher of biology, Chuck Dyke tries to clarify the underlying logic and methodology of Bourdieu's social theory through two complementary ways: first, by analogy with new non-linear methodologies of explanation in the natural sciences; but, secondly, by applying Bourdieuean theory in a concrete historical case study of American social dynamics.

Dyke underlines the striking affinities between Bourdieu's logic of social explanation and the fractal logic of nonlinear dynamic systems that has recently been introduced to explain a wide variety of "formations of organized diachronic complexity" in the natural world (e.g. weather systems and other phenomena associated with "chaos theory", formations that despite being causally determined nonetheless resist absolute linear predictability. Bourdieu's theory of the dynamics of *habitus* (not a rigidly fixed or mechanical habit) and of *field* (not a stationary space but a dynamic field constituted by struggles over changing positions) demonstrates that social structures and identities must be understood not as static, typological, and hard-edged categories but rather as dynamic formations of organized diachronic complexity, poised between stability and change, whose edges are best construed (in terms of non-linear dynamics) as fuzzy, shifting fractal basin boundaries between complex attractors with relatively hard cores. To clarify this dynamic logic and terminology, Dyke examines a concrete case of complex diachronic social formation by exploring some of the cultural attractors and factors that contributed to the self-organization of the American middle-class in the nineteenth century. Dyke's particular prism is the importation and deployment of John Ruskin's ideals of art, architecture, and culture.

In raising these themes, Dyke brings us toward the topic of aesthetics, a philosophical field to which Bourdieu has dedicated much attention and made important contributions. Because of limited space and the relative marginality of aesthetics in Anglo-American philosophy, this collection of essays concentrates on Bourdieu's contributions to issues more central to the Anglo-American philosophical field. But Arthur Danto, eminent master of analytic philosophy of art, provides a brief appreciation of Bourdieu's aesthetics, focusing on the explanatory merits and limits of Bourdieu's notion of the field.

Danto argues that this notion shows the inadequacy of analytic aesthetics' standard Institutional Theory of Art, which leaves the powers of art making to the intentions of artists and other agents in the institutions of the art world without recognizing the wider historical and social forces that limit and structure the very form such intentions (and even such institutions) can take. Beginning with Bourdieu's own use of "the field" to critique Sartre's existential analysis of Flaubert, Danto goes on to show this concept's usefulness for understanding the different possible options of position-taking available at certain periods in the history of philosophy and also at the crisis of mid-twentieth century art which Danto knows so well. But Danto resists what he sees as Bourdieu's suggestion that the genius or greatness of an artist must be explained simply as a function of the environing artistic field. Art, argues Danto, involves "autonomous experiences", even if art is not fully autonomous.

The final essay in this volume is by Pierre Bourdieu. Rather than responding directly to any of the previous essays that relate his work to the English-speaking philosophical world, Bourdieu's contribution offers an eye-opening perspective through which to understand *any* attempt to treat his work in a foreign field like Anglo-American philosophy. In "The Social Conditions of the International Circulation of Ideas", Bourdieu exposes the unarticulated social factors, deep structural constraints, unthematized problems, and typically hidden motives involved in importing intellectual ideas from one national field to another.[4] He explains, for example, the structural reasons why Heidegger became so important for French academic philosophy in terms of its struggle against Sartre's domination; and how Chomsky's linguistic theory had its meaning altered through the context of its importation in France, where it was deployed by left-wing Catholic thought to oppose the dominant structuralism which was felt to be "subjectless", thus leaving no place for generative agency or a creative soul. Bourdieu has elsewhere complained how American cultural and literary theorists often deeply distort his theory by linking it with the French postmodernism of Baudrillard, Lyotard, and Derrida, and then deploying it as one more trendy French philosophical flavor of the month with which to perform exercises of transgressive textual interpretation.[5] One central aim of this collection is to displace such misreadings by providing a collection of careful philosophical readings of Bourdieu's work.

Bourdieu's analysis of the problems, motives, and transformations that attend the importation of philosophical ideas should encourage readers of this volume to reflect further on the difficulties, strategic purposes, and philosophical stakes that shape the different essays here published and that indeed inform the very project of marking Bourdieu's philosophical importance by devoting a critical collection to his philosophy with a premier English publisher of analytic philosophy. In short, Bourdieu's essay can be seen as a metaphilosophical reflection on the problems of international philosophical understanding, a reflexive comment on this very book's attempt to advance such international dialogue through the importation of Bourdieu's work into the Anglo-American philosophical field. Such critical reflexivity is an explicit emblem of Bourdieu's thought, but also a traditional hallmark of philosophy itself.

III

Thus, even disregarding Bourdieu's work as a systematic philosopher proposing theories (of language, action, knowledge, art, subject and society, mind and body) and formulating them through an original set of interlocking theoretical concepts like *habitus*, *illusio*, field, symbolic capital, etc., there remains a strong case for Bourdieu as a *metaphilosopher*. In affirming Pascal's view that philosophy must be self-critical ("the true philosopher pokes fun at philosophy", MP 11), Bourdieu offers a very sustained critique of the limits of philosophical reason by examining the historical and social conditions, professional strategies, and disciplinary stakes and constraints that structure philosophy's reasonings and theories. This is most explicit in recent works like *Raisons pratiques* and *Méditations pascaliennes* where he formulates his "critique of scholastic reason" and his analysis of the historical genesis and social conditions of objective theoretical knowledge. But such philosophical critique is also evident in Bourdieu's study of the logic of practice (which attacks the universal claims of philosophical intellectualism) and in works like *Homo Academicus* (which expose the structures, strategies, and limits of the social world in which academic philosophy is practiced).[6]

Moreover, one could argue that Bourdieu's metaphilosophical project of tracing philosophy's limits is advanced by his very practice of going outside philosophy's conventional limits (as if to view them from the outside) in pursuing his theoretical inquiries through the methods of sociology and anthropology. In contrast to other models of philosophical criticism that are either confined to the solitary introspective subject of self-critique or to a dialogical set of subjects questioning each other through a web of intersubjectivity, Bourdieu's model of philosophical critique construes its "reflexivity as a collective enterprise" that goes still deeper (MP 12). Beyond both subject-centered and intersubjective dialogical thought, it reveals the unarticulated, typically unconscious social conditions and bodily habits that structure both subjectivity and the relations of intersubjective thought.

Because of Bourdieu's defense of scientific objectivity (albeit in a distinctly historicized form) and the empirical, often statistical, research methods that he uses, it is tempting to see his theoretical project as rigidly scientific and impersonal. This would be a mistake. It ignores some of the strategic motives for Bourdieu's brandishing of science's symbolic capital. It also ignores a philosophical dimension of Bourdieu's work that is deeply personal (though in no way sentimental), a dimension emerging from philosophy's ancient definition as the persistent quest for self-knowledge through self-critique in the aim of self-improvement and emancipation. Critical of the intellectualist privilege accorded to self-consciousness, Bourdieu realizes that traditional self-conscious-centered forms of philosophical self-examination (e.g. introspective meditations, confessions, phenomenological narratives, autobiographical memoirs, etc.) will not penetrate to the deeper, unconscious, socially structured strata of the self that in fact shape individual consciousness. Impersonal sociological analysis can help here by circumventing the selective memory and defensive mechanisms of personal recollection and its protective self-affirming narrative fictions. This, as Bourdieu remarks, is the motivating logic behind his critical analyses of his own social worlds, analyses which could be reflexively turned against his own work and person. "I have thus learned much from two studies which, dealing with two socially very different worlds – my childhood village and Parisian academia – allowed me to explore as an objectivist observer some of the most obscure regions of my own subjectivity" (MP 12–13).

For Bourdieu, it is only by exceeding the limits of introspective self-conscious self-analysis that one can glimpse the limits of one's thought and then struggle to transcend them, even if that struggle cannot be completely successful. Bourdieu's reflexive *askesis* of self-examination through impersonal sociological research thus has an ethical dimension of ameliorative care for the self that links his work to philosophy's ancient self-definition and to the work of his Collège de France colleagues, Michel Foucault and Pierre Hadot.[7] "I have never truly felt justified to exist as an intellectual", Bourdieu confesses in his recent book. "And I have always tried – and here as well – to exorcise all in my thought that could be tied to that status, like philosophical intellectualism. I don't like the intellectual in me, and what may sound like anti-intellectualism in my writings is especially directed at what remains, despite all my efforts, of intellectualism or intellectuality in me, as the difficulty, so typical of intellectuals, that I have of truly accepting that my liberty has its limits" (MP 16).

We should not conclude without reminding readers that philosophy's self-examination and self-amelioration has more than selfish motives. As Socrates insisted, philosophy's benefits of self-care (cognitive and moral) should extend to the society in which the self is situated and through which it is shaped. In Bourdieu's theory, the practical purposes of democratic social emancipation are no less evident. By exposing the concealed social conditions, presuppositions, strategies, and *illusio* of certain elite social worlds (e.g. of art and academia), Bourdieu provides a tool of liberation for people laboring under their social spell of domination but who cannot, through their own experience (and especially because of their own social position) know the inner, unarticulated, workings of these dominating social worlds.

Such critical demystifications belong to the tradition of philosophical critique, even when directed at philosophy itself. But since professions, no less than individuals, do not like having their secrets exposed, it would be strange if Bourdieu's work encountered no philosophical resistance. One form of resistance that philosophers have directed at his work is willful denial by an ignoring silence or *Totschweigen*, as the Germans like to call it. Another frequent strategy of professional philosophical orthodoxy is to summarily dismiss all kinds of threatening facts and theories by simply labelling them nonphilosophical. But the premise of this collection is that philosophical understanding is better promoted by more open and reciprocal critical confrontation. In exposing philosophy to Bourdieuean critique by granting him entry into the philosophical field, we are in turn exposing his theories to the rigorous critique of those who profess philosophy as their (and implicitly *the*) chosen profession.

New York City
December 1997

Notes

1   See, for example, the collection of essays, *Bourdieu: Critical Perspectives* edited by the the sociologists Craig Calhoun and Moishe Postone and the anthropologist Edward LiPuma (Chicago: University of Chicago Press, 1993). The two philosophical contributions to that volume (by Charles Taylor and by Hubert Dreyfus and Paul Rabinow) are reprinted in this present collection, whose other essays appear here for the first time in English and were mostly written specifically for this critical collection. For a further bibliography of writings on Bourdieu, see "Appendix 3" of Pierre Bourdieu and Loic J. D. Wacquant, *An Invitation to Reflexive Sociology* (Chicago: University of Chicago Press, 1992).

2   Pierre Bourdieu, *Raisons pratiques: sur la théorie de l'action* (Paris: Seuil, 1994); and *Méditations pascaliennes* (Paris: Seuil, 1997), henceforth referred to in this introduction with the abbreviation MP.

3   This series entitled "Le sens commun", also published the French translation of my *Pragmatist Aesthetics* as *L'art à l'état vif* late in 1991.

4   An earlier version of this essay (based on an oral address in Freiburg, Germany and containing a great many details pertaining specifically to French-German cultural relations) was published as "Les conditions sociales de la circulation internationale des idées," in *Romantische Zeitschrift für Literaturgeschichte*, 1 (1990), 1–10. It has been abridged by the editor in collaboration with Pierre Bourdieu.

5   See Pierre Bourdieu, "Passport to Duke", *Metaphilosophy*, 28:4 (1997), 449–455, in a special issue of the journal entitled *Internationalism in Philosophy*.

6   Pierre Bourdieu, *Homo Academicus* (Cambridge: Polity Press; Stanford: Stanford University Press, 1988).

7   For an account of the recent revival of philosophy as a personal quest of self-improvement through self-knowledge and self-critique in Foucault and other philosophers (in both continental and Anglo-American traditions), see Richard Shusterman, *Practicing Philosophy: Pragmatism and the Philosophical Life* (London and New York: Routledge, 1997).

1

Bourdieu and Anglo-
American Philosophy

Richard Shusterman

I

The views of a thinker are essentially structured by the particular social field in which he thinks. This is true even for such putatively abstract, transcendental, and universal domains as philosophy; and it is just as true for the iconoclast who opposes that field (and thus logically depends on it) as for the traditionalist who endorses it (often without recognizing it as such). No one has pressed these points more strongly than Pierre Bourdieu, who also insists that the social nature of an intellectual field (and hence the full meaning of its intellectual products) must be grasped in terms of concrete social details (particular stakes, positions, interests, powers) rather than by vague appeal to general notions of "the social" as typically found in philosophy's abstract concepts of *tradition* and *practice*.

Granting these points suggests that an adequate account of Bourdieu's relationship to Anglo-American philosophy requires a very complex socio-analysis involving a number of interacting, overlapping, and contesting (as well as contested) fields: not only French philosophy and social thought but Anglo-American philosophy and non-French continental theory. I shall not attempt such an analysis. Nor shall I simply offer the standard excuses – that such a project obviously exceeds the space I have been given and departs from the philosopher's role I am expected to perform. Instead, I appeal to the pragmatic point made by Dewey and Wittgenstein that the concept of adequacy (like that of exactness or precision) has no absolute standard but depends on the purposes in view.

What are my prime purposes here? Obviously, in the opening essay of a collection of this sort, there is the ritual aim of paying homage to a master thinker who deeply influenced my thought, a ritual act whose conditions of successful performance paradoxically require that I do more than simply pay homage by asserting his eminence and achievement. So beyond this act, I hope to clarify some central features of Bourdieu's use of Anglo-American philosophy that may initially seem puzzling, including the very fact that he insists so much on this philosophy's great importance to his work.

Since his attitude is unfortunately not yet sufficiently reciprocated by Anglo-American philosophers (who, by the complex logic of national philosophical fields, are not exactly equivalent to philosophers in the Anglophone world[1]), I hope to show why Anglo-American philosophy should indeed recognize Bourdieu's approach as not only congenial but as a logical and necessary next step toward some of its own central goals. This will be shown for both major trends of Anglo-American philosophy: analysis and pragmatism. Finally, by noting the particular strategies of Bourdieu's deployment of Anglo-American philosophy, I hope to illuminate the differences that remain between his philosophical position and the pragmatism I favor.

II

Bourdieu makes a special point of highlighting his rapport to analytic philosophy, most particularly to Austin and Wittgenstein. He invokes them in the most salient places and with terms of highest praise. From Austin, "who is no doubt one of the philosophers I most admire", Bourdieu outspokenly takes the very titles of two important articles "Fieldwork in Philosophy" and "The Scholastic Point of View". Wittgenstein, he likewise affirms, "is no doubt the philosopher who has helped me most in moments of difficulty".[2]

These confessions are no doubt sincere, but they are initially puzzling for two reasons. First, if a theorist's thought is essentially formed by the intellectual field in which he is situated, one would expect that Austin and Wittgenstein would be much less influential than other philosophers who were far more central to the French field of Bourdieu's intellectual production (e.g. Heidegger, Sartre, Husserl, Merleau-Ponty). Secondly, Austin and Wittgenstein actually receive much less discussion in Bourdieu's *corpus* than the work of some of these other theorists. The puzzlement is apt to be reinforced by the back cover blurb of Bourdieu's recent philosophical book, *Raisons Pratiques* (1994), where only analytic philosophers are thought worthy of specific mention ("he puts to the test the analyses of Strawson, Austin, Wittgenstein, Kripke"). Yet these philosophers do not form the philosophical core of the book (and Strawson, for example, is hardly visible at all, not even appearing in the index).

This puzzlement may be partly relieved by distinguishing between "oppositional" and "positive" usefulness, and by recognizing that if one's goal is the intellectual distinction of one's work by its specific originality and hence contrast with other work in the field, then it is more useful to discuss authors and views one opposes than those one accepts. Moreover, given the same goal of distinction (which is always in terms of a given social field), it seems more profitable to positively highlight (e.g. by praise or confessions of debt) authors that lie outside one's immediate field than authors within it who are thus closer, more dangerous rivals. Outside the dominating center of the French philosophical field, but itself the dominating center of the Anglo-American field, analytic philosophy was an excellent source for importing ideas that could help Bourdieu challenge the dominant structure of the French field and thus achieve, for his own work, greater power.

Indeed, as Bourdieu well knows, one of the prime motives in importing foreign ideas is precisely to undermine the dominating authority of the home field.[3] In the French philosophical field, Bourdieu's particular professional trajectory would tend to marginalize him. By going beyond philosophy and adopting the *métier* of a sociologist, he deprived himself of the institutional identification/ authorization as a professional or "real" philosopher. To the extent that philosophy remains dominant in the larger French intellectual field, this could have a more general limiting effect on Bourdieu's work, were it to be excluded from the field of philosophy.

What better way to frustrate the possible marginalization of his philosophical theories by the French philosophical field than to out-flank that field by enlisting the symbolic power of the rival philosophical field of analytic philosophy? What makes this strategy all the more appealing is the scientific, empirical reputation of analytic philosophy.[4] This not only seems to endorse Bourdieu's empirical approach and so assimilate it into the tradition of "rigorous philosophy" (as does his invocation of Bachelard and Canguilhem) but also provides him a way of damning by contrast the institutionally dominant French philosophy as unscientific "babble" or "sanctified stupidity" (*Choses dites* 14–15: IOW 4–5).

If the outflanking strategy of rigorous, empirical scientific philosophy makes analytic philosophy a powerful symbolic weapon to cite and brandish, why specifically focus on Austin and Wittgenstein, who are, after all, the champions of ordinary language rather than scientific discourse and who are often criticized by the more scientistic voices of the analytic community for (accepting and hence promoting) a consequent vagueness? Why did Bourdieu not turn instead to Russell and Carnap or Quine, who offer more hard-core examples of scientific philosophy?

Here, Bourdieu's choice reveals itself as more than a clever symbolic strategy but a real affinity with Austin and Wittgenstein – not so much as exemplars of scientific empiricism in philosophy (at least in the standard English sense of the term) but as social philosophers, theorists of practice. Austin and Wittgenstein are exemplary in analytic philosophy for insisting on the essential, constitutive role of social context and history, by arguing that language (hence all thought of which language is the medium) is essentially social. Its meaning and import derive not from autonomous referents or facts in the extra-social world (if such a notion is indeed intelligible), but rather from the complex and context-dependent social practices and conventions that help constitute the lived world and that vary with social and historical context.

Opposing the analytic approach of Russell and Moore which focused on the individual proposition, both Austin and Wittgenstein claim that the meaning of an utterance depends not so much on the words said but on the specific *context* in which they are said, a context which is obviously structured and enabled by social conditions, not the least of which is the socially learned practice of speaking a language.

As Austin argues, since linguistic utterances are not mere products of reference or intention but are essentially constituted "by convention", i.e. by social norms of proper performance that vary with social context, "what we have to study is not the sentence but the issuing of an utterance in a speech situation".[5] His original doctrine of performatives was meant to show that certain utterances (promises, marriage vows, christenings) are more appropriately thought of as social action than as linguistic statement, more as *doing something* than as *saying something*. In such highly ritualized acts of symbolic expression what counts is not so much the words but the background institutions, conventions, social roles, and the given context in which the words' bare "linguistic" meaning plays only a negligible part. We could, for example, imagine such acts successfully performed without words at all, but simply by gestures. If Austin's later, more general theory of speech acts challenges the performative/constative distinction, it is only to highlight the fact that all speech is a form of social action, since all illocutionary acts are partly constituted by convention.

The later Wittgenstein also grounds language in social practice, "not agreement in opinions but in form of life". Such forms of life are "what has to be accepted, the given"; thus "conventions" constitute a philosophical "rock bottom".[6] Not merely insisting, like Austin, that linguistic meaning is more a matter of social context than of words, Wittgenstein also adds a crucial historical dimension to the notion of changing social context and applies this idea to the domain of aesthetics in which Bourdieu has been so interested.[7]

For a philosophical understanding of the meaning of an aesthetic judgement, we should be "concentrating, not on the words 'good' or 'beautiful', which are entirely uncharacteristic,... but on the occasions on which they are said – on the enormously complicated situation in which the expression has a place, in which the expression itself has a negligible place". Aesthetic judgements and predicates "play a very complicated role, but a very definite role in what we call a culture of a period. To describe their use or to describe what you mean by a cultured taste, you have to describe a culture". Moreover, such descriptions must be sensitive to historical change, since "an entirely different game is played in different ages".[8] One could hardly find a better philosophical endorsement for Bourdieu's analysis of legitimate aesthetic taste through a full-scale study of the entire cultural field, as well as for his project of exposing "the historical genesis of the pure aesthetic" and *"le champ littéraire"*.

These and other projects of Bourdieu show that he does not simply follow Austin and Wittgenstein but goes beyond them. Though their analytic project was to clarify the meaning of language by seeing it in terms of the social forms and contexts in which it is used, Austin and Wittgenstein never really provide a systematic, ramified analysis of the actual social forces, positions, stakes, roles, and strategies which shape the social field and thus structure context. "The total speech act in the total speech situation", says Austin, is what linguistic philosophy should aim to elucidate (HT 147). Since this total act and situation are structured by enduring social factors, such factors should be elucidated in a rigorous, perspicuous, and reasonably systematic way.

Wittgenstein and Austin were perceptive masters of the social space governing language, yet neither ever went on to theorize this social space and articulate its network of factors so as to provide a general conceptual scheme, a reasonably ordered tool-box of categories and principles, to elucidate the social situations that give language its meaning. Instead, they give only piecemeal analysis of certain philosophically-centered issues. Despite its insight and rigor, such work remains too fragmented and often too impressionistic to serve as a general model for analysing the total speech situation and hence the meaning of linguistic practice.

Bourdieu provides such a model by going more deeply and daringly into the social, and thus realizes one line of analytic philosophy better than the analysts, who perhaps feared (perhaps justly and unreflectively) that the social status of philosophy would itself be threatened by its sociological realization. If it cannot be naïveté, is it denial that explains the limits to which Austin was willing to probe the social? How, indeed, should one take this distinguished Oxford professor's strategic identification of himself (and his elite readers and disciples) with "the ordinary man" and in opposition to what he calls "the scholastic view" of philosophers? To what extent did Austin critically, reflexively, consider the scholastic nature and the social space of his own practice of painstaking analysis of ordinary language? After apologizing for wrongly blaming Austin for the faults of his formalist epigoni, Bourdieu praises him for having gone "as far as he could" in Bourdieu's direction of social fieldwork (*Choses Dites* 40; IOW 29). Is this simply praise for Austin's achievement of his limited aims or is its qualification also an implicit critique of the limits of philosophy?

Wittgenstein is another example of how philosophy can recognize the social (and other natural) grounds that shape language but then couple and counter this recognition with a will to keep philosophy essentially independent of the claims of empirical science by confining philosophical inquiry to the grammatical, conceptual level. "Our interest does not fall back upon these causes of the formation of concepts; we are not doing natural science; nor yet natural history – since we can also invent fictitious natural history for our purposes" (PI, II, p. 230). For certain philosophical purposes this may be sufficient, but as Wittgenstein himself elsewhere saw, not for the purposes of explicating the meaning of judgments in aesthetics, ethics, and other cultural domains. Though more recent analytic philosophers (e.g. Searle) show continued recognition of the constitutive importance of the social *background* – not only for linguistic action but for consciousness itself – they tend to leave its study too complacently in the background, while Bourdieu actually brings this background to the foreground through a systematic analysis that allows its theoretical importance to be understood and thus deployed more effectively.

To support the view that Bourdieu develops the central line of inquiry projected by Austin and Wittgenstein's philosophy of language, I can add my personal testimony that this is what initially made his work both accessible and attractive to me. Having devoted my studies at St John's College, Oxford to these analytic philosophers (working with the Wittgenstein specialist P. M. S. Hacker and writing

my dissertation under Austin's disciple, editor, and literary executor
J. O. Urmson), I began to appreciate just how deeply social structures
and practical interests of action shape even the most seemingly
abstract of philosophical notions (e.g. meaning, truth, validity). Yet
I felt that philosophy never really explored this social and practical
dimension in a sufficiently systematic manner, not even in Austin and
Wittgenstein. I therefore turned to Bourdieu, but also to the pragmatist philosophy of John Dewey. Dewey's appreciation of the philosophical import of social science (an appreciation far greater than
Austin's and Wittgenstein's) not only enriched his thought but led to
the establishment of a fruitful tradition of pragmatist social science
that thrived particularly in Chicago (through the collaborative impact
of Mead) and also elsewhere.[9]

III

Dewey, of course, insists that all meaning (hence all thought) is social,
contextual, and ultimately grounded in practices that we embodied
creatures develop. We develop these practices in order to cope with
our (social as well as natural) environment (by both adjustment to it
and transformation of it) and in order to advance our purposes which
themselves are shaped by that environment, itself a changing and
changeable product of history. Dewey, moreover, explains how these
social practices that constitute practical sense are incorporated and
maintained through habits that work on a prereflective non-linguistic
level, how they can be non-mechanical, intelligent, and even creative
without being reflective, and how they can be changed through changing conditions.

Dewey's approach is not only social but genealogical. The first part
of his *Ethics* is thus devoted to a study of the *Sitten* and structures of
earlier societies which have shaped our own. Arguing that philosophy's problems are primarily the intellectual response to problems
in social life, Dewey also explains how some of philosophy's most
basic concepts and distinctions derive from social formations and
interests. He traces the nature of the theory/practice and end/means
distinctions to hierarchies in Greek social life, and also shows how
our elitist "museum concept of art" is no ontological conceptual
necessity but simply the unhappy product of social, political, and
economic forces that isolate art from the popular life of the community so as to afford art's partakers a particular distinction.[10]

The close affinity of these views to Bourdieu's own are "quite
striking", as Bourdieu himself has recently noted;[11] and his work

could indeed be integrated into the current development of pragmatism. As in the case of analytic philosophy, Bourdieu can be used not simply to affirm pragmatist views but to improve them by providing a more precise, sophisticated, and empirically validated system of concepts for the analysis of society's structure and its strategies and mechanisms of reproduction and change. One brief example (I elsewhere elaborate) should suffice.[12] Though Dewey was right to insist that our concept of art is largely shaped by historical and socio-economic factors, Bourdieu's work (with its more fine-grained analysis of class and class fragments, economic and cultural capital) makes clear that the relations between wealth and social class and between economic and cultural capital are far more complex than Dewey accounts for. Moreover, Bourdieu's Nietzschean strain of emphasizing the intrinsic social conflict over power and prestige provides a useful balance to Dewey's excessive faith that all conflict could somehow be reconciled in an organic social whole.

So far I have argued that Bourdieu advances the central projects of both analytic and pragmatist philosophy by articulating in a more systematic and empirically richer way the basic structures constituting "the social" that for Austin, Wittgenstein, and Dewey are constitutive of language, thought, and action. Does this mean that philosophy itself must probe more deeply into the (changing) social background that constitutes all discourse, including its own? And does this further mean that philosophers must become sociologists like Bourdieu?

Philosophy, one could argue, involves so many different problems at so many different levels, that such radical conclusions need not be drawn. But the very fact that such disturbing conclusions even arise to challenge the philosopher's self-image must surely account for some of the philosophical resistance to Bourdieu. In any case, it seems reasonable that philosophies which explicitly affirm the crucial role of "the social" should themselves take the actual study of society far more seriously; and Bourdieu's amalgam of theory with concrete, comprehensive empirical research provides an excellent, enviable example. I often wish that philosophers like myself had the research resources (including those of legitimizing professional definition) to undertake such an extensive program of fieldwork.

IV

My close philosophical affinities to Bourdieu do not preclude some strong disagreements. Rather than tastelessly rehashing them in this opening essay,[13] I shall try to portray some of our differences in a more oblique manner by returning to the central topic of Bourdieu's relation to Anglo-American philosophy and by explaining his clear preference for Austin and Wittgenstein over Dewey, whose richer analyses of habit, history, society, and politics could have made him the most congenial and useful for Bourdieu's projects.[14] Bourdieu's preference for Austin and Wittgenstein is not merely due to the greater institutional power and symbolic capital of analytic philosophy over pragmatism (not just in the English-speaking philosophical world but also in France). There are also other reasons.

Before exploring them, we should first note another reason for Bourdieu's choice of Austin and Wittgenstein over other *analytic* philosophers. It is not only because of their appreciation of the social, the practical, the contextual, and the historical. It is also their appreciation of *the ordinary* – as expressed in their careful, devoted attention to ordinary language. Though recognizing that ordinary language can be misleading when driven beyond its practical context by philosophers pursuing their own theoretical purposes, Wittgenstein and Austin do not think it needs to be replaced by a more logical, rationally reconstructed language. Philosophy's job is to analyze and give a perspicuous overview of our ordinary concepts; and it may for that purpose invent its own technical terms (like "illocutionary act" or "language game"). But it should not (*pace* Carnap and other constructivists) try to replace or transform our ordinary practical concepts by artificial, rationally reconstructed ones that meet the standards of scientific, theoretical discourse. To do so would be to lose the effective common forms of speaking and acting on which successful theoretical activity (and ordinary life practices) ultimately rely.

Bourdieu shares this appreciation of the ordinary. It is evident in his critique of what (paraphrasing Austin) he calls "the scholastic point of view" and in his masterful advocacy for an elementary but socially inculcated "practical sense" (*sens pratique*) that has its own effective logic that can neither be adequately represented nor replaced by theoretical reconstruction. This recognition of the ordinary is a point of *theory*, but it also expresses (at least for Wittgenstein and Bourdieu) a strong and noble democratic purpose. Paradoxically, however, a complete respect for ordinary language helps to preserve the *status quo* of the social forces which shape it, and these can be far from democratic. The contrast between Wittgenstein's democratic ideals and the conservative, elite scholasticism that his work generated at Oxbridge's "High Tables" caused him bitter frustration.

In both Austin and Wittgenstein, there is not only respect for the ordinary but also a further commitment to the traditional notion of disinterested objectivity – that philosophy should just portray correctly or clarify things rather than change them. Such commitments suggest a distinct quietism in Austin's and Wittgenstein's philosophical approach. In exposing the fallacies arising from misuse of language, philosophical analysis, says Austin, simply "leaves us, in a sense, just where we began". Though shrewdly admitting that ordinary language is not "the last word" and can "in principle" be "improved upon and superseded", he insists that we "remember it is the first word", whose endless, and ever regenerating complexities must first be adequately clarified before venturing any improvements.[15] The practical upshot of such prioritizing is the constant deferral of philosophy's attempts at linguistic revision, which, given the reciprocal links between "the linguistic" and "the social", can promote social revision as well. Wittgenstein is even more explicit. "Philosophy may in no way interfere with the actual use of language; it can in the end only describe it . . . It leaves everything as it is" (PI 124).

Dewey is surely as much a philosopher of ordinary practice as Austin and Wittgenstein; and surely a greater champion of democracy. More sensitive to the needs of ordinary people and to the class relations that structure "the social" of language, he realized that ordinary language is often a tool through which ordinary people are subjected and oppressed by the social masters of discourse, who may themselves become ensnared and hindered by linguistic modes that have outlived their use in the flux of social change. Dewey was therefore not a fetishist of ordinary language and practice but a pragmatic, meliorist about them, arguing that ordinary concepts should be revised, replaced, or abandoned when they systematically hinder inquiry, limit freedom, or diminish potentialities of improvement. The philosopher, like the poet and scientist, can offer conceptual revisions, which can be tried and tested in the complex, contested, and changing fields of discourse. More than the poet (though less than the scientist), the philosopher is constrained by "the facts" which, however, are themselves largely shaped by our concepts. For Dewey, conceptual revisions (in science as well as philosophy) are based not merely on facts but on perceived *needs*.

Often Dewey's sense of need too far exceeds his sense of fact. His attempt to remedy the oppressive, impoverishing distortions of the aesthetic field by means of a revisionary global definition of art as experience is, as I show in *Pragmatist Aesthetics*, as quixotic as it is unnecessary. Nonetheless, he seems right that philosophy can play a useful revisionary role and that philosophers should not confine themselves to accepting ordinary usage and the ordinary positive facts it expresses. Of course, theoretical persuasion cannot replace reform of material conditions, for which Dewey also tirelessly worked. But, through the reciprocal constitution of language and practice, new ways of talking can influence attitudes and action, and thus can help bring about more substantive, material reform. To suppose that theoretical interventions can in no way promote or guide such reform is, for pragmatism, to accept an implausible, pernicious dichotomy between theory and practice.

While sharing Dewey's democratic drive and vigorous political concern for ordinary people and their problems,[16] Bourdieu displays a politics of theory that seems much closer to Austin's and Wittgenstein's. In fact, he explicitly rebukes as false "magic" some Deweyan challenges to certain confused, oppressive categories in the "ordinary language" of cultural discourse. It is not our categories that need fixing, complains Bourdieu, but the material and institutional "conditions" that generate them and other suffering.[17] But why can't Bourdieu recognize the pragmatist strategy of working simultaneously on both fronts, for discursive as well as more material and institutional change? Why can't one combine revisionary theory and practice, as the double-barrelled Deweyan pragmatist policy recommends?

Rather than turn these questions into mere rhetorical critique, let me try to answer them by suggesting what could be Bourdieu's best reasons for rejecting pragmatism's theoretical activism, reasons that even a pragmatist like myself can appreciate and that express the pragmatic character of Bourdieu's own thinking.[18] These reasons cannot lie in foundational objectivism or naive positivism, for no one knows better than Bourdieu the interested social powers that shape language and science.

One pragmatist argument against theoretical revisionism is that linguistic change can lead only to confusion that threatens our solid sense of reality – our sense of the facts on which substantive material reforms must rely for their data, direction, and instruments. Theoretical tinkering thus does not enable but disables real material reform. Moreover, since the socially disempowered seem generally more vulnerable and less equipped to respond to new changes, the uncertainty and confusion that may arise from challenging oppressive categories may turn out to be far more oppressive, while the better-equipped, entrenched elites may simply appropriate the conceptual change for their own undemocratic purposes. This argument, which Bourdieu seems to suggest by his condemnation of "radical chic", has undeniable power. The fact that such arguments are deployed effectively by pragmatic conservatives like T. S. Eliot does not preclude their use for Bourdieu's more progressive social aims.[19]

The force of these arguments, however, seems limited. Very radical and global change may dangerously upset social and cognitive stability, but modest and site-specific conceptual revision need not do this, especially given the degree of conservatism already built into our habitual social selves. Experiments of change are essential to the pragmatist notion of progress, although the dangers of such experiments need to be carefully assessed and minimized, so that change may be balanced with stability. But again, only experiment can teach us how to do this.

Bourdieu could have another good reason for refusing revisionary theory and insisting that one's aim, *qua* theorist, is simply to reveal the facts (however ugly and painful) rather than to try to change them. Adopting this position (the traditional hallmark of scientific objectivity) allows Bourdieu to assume all the symbolic power of the natural science tradition and its conventialy hallowed (though increasingly questioned) objectivist ideology of disinterested description of the naked truth. Still wielding enormous power in the intellectual field (even on philosophy itself), the natural science tradition of objectivism seems to have the most influence in politics. By assimilating this symbolic power and so enhancing his own, Bourdieu can give his views greater authority in the political sphere and thereby improve his efficacy as an agent for socio-political reform. Conversely, since Bourdieu's professional status belongs to social science (which lacks the symbolic capital of natural science, largely through doubts about its objectivity), to flirt with revisionary theory could be fatal. Adopting revisionary theory, even in a limited way, would risk discrediting the objectivity of his work, the veracity of all his painstakingly gathered and processed empirical research, the entire credibility of his views.

The philosopher, in contrast, occupies a different place in our intellectual tradition and cultural imagination, drawing his symbolic power from somewhat different sources than the scientist. Though acquiring the academic title of philosopher only through an educational system committed to the ideology of objectivism and rigorous science, the symbolic power of the name *philosopher* derives from a tradition older and broader than modern science. The philosopher's legendary social role is not simply the describer of facts; it is just as much the revisionary prophet, utopian myth-maker, and transcendental sage, who all, to some extent, defy ordinary facts and conventions even when advocating something humbly down-to-earth like

"the simple life". The strength of this tradition in our social unconscious is very strong (how else could society not only tolerate but
celebrate so much mystifying philosophical nonsense!). This tradition
gives a symbolic power to the philosopher as revisionist that the social
scientist cannot claim. Indeed, given philosophy's shrinking authority
to speak for empirical science, revisionary theory may be where the
philosopher can wield the most effective symbolic power, and he can
wield it without resorting to an extremist revisionism that has no
respect for empirical findings.

If revisionary theory is worth trying,[20] then the philosopher has
perhaps a role to play beyond and against the limits of Bourdieu's
project, even though Bourdieu's productive analysis of the social
should enrich and guide the philosopher's perhaps quixotic, perhaps
dangerous, attempts at revision. Such attempts may even be useful to
Bourdieu – at least as foils that make his own theorizing look all the
more robust and scientific.

Notes

1   For a discussion of the complexities of individuating national philosoph-
    ical traditions, see Richard Shusterman, "Internationalism in Philo-
    sophy", *Metaphilosophy*, 28: 4 (1997), 289–301. North American
    philosophers like Charles Taylor, Hubert Dreyfus, and Judith Butler
    (who contributed articles to this volume) are typically considered "con-
    tinental philosophers". The growing appreciation of Bourdieu by analytic
    philosophers is evident not only in this volume's contributions from
    Danto, Margolis, and others, but in the respectful attention that a hard-
    core analyst like Searle pays to Bourdieu's theory of habitus. See John
    Searle, *The Rediscovery of the Mind* (Cambridge: MIT, 1992) and *The
    Construction of Social Reality* (New York: Free Press, 1995).
2   See P. Bourdieu, *Choses Dites* (Paris: Minuit, 1987), pp. 19, 40. "Field-
    work in Philosophy" originally appeared (in French) in *Choses Dites* and
    "The Scholastic Point of View" was originally written in French and can
    be found in *Raisons Pratiques* (Paris: Seuil, 1994). Its English translation
    appeared in *Cultural Anthropology*, 5 (1990), 380–91. The Austinian
    phrases for these titles come from "A Plea for Excuses" and *Sense and
    Sensibilia*. *Choses Dites* appears in English translation as *In Other
    Words: Essays towards a Reflexive Sociology* (Stanford: Stanford Uni-
    versity Press, 1990). The quotations cited above are on pages 9, 28. I have
    slightly altered the translation, rendering "sans doute" as "no doubt"
    rather than as the weaker "probably" in the published English transla-
    tion. Reference to this translation will be by the abbreviation IOW.
3   For Bourdieu's recognition of this strategy of importation, see his essay
    "The Social Conditions of the International Circulation of Ideas" revised

and reprinted in this collection. For a detailed case study of this phenomenon with respect to aesthetics, see Richard Shusterman, "Aesthetics Between Nationalism and Internationalism", *Journal of Aesthetics and Art Criticism*, 51 (1993), 157–67.

4 Doubts can be raised, however, as to whether this reputation is still deserved or whether (as Hilary Putnam has recently complained) analytic philosophy has become exceedingly metaphysical.

5 J. L. Austin, *How To Do Things With Words* (Oxford: Oxford University Press, 1970), 127, 138; henceforth referred to as HT.

6 See Ludwig Wittgenstein, *Philosophical Investigations* (Oxford: Basil Blackwell, 1968), I. para. 241, II, p. 226; henceforth PI, and *The Blue and Brown Books* (New York: Harper, 1958), 24.

7 Bourdieu's important contributions to aesthetics include *Distinction: A Social Critique of the Judgement of Taste* (Cambridge, Mass: Harvard University Press, 1984); *Photography: A Middle-brow Art* (Cambridge: Polity Press, 1990); *The Rules of Art: Genesis and Structure of the Literary Field* (Cambridge: Polity Press, 1996). His specific interest in Anglo-American aesthetics is shown by his contribution to a collection on analytic aesthetics. See Pierre Bourdieu, "The Historical Genesis of a Pure Aesthetic" in Richard Shusterman (ed.), *Analytic Aesthetics* (Oxford: Blackwell, 1989), 147–60.

8 Ludwig Wittgenstein, *Lectures and Conversations on Aesthetics, Psychology, and Religious Belief* (Oxford: Blackwell, 1970), 2, 8. I provide a detailed analysis of the nature and consequences of Wittgenstein's aesthetics in "Wittgenstein and Critical Reasoning", *Philosophy and Phenomenological Research*, 47 (1986), 91–110.

9 For a detailed discussion of Mead's work and its relation to Bourdieu's, see chapter 9 in this volume.

10 See John Dewey, *Art as Experience* (Carbondale: Southern Illinois University Press, 1987), 12–16.

11 See Pierre Bourdieu and Loic Wacquant, *An Invitation to Reflexive Sociology* (Chicago: University of Chicago Press, 1992), 122. Bourdieu converges with Deweyan pragmatism not only in highlighting the social, historical, and practical, but also in underlying the crucial role of embodiment and non-reflective experience. In recognizing how a philosopher's thought is shaped by society, Dewey also appreciated the theorist's duty to study the ills of that society in the hope of finding remedies. Possessed by a powerful democratic impulse, he played an active political role to advance it. The affinities to Bourdieu are here also quite striking.

12 See Richard Shusterman, *Pragmatist Aesthetics: Living Beauty, Rethinking Art* (Oxford: Blackwell, 1992), 21–5.

13 They appear quite pointedly in *Pragmatist Aesthetics*' defense of popular art, Bourdieu's condemnation of the radical chic of such intellectual efforts to appreciate popular culture, and my response in "Légitimer la légitimation de l'art populaire", *Politix*, 24 (1993), 153–7. See also Richard Shusterman, "Popular Art and Education", *Studies in*

Philosophy and Education, 13 (1995), 203–12; and "Rap Remix: Pragmatism, Postmodernism and Other Issues in the House", *Critical Inquiry*, 22 (1995), 150–8.

14 These analyses certainly made Dewey a favorite with the great French social theorists whom Bourdieu most admires – Durkheim and Mauss. Dewey, claimed Mauss, is the American philosopher "whom Durkheim put ahead of all the others, and it is a great regret of mine not to have been able to attend the last great philosophy lecture of Durkheim, dedicated in great part to Professor Dewey". See John Dewey: The Later Works, vol. 5 (Carbondale: Southern Illinois University Press, 1985), 500–1.

15 J. L. Austin, *Sense and Sensibilia* (Oxford: Oxford University Press, 1962), 5; "A Plea for Excuses", in *Philosophical Papers* (Oxford: Oxford University Press, 1970), 185.

16 See, for instance, his monumental and deeply moving *La Misère du Monde* (Paris: Seuil, 1993).

17 *An Invitation to Reflexive Sociology*, 84.

18 Bourdieu stresses his "pragmatic" view in treating culture, "especially the culture *par excellence*, namely philosophy" (*Choses Dites* 41; IOW 29).

19 For Bourdieu's critique of "radical chic", see *Raisons Pratiques*, 232–3, and *An Invitation to Reflexive Sociology*, 84.

20 A more detailed defense of pragmatist revisionary theory can be found in *Pragmatist Aesthetics* (especially ch. 2), while the idea of philosophy as not mere scientific theory but revisionary and visionary life-practice is developed in my *Practicing Philosophy: Pragmatism and the Philosophical Life*. (New York: Routledge, 1977).

2

To Follow a Rule...

Charles Taylor

Great puzzlement has arisen about rules and conventions, as we try to understand their place in human life in the light of modern philosophy. One fact of this was pressed most acutely and famously by Wittgenstein in his *Philosophical Investigations*[1] and further elaborated by Saul Kripke in his book on the subject. It concerns what it means to understand a rule. Understanding seems to imply knowledge or awareness; yet Wittgenstein shows that the subject not only isn't but *couldn't* be aware of a whole host of issues which nevertheless have a direct bearing on the correct application of a rule.

Wittgenstein shows this by raising the possibilities of misunderstanding. Some outsider, unfamiliar with the way we do things, might misunderstand what to us are perfectly clear and simple directions. You want to get to town? Just follow the arrows. But suppose that what seemed the natural way of following the arrow to him or her was to go in the direction of the feathers, not of the point? (i: 85). We can imagine a scenario: there are no arrows in the outsider's culture, but there is a kind of ray gun whose discharge fans out like the feathers on our arrows.

Now this kind of example triggers off a certain reaction in our intellectualist philosophical culture. What the stranger fails to understand (you follow arrows towards the point), we must understand. We *know* how to follow arrows. But what does this mean? From the intellectualist perspective, it must be that somewhere in our mind, consciously or unconsciously, a premise has been laid down about how you follow arrows. From another angle, once we see the

From *Bourdieu: Critical Perspectives*, ed. C. Calhoun, E. LiPuma and M. Postone, University of Chicago Press, Chicago, and Polity Press, Cambridge, 1993.

stranger's mistake, we can explain what he or she ought to do. But if we can give an explanation, we must already *have* an explanation. So the thought must reside somewhere in us that you follow arrows this way.

Or we could come at the same point from another direction. Suppose we didn't have such a thought. Then when the issue arises as to whether we really ought to follow arrows towards the point, we would be in doubt. How would we know that this was right? And then how would we follow the directions?

Now this kind of reply runs into insuperable difficulties, because the number of such potential misunderstandings is endless. Wittgenstein makes this point over and over again. There are an indefinite number of points at which, for a given explanation of a rule and a given run of paradigm cases, someone could nevertheless misunderstand, as our stranger did the injunction to follow the arrows. For instance (i: 87), I might say that by "Moses" I mean the man who led the Israelites out of Egypt, but then my interlocutor might have trouble with the words "Egypt" and "Israelites". "Nor would these questions come to an end when we get down to words like 'red', 'dark', 'sweet'." Nor would even mathematical explanations be proof against this danger. We could imagine someone to whom we teach a series by giving a sample range, say: 0, 2, 4, 6, 8. The person might carry on quite well till 1,000, and then go 1,004, 1,008, 1,012. He or she is indignant when we say that this is wrong. The person understood our sample range to be illustrating the rule: "Add 2 up to 1,000, 4 up to 2,000, 6 up to 3,000, and so on" (i: 185).

If in order to understand directions or know how to follow a rule, we have to know that all these deviant readings are deviant, and if this means that we have to have formulated thoughts to this effect already, then we need an infinite number of thoughts in our heads to follow even the simplest instructions. Plainly this is crazy. The intellectualist is tempted to treat all these potential issues as though they would have to be *resolved* by us already, if we are to understand the directions. ("It may easily look as if every doubt merely *revealed* an existing gap in the foundations; so that secure understanding is only possible if we first doubt everything that *can* be doubted, and then remove all these doubts" [i: 87]. But since any explanation leaves some potential issues unresolved, it stands in need of further explanations to back it up. And further explanations would have the same lack and so the job of explaining to somebody how to do something would be literally endless. " 'But then how does an explanation help me to understand, if after all it is not the final one? In that case the explanation is never completed; so I still don't understand what he means, and never shall!' – As though an explanation as it were hung in the air unless supported by another one" (i: 87).

The last remark, the one not in single quotes, is Wittgenstein's reply to his interlocutor. It hints at the mind-set of the intellectualist. This outlook seeks securely founded knowledge. We recognize an obsession of the modern intellectual tradition, from Descartes. It didn't see this as a problem, because it thought we could find such secure foundations, explanations in terms of features which were self-explanatory or self-authenticating. That's why the imagined interlocutor placed his hopes in words like "red", "dark", "sweet", referring to basic empirical experiences on which we can ground everything else. The force of Wittgenstein's argument lies in its radical undercutting of any such foundationalism.

Why can someone always misunderstand? And why don't we have to resolve all these potential difficulties before we can understand ourselves? The answer to these two questions is the same. Understanding is always against a background of what is taken for granted, just relied on. Someone who lacks this background can always come along and so the plainest things can be misunderstood, particularly if we let our imagination roam and imagine people who have never even heard of arrows. But at the same time, the background, as what is simply relied on, isn't the locus of resolved questions. When the misunderstanding stems from a difference of background, what needs to be said to clear it up articulates a bit of the explainer's background which may never have been articulated before.

Wittgenstein stresses the unarticulated – at some points even unarticulable – nature of this understanding. "'[O]beying a rule' is a practice" (i: 202). Giving reasons for one's practice in following a rule has to come to an end. "My reasons will soon give out. And then I shall act, without reasons" (i: 211). Or later, "If I have exhausted my justifications I have reached bedrock, and my spade is turned. Then I am inclined to say: 'This is simply what I do'" (i: 217). More laconically, "When I obey a rule, I do not choose. I obey the rule *blindly*" (i: 219).

There are two broad schools of interpretation of what Wittgenstein is saying here, which correspond to two ways of understanding the phenomenon of the unarticulated background. The first would interpret the claim that I act without reasons as involving the view that no reasons can be given here, that no demand for reasons can arise. This is because the connections which form our background are just *de facto* links, not susceptible of any justification. For instance, they are simply imposed by our society; we are conditioned to make them. They become "automatic," which is why the question never arises. The view that society imposes these limits is the heart of Kripke's interpretation of Wittgenstein. Or else they can perhaps be considered as "wired in." It's just a fact about us that we react this way, as it is that we blink when something approaches our eyes, and no justification is in order.

The second interpretation takes the background as really incorporating *understanding*; that is, as a grasp on things which, although quite unarticulated, may allow us to formulate reasons and explanations when challenged. In this case, the links are not simply *de facto*, but make a kind of sense, which is precisely what one would be trying to spell out in the articulation.

On the first view, then, the "bedrock" on which our explicit explanations rest is made up of brute connections; on the second, it is a mode of understanding and thus makes a kind of unarticulated sense of things.

What suggest the first interpretation are phrases like "I obey the rule blindly," and perhaps even the image of bedrock itself, whose unyielding nature implies that nothing further *can* be said. What tell against it are other passages in which Wittgenstein says, for example, that following a rule is not like the operations of a machine (i: 193–4), or that "To use a word without justification does not mean to use it without right" (i: 289 – although I can imagine an interpretation of this compatible with the first view). Above all, I want to say that it is his insistence that following rules is a *social* practice. Granted, this also fits, perhaps, with Kripke's version of the first view. But I think that, in reality, this connection of background with society reflects an alternative vision, which has jumped altogether outside the old monological outlook which dominates the epistemological tradition.

Whatever Wittgenstein thought, this second view seems to me to be right. What the first cannot account for is the fact that we do give explanations, that we can often articulate reasons when challenged. Following arrows towards the point is not just an arbitrarily imposed connection; it makes sense, granted the way arrows move. What we need to do is follow a hint from Wittgenstein and attempt to give an account of the background as understanding, which also places it in social space. This is what I would now like to explore.[2]

The exploration that follows runs against the grain of much modern thought and culture; in particular, of our scientific culture and its associated epistemology, which in turn, have molded our contemporary sense of self.

Among the practices which have helped to create this modern sense are those which discipline our thought to disengagement from embodied agency and social embedding. Each of us is called upon to become a responsible, thinking mind, self-reliant for his or her judgments (this, at least, is the standard). But this ideal, however admirable in some respects, has tended to blind us to important facets of the human condition. There is a tendency in our intellectual tradition to read it less as an ideal than as something which is already established in our constitution. This reification of the disengaged first-person-singular self is already evident in the founding figures of the modern epistemological tradition – for instance, Descartes and Locke.

It means that we easily tend to see the human agent as primarily a subject of representations: representations about the world outside and depictions of ends desired or feared. This subject is a monological one. She or he is in contact with an "outside" world, including other agents, the objects she or he and they deal with, her or his own and others' bodies, but this contact is through the representations she or he has "within." The subject is first of all an "inner" space, a "mind" to use the old terminology, or a mechanism capable of processing representations if we follow the more fashionable computer-inspired models of today. The body, other people or objects may form the content of my representations. They may also be causally responsible for some of these representations. But what "I" am, as a being capable of having such representations, the inner space itself, is definable independently of body or other. It is a center of monological consciousness.

It is this stripped-down view of the subject which has made deep inroads into social science, breeding the various forms of methodological individualism, including the most recent and virulent variant, the current vogue of rational choice theory. It stands in the way of a richer, more adequate understanding of what the human sense of self is really like and hence of a proper understanding of the real variety of human culture and so of a knowledge of human beings.

What this kind of consciousness leaves out are: the body and the other. Both have to be brought back in if we are to grasp the kind of background understanding which Wittgenstein seems to be adverting to. And in fact, restoring the first involves retrieving the second. I want to sketch briefly what is involved in this connection.

A number of philosophical currents in the last two centuries have tried to get out of the cul-de-sac of monological consciousness. Prominent in this century are the works of Heidegger (1927), Merleau-Ponty (1945), and of course, Wittgenstein (1953) himself. What all these have in common is that they see the agent not primarily as the locus of representations, but as engaged in practices, as a being who acts in and on a world.

Of course, no one has failed to notice that human beings act. The crucial difference is that these philosophers set the primary locus of the agent's understanding in practice. In the mainline epistemological view, what distinguishes the agent from inanimate entities which can also affect their surroundings is the former's capacity for inner representations, whether these are placed in the "mind" or in the brain understood as a computer. What we have which inanimate beings don't have – understanding – is identified with representations and the operations we effect on them.

To situate our understanding in practices is to see it as implicit in our activity, and hence as going well beyond what we manage to frame representations of. We do frame representations: we explicitly formulate what our world is like, what we aim at, what we are doing. But much of our intelligent action in the world, sensitive as it usually is to our situation and goals, is carried on unformulated. It flows from an understanding which is largely inarticulate.

This understanding is more fundamental in two ways: first, it is always there, whereas sometimes we frame representations and sometimes we do not, and, second, the representations we do make are only comprehensible against the background provided by this inarticulate understanding. It provides the context within which alone they make the sense they do. Rather than representations being the primary locus of understanding, they are similarly islands in the sea of our unformulated practical grasp on the world.

Seeing that our understanding resides first of all in our practices involves attributing an inescapable role to the background. The connection figures, in different ways, in virtually all the philosophies of the contemporary counter-current to epistemology, and famously, for example, in Heidegger and Wittgenstein.

But this puts the role of the body in a new light. Our body is not just the executant of the goals we frame or just the locus of the causal factors which shape our representations. Our understanding itself is embodied. That is, our bodily know-how and the way we act and move can encode components of our understanding of self and world. I know my way around a familiar environment in being able to get from any place to any place with ease and assurance. I may be at a loss when asked to draw a map or even to give explicit directions to a stranger. I know how to manipulate and use the familiar instruments in my world, usually in the same inarticulate fashion.

But it is not only my grasp on the inanimate environment which is thus embodied. My sense of myself and of the footing I am on with others are in large part embodied also. The deferrence I owe you is carried in the distance I stand from you, in the way I fall silent when you start to speak, in the way I hold myself in your presence. Or alternatively, the sense I have of my own importance is carried in the way I swagger. Indeed, some of the most pervasive features of my attitude to the world and to others are encoded in the way I carry myself and project in public space: whether I am "macho" or timid or eager to please or calm and unflappable.

In all these cases, the person concerned may not even possess the appropriate descriptive term. For instance, when I stand respectfully and defer to you, I may not have the word "deference" in my vocabulary. Very often, words are coined by (more sophisticated) others to describe important features of people's stance in the world. (Needless to say, these others are often social scientists.) This understanding is not, or is only imperfectly, captured in our representations. It is carried in patterns of appropriate action: that is, action which conforms to a sense of what is fitting and right. An agent with this kind of understanding recognizes when he or she or others "have put a foot wrong." His or her actions are responsive throughout to this sense of rightness, but the "norms" may be quite unformulated, or formulated only in fragmentary fashion.

In recent years, Pierre Bourdieu (1977c, 1990e) has coined a term to capture this level of social understanding – the *"habitus."* This is one of the key terms necessary to give an account of the background understanding invoked in the previous section. I will return to this in a minute. But first I want to make the connection between the retrieval of the body and that of the other.

In fact, one can see right away how the other also figures. Some of these practices which encode understanding are not carried out in acts of a single agent. The above example of my deference is a case in point. Deferent and deferred-to play out their social distance in a conversation, often with heavily ritualized elements. And indeed, conversations in general rely on small, usually focally unnoticed rituals.

But perhaps I should say a word first about this distinction I'm drawing between acts of a single agent – (let's call them "monological" acts) – and those of more than one – ("dialogical" acts). From the standpoint of the old epistemology, all acts were monological, although often the agent coordinated his or her actions with those of others. But this notion of coordination fails to capture the way in which some actions require and sustain an integrated agent. Think of two people sawing a log with a two-handed saw or a couple dancing. A very important feature of human action is rhythmizing, cadence. Every apt, coordinated gesture has a certain flow. When this is lost, as occasionally happens, one falls into confusion; one's actions become inept and uncoordinated. Similarly, the mastery of a new kind of skilled action goes along with the ability to give one's gestures the appropriate rhythm.

Now in cases like the sawing of the log and ballroom dancing, it is crucial to their rhythmizing that it be shared. These activities only come off when we can place ourselves in a common rhythm, in which our component action is taken up. This is a different experience from coordinating my action with yours, as when I run to the spot on the field where I know you are going to pass the ball.

Sawing and dancing are paradigm cases of dialogical actions. But there is frequently a dialogical level to actions that are otherwise merely coordinated. A conversation is a good example. Conversations with some degree of ease and intimacy move beyond mere coordination and have a common rhythm. The interlocutor not only listens, but participates by nodding his or her head and by saying "unh-hunh," and the like, and at a certain point the "semantic turn" passes to him or her by a common movement. The appropriate moment is felt by both partners, in virtue of the common rhythm. The bore and the compulsive talker thin the atmosphere of conviviality because they are impervious to this. There is a continuity between ordinary, convivial conversation and more ritualized exchanges: litanies or alternate chanting, such as one sees in many earlier societies.[3]

I have taken actions with a common rhythmizing as paradigm cases of the dialogical, but they are only one form of these. An action is dialogical, in the sense that I'm using the word here, when it is effected by an integrated, nonindividual agent. This means that for those involved in it, its identity as this kind of action essentially depends on the agency being shared. These actions are constituted as such by a shared understanding among those who make up the common agent. Integration into a common rhythm can be one form that this shared understanding takes. But it can also come into being outside the situation of face-to-face encounter. In a different form it can also constitute, for instance, a political or religious movement whose members may be widely scattered but are animated by a sense of common purpose – such as that which linked the students in Tionanmen Square with their colleagues back on the campuses and, indeed, with a great part of the population of Peking. This kind of action exists in a host of other forms, and on a great many other levels as well.

The importance of dialogical action in human life shows the utter inadequacy of the monological subject of representations which emerges from the epistemological tradition. We can't understand human life merely in terms of individual subjects who frame representations about and respond to others, because a great deal of human action happens only insofar as the agent understands and constitutes him or herself as an integrall part of a "we."

Much of our understanding of self, society, and world is carried in practices which consist in dialogical action. I would like to argue, in fact, that language itself serves to set up spaces of common action, on a number of levels, intimate and public.[4] This means that our identity is never defined simply in terms of our individual properties. It also places us in some social space. We define ourselves partly in terms of what we come to accept as our appropriate place within dialogical actions. In the case that I really identify myself with my deferential attitude towards wiser people like you, then this conversational stance becomes constituent of my identity. This social reference figures even more clearly in the identity of the dedicated revolutionary.

The background understanding invoked in the first section, which underlies our ability to grasp directions and follow rules, is to a large degree embodied. This helps to explain the combination of features it exhibits: that it is a form of *understanding*, a making sense of things and actions, but at the same time is entirely unarticulated, and, thirdly, can be the basis of fresh articulation. As long as we think of understanding in the old intellectualist fashion, as residing in thoughts or representations, it is hard to explain how we can know how to follow a rule or in any way to behave rightly without having the thoughts which would justify this behavior as right. We are driven either to a foundationalist construal, which would allow us to attribute only a finite list of such thoughts justifying an action from scratch, as it were, or else, abandoning this, to conceive of a supporting background in the form of brute, *de facto* connections. This is because intellectualism leaves us with the choice only of an understanding which consists of representations or of no understanding at all. Embodied understanding provides us with the third alternative we need to make sense of ourselves.

At the same time, it allows us to show the connections of this understanding with social practice. My embodied understanding doesn't exist only in me as an individual agent; it also exists in me as the co-agent of common actions. This is the sense we can give to Wittgenstein's claim that "obeying a rule" is a practice (i: 202), by which he means a social practice. Earlier (i: 198) he asks: "What has the expression of a rule – say a sign-post – got to do with my actions? What sort of connection is there?" His answer is: "Well, perhaps this one: I have been trained to react to this sign in a particular way, and now I do so react." This may sound at first like the first interpretation I mentioned above: the training would set up a brute *de facto* tendency to react. The connection would be merely causal. But Wittgenstein moves right away to set aside this reading. His imaginary interlocutor says: "But that is only to give a causal connection"; and the Wittgensteinian voice in the text answers: "On the contrary; I have further indicated that a person goes by a signpost only insofar as there exists a regular use of sign-posts, a custom [*einen ständigen Gebrauch, eine Gepflogenheit*]."

This standing social use makes the connection, which is not to be understood as a merely causal connection. This is perhaps because the standing use gives my response its *sense*. It doesn't merely bring it on through a brute causal link. But the sense is embodied, not represented. That is why Wittgenstein can ask in the immediately following passage (i: 199): "Is what is called 'obeying a rule' something it would be possible for only *one* man to do only *once* in his life?" This rhetorical question demanding a negative answer is understood by Wittgenstein to point not just to a factual impossibility, but to something which doesn't even make sense. "This is a note," he adds, "on the grammar of the expression 'to obey a rule'." But if the role of society were just to set up the causal connections underlying my reactions, then it couldn't be senseless to suppose that those connections held only for one person at one time, however bizarrely unlikely. In fact, the social practice is there to give my actions the meaning they have, and that's why there couldn't just be one action with this meaning.

Because the wrong, intellectualistic epistemology has made deep inroads into social science, to ill effect, it is important that the scientific consequences of embodied understanding be developed. This is what makes Bourdieu's notion of *habitus* so important and potentially fruitful.

Anthropology, like any other social science, can't do without some notion of rule. Too much of human social behavior is "regular," in the sense not just of exhibiting repeated patterns but also of responding to demands or norms which have some generalizable form. In certain societies, women defer to men, young to old. There are certain forms of address and marks of respect which are repeatedly required. Not conforming is seen as wrong, as a "breach." So we quite naturally say for example, that women use these forms of address not just haphazardly and not (in the ordinary sense) as a reflex, but "following a rule."

Suppose we are trying to understand this society. We are anthropologists, who have come here precisely to get a picture of what the people's life is like. Then we have to discover and formulate some definition of this rule; we identify certain kinds of predicament – say, a woman meeting her husband or meeting a man who is not her husband in the village or meeting this man in the fields – and define what appears to be required in each of these situations. Perhaps we can even rise to some more general rule from which these different situational requirements can be deduced. But in one form or another, we are defining a rule through a *representation* of it. Formulating in this case is creating a representation.

So far, so necessary. But then intellectualism enters the picture, and we slide easily into seeing the rule-as-represented as somehow causally operative. We may attribute formulations of the rule as thoughts to the agents. But more likely, since this is very implausible in some cases, we see the rule-as-represented as defining an underlying "structure." We conceive this as what is really causally operative, behind the backs of the unsophisticated agents, as it were.

So argues Bourdieu. "Intellectualism is inscribed in the fact of introducing into the object the intellectual relation to the object, of substituting the observer's relation to practice for the practical relation to practice" (1990e: 34).[5] Of course, writing on the French scene, Bourdieu naturally gives an important place to structuralism, which is his main target here. It bulks less large in the English-speaking world. But the reified understanding of rule-as-representation doesn't haunt only the school of Lévi-Strauss. It obtrudes in a confused and uncertain form wherever the issue Bourdieu wants to pose has not been faced: just how do the rules *we* formulate operate in *their* lives? What is their *Sitz im Leben*? So long as this issue is not resolved, we are in danger of sliding into the reification that our intellectualist epistemology invites, in one or other of the two ways mentioned. "To slip from *regularity*, i.e. from what recurs with a certain statistically measurable frequency and from the formula which describes it, to a consciously laid down and consciously respected *ruling* (*règlement*), or to unconscious *regulating* by a mysterious cerebral or social mechanism, are the two commonest ways of sliding from the model of reality to the reality of the model" (p. 39).

There's a mistake here, but is it important? If we have to represent the rules to grasp them and we define them right, what does it matter how exactly they operate in the lives of the agents? Bourdieu argues that an important distortion occurs when we see the rule-as-represented as the effective factor. The distortion arises from the fact that we are taking a situated, embodied sense and providing an express depiction of it. We can illustrate the difference in the gap which separates our inarticulate familiarity with a certain environment, enabling us to get around in it without hesitation, on one hand, and a map of this terrain, on the other. The practical ability exists only in its exercise, which unfolds in time and space. As you get around a familiar environment, the different locations in their interrelation don't all impinge at once. Your sense of them is different, depending on where you are and where you are going. And some relations never impinge at all. The route and the relation of the landmarks look different on the way out and the way back; the way stations on the high road bear no relation to those on the low road. A way is essentially something you go through in time. A map, on the other hand, lays out everything simultaneously and relates every point to every point, without discrimination (pp. 34–5).

Maps or representations, by their very nature, abstract from lived time and space. To make something like this the ultimate causal factor is to make the actual practice in time and space merely derivative, a mere application of a disengaged scheme. It is the ultimate in Platonism. But this is a constant temptation not only because of the intellectualist focus on the representation, but also because of the prestige of the notion of law as it figures in natural science. The inverse square law is such a timeless, aspatial formula which "dictates" the behavior of all bodies everywhere. Shouldn't we be seeking something similar in human affairs? This invitation to imitate the really successful modern sciences also encourages the reification of the rule.

But this reification crucially distorts, and this in three related ways: it blocks out certain features that are essential to action; it does not allow for the difference between a formula and its enactment; nor does it take account of the reciprocal relation between rule and action, that the second doesn't just flow from the first, but also transforms it.

Abstracting from lived time and space means abstracting from action, because the time of action is asymmetrical. It projects a future always under some degree of uncertainty. A map or a diagram of the process imposes symmetry. Take a society, such as those described by Marcel Mauss or the Kabyle communities studied by Bourdieu, where a reciprocal exchange of gifts plays an important role in defining and confirming relationships. One can make an atemporal schema of these exchanges and of the "rules" which they obey. One may then be tempted to claim, as Lévi-Strauss does, that "'the primary, fundamental phenomenon is exchange itself, which gets split up into discrete operations in social life'" (p. 98).[6]

But this leaves out of account the crucial dimension of action in time. Bourdieu points out several ways in which this might matter. Not all of them directly back up his main point. For instance, he points out that there is a proper time (a *kairos*) for reciprocating a favor. If one gives something back right away, it stands as a rebuff, as though one didn't want to be beholden to the original giver. If one delays too long, it's a sign of neglect. But this is an aspect of time which could itself be expressed in some abstract formula. Where the time of action becomes crucial is where we have to act in uncertainty and our action will irreversibly affect the situation. In the rule book of exchanges (which would be an anthropologist's artifact), the relations look perfectly reversible. But on the ground, there is always uncertainty, because there are difficult judgment calls. In Kabylia, the gift relation is a recognition of rough equality of honor between the participants. So you can make a claim on a higher-ranked person by giving him a gift and expose yourself to the danger of a brutal refusal if you have presumed too much (or have your prestige raised if your gamble pays off). At the same time, you dishonor yourself if you initiate a gift to someone too far below you.

What on paper is a set of dictated exchanges under certainty is lived on the ground in suspense and uncertainty. This is partly because of the asymmetrical time of action, but also because of what is involved in actually acting on a rule. A rule doesn't apply itself; it has to be applied, and this may involve difficult, finely tuned judgments. This was the point made by Aristotle and underlay his understanding of the virtue of *phronsis*. Human situations arise in infinite varieties. Determining what a norm actually amounts to in any given situation can take a high degree of insightful understanding. Just being able to formulate rules will not be enough. The person of real practical wisdom is marked out less by the ability to formulate rules than by knowing how to act in each particular situation. There is, as it were, a crucial "phronetic gap" between the formula and its enactment, and this too is neglected by explanations which give primacy to the rule-as-represented.

These two points together yield the uncertainty, the suspense, the possibility of irreversible change that surrounds all significant action, however "rule-guided." I give you a gift in order to raise myself to your level. You pointedly ignore it, and I am crushed. I have irremediably humiliated myself; my status has declined. But this assumes added importance, when we take into account the way in which the rules are transformed through practice. This latter is not the simple putting into effect of unchangeable formulae. The formula as such exists only in the treatise of the anthropologist. In its operation, the rule exists in the practice it "guides." But we have seen that the practice not only fulfills the rule, but also gives it concrete shape in particular situations. Practice is, as it were, a continual "interpretation" and reinterpretation of what the rule really means. If enough of us give a little "above" ourselves and our gesture is reciprocated, we will have altered the generally understood margins of tolerance for this kind of exchange between equals. The relation between rule and practice is like that between *langue* and *parole* for Saussure: the latter is possible only because of the preexistence of the former, but at the same time the acts of *parole* are what keep the *langue* in being. They renew it and at the same time alter it. Their relation is thus reciprocal. *Parole* requires *langue*, but at the same time, in the long run what the *langue* is, is determined by the multiplicity of acts of *parole*.

It is this reciprocity which the intellectualist theory leaves out. In fact, what this reciprocity shows is that the "rule" lies essentially *in* the practice. The rule is what is animating the practice at any given time, not some formulation behind it, inscribed in our thoughts or our brains or our genes or whatever. That is why the rule is, at any given time, what the practice has made it. But this shows how conceiving the rule as an underlying formula can be scientifically disastrous. We miss the entire interplay between action under uncertainty and varying degrees of phronetic insight, on one hand, and the norms and rules which animate this action, on the other. The map gives only half the story; to make it decisive is to distort the whole process.

A rule which exists only in the practices it animates, which does not require and may not have any express formulation – how can this be? Only through our embodied understanding. This is what Bourdieu is trying to get at with his *habitus*. The habitus is a system of "durable, transposable dispositions" (p. 53); that means, dispositions to bodily comportment, say, to act or to hold oneself or to gesture in a certain way. A bodily disposition is a *habitus* when it encodes a certain cultural understanding. The habitus in this sense always has an expressive dimension. It gives expression to certain meanings that things and people have for us, and it is precisely by giving such expression that it makes these meanings exist for us.

Children are inducted into a culture, are taught the meanings which constitute it, partly through inculcation of the appropriate habitus. We learn how to hold ourselves, how to defer to others, how to be a presence for others, all largely through taking on different styles of bodily comportment. Through these modes of deference and presentation, the subtlest nuances of social position, of the sources of prestige, and hence of what is valuable and good are encoded.

Adapting a phrase of Proust's, one might say that arms and legs are full of numb imperatives. One could endlessly enumerate the values given body, *made* body, by the hidden persuasion of an implicit pedagogy which can instill a whole cosmology, through injunctions as insignificant as "sit up straight" or "don't hold your knife in your left hand," and inscribe the most fundamental principles of the arbitrary content of a culture in seemingly innocuous details of bearing or physical and verbal manners, so putting them beyond the reach of consciousness and explicit statement. (p. 79)

This is one way in which rules can exist in our lives, as "values made flesh." Of course, it is not the only way. Some rules *are* formulated. But these are in close interrelation with our *habitus*. The two normally dovetail and complement each other. Bourdieu speaks of habitus and institutions as "two modes of objectification of past history" (p. 57). The latter are generally the locus of express rules or norms. But rules aren't self-interpreting; without a sense of what they're about and an affinity with their spirit, they remain dead letters or become a travesty in practice. This sense and this affinity can only exist where they do in our unformulated, embodied understanding. They are in the domain of the *habitus*, which "is a practical sense which reactivates the sense objectified in institutions" (p. 67).

We return here to the question we started with, the place of rules in human life. We started with the puzzle of how an agent can understand a rule and be guided by it without having even an inkling of a whole host of issues which must (it would appear) be resolved before the rule can "guide" him properly. The intellectualist bent of our philosophical culture made this seem paradoxical. But the answer is to be found in a background understanding which makes these issues irrelevant and so keeps them off our agenda. Rules operate in our lives, as patterns of reasons for action, as against just constituting causal regularities. But express reason-giving has a limit and in the end must repose in another kind of understanding.

What is this understanding? I have been arguing that we should see it as embodied. Bourdieu has explored how this kind of understanding can arise and how it can function in our lives, along with the institutions which define our social existence. So he too recurs to a picture, very much like the one I would like to attribute to Wittgenstein. Express rules can function in our lives only along with an inarticulate sense which is encoded in the body. It is this habitus which "activates" the rules. If Wittgenstein has helped us to break the philosophical thrall of intellectualism, Bourdieu has begun to explore how social science could be remade, once freed from its distorting grip.

Notes

1   References to this book are included parenthetically in the text, by part and paragraph number (e.g. i: 258).

2 This question of how to understand Wittgenstein's argument is discussed at greater length in Fultner 1989.
3 See, e.g. Urban 1986, from which I have drawn much of this analysis.
4 I have tried to argue this in Taylor 1985.
5 Unstipulated page references in the text henceforth are to this work.
6 Bourdieu quotes here from Lévi-Strauss 1987: 47.

References

Fultner, Barbara 1989: Rules in context: a critique of Kripke's interpretation of Wittgenstein. M. A. thesis, McGill University.
Heidegger, Martin 1927: *Sein und Zeit*. Tübingen: Niemeyer.
Kripke, Saul 1972: *Wittgenstein on Rules and Private Language*. Cambridge, Mass.: Harvard University Press.
Lévi-Strauss, Claude 1987: *Introduction to the Work of Marcel Mauss*, trans. F. Baker. London: Routledge & Kegan Paul. (First French edn 1950).
Merleau-Ponty, Maurice 1945: *La Phénoménologie de la perception*. Paris: Gallimard.
Taylor, Charles 1985: Theories of meaning. In *Human Agency and Language*, New York: Cambridge University Press.
Urban, Greg 1986: Ceremonial dialogues in South America. *American Anthropologist*, 88, 371–86.
Wittgenstein, Ludwig 1973: *Philosophical Investigations*, trans. G. E. M. Anscombe. Oxford: Basil Blackwell.

3

Rules, Dispositions, and the *Habitus*

Jacques Bouveresse

I

If there is any common ground between Bourdieu and Wittgenstein, it is probably in their consciousness of the ambiguity of the world "rule", or rather their awareness of the sometimes widely differing senses in which the word "rule" is used. Bourdieu is highly conscious of this, and in *Outline of a Theory of Practice* (Cambridge: Cambridge University Press, 1977) he quotes the passage from *Philosophical Investigations* where Wittgenstein asks in what sense one may talk of the "rule by which someone proceeds", and whether it is possible to talk of such a thing at all when a word is used:

What do I call "the rule by which he proceeds?" – The hypothesis that satisfactorily describes his use of words, which we observe; or the rule which he looks up when he uses signs; or the one which he gives us in reply when we ask him what his rule is? – But what if observation does not enable us to see any clear rule, and the question brings none to light? – For he did indeed give me a definition when I asked him what he understood by "N", but he was prepared to withdraw and alter it. – So how am I to determine the rule according to which he is playing? He does not know it himself. – Or to ask a better question: What meaning is the expression "the rule by which he proceeds" supposed to have left to it here?[1]

There are, it would appear, at least two levels which should be clearly distinguished in the Wittgensteinian attack on what we might term the "mythology of rules". The above passage comes in the context of a critique of the idea of language as calculus, an idea still attractive to Wittgenstein at the time of the *Tractatus*, which he defined as the supposition that when "anyone utters a sentence and *means* or *understands* it he is operating a calculus according to definite rules" (ibid., § 81). Wittgenstein remarks that it is simply not true to say that in the use of a word like "chair", for example, "we are equipped with rules for every possible application of it" (ibid., § 80); but that obviously does not mean that we do not as a result attach any meaning to it. The use of a word can be quite regular without "being everywhere bounded by rules" (ibid., § 84).

But Wittgenstein is equally critical of what might be termed a mechanistic conception of what happens in cases where we do actually refer to a sort of calculus that follows a set of rules quite strictly. When we apply rules that are perfectly explicit and unambivalent, like the rules that we apply in mathematics, it seems that an understanding of the rule has somehow been fixed forever in advance regarding what is to be done in each one of the possible cases that may occur. In order to dispute these ideas, Wittgenstein uses the metaphor of parallel rails that have been laid down for an infinite distance, and along which any application will naturally glide. Now the rails can only be of some use if the experience of understanding can provide us with a non-ambiguous representation of the invisible part which goes beyond the envisaged examples, and so on until infinity. And this is precisely where the problem lies. If it is not possible to consider that all possible transitions have already been somehow instantaneously carried out in the act of comprehension, then it would appear that one is obliged to rely on intuition, or the impression of a single moment, to determine each time the way in which the rails proceed, and hence the manner in which one should carry on in order to apply the rule correctly. What one would like to understand is the manner in which comprehension could provide for the user of the rule the certainty (which would be justified most of the time and subsequently confirmed by the manner in which he correctly applies the rule) that he is at present, and will remain in all circumstances, on the right track regarding correct use. Even if the use of a word obeyed quite strict rules, there would still remain the question resulting from what could be called Wittgenstein's "paradox", but that perhaps should be more correctly attributed to Kripke.[2]

For obvious reasons, Bourdieu is particularly sensitive to the confusion that often reigns (notably among sociologists) between two very different uses of the word "rule": rule as an explanatory hypothesis formulated by the theorist in order to explain what he sees, and rule as the principle which really governs the practice of the agents concerned. It is this confusion which leads to "giving as the source of agents' practice the theory that [has] to be constructed in order to explain it".[3] It is mainly on account of this almost inevitable confusion that Bourdieu usually prefers to express his ideas in terms of strategies, *habitus* or dispositions, rather than in terms of rules. In *Choses dites*, he explains that one should not mistake the existence of some sort of regularity for the presence of a rule:

> The social game is regulated, it is the locus of certain regularities. Things happen in regular fashion in it: rich heirs regularly marry rich younger daughters. That does not meant that it is a rule saying that rich heirs must marry rich younger daughters, even if you may think that marrying an heiress (even a rich one, and *a fortiori* a poor younger daughter) is an error, or even in the parents' eyes for example, a misdeed. I can say that all my thinking started from this point: how can behaviour be regulated without being the product of obedience to set rules? ... In order to construct a model of the game, which will not be the mere recording of explicit norms, nor a statement of regularities, while synthesising both norms and regularities, one has to reflect on the different modes of existence of the principles of regulation and the regularity of different forms of practice; there is of course the habitus, that regulated disposition to generate regulated and regular behaviour outside any reference rules; and in societies where the work of codification is not particularly advanced, the habitus is the principle of most modes of practice.[4]

Leibniz thought that one has a *habitus* for a thing when the thing is normally done because of a disposition found in the agent: "*Habitus est ad id quod solet fieri ex agentis dispositione*", he says, and defines the *spontaneous* as that for which the principle is to be found in the agent: "*Spontaneum est, cum principium agentis in agente*".[5] What freedom, or free will, adds to spontaneity is the idea of a decision based on a process of deliberation. Free will can be defined as "spontaneity coupled with deliberation" (*libertas spontaneitas consultantis*), or again as rational, intelligent spontaneity. Animals have spontaneity, but lacking reason, they are not capable of actions that are truly free. The fact that the behavior of an agent is the product of a *habitus* is obviously not a threat to the spontaneity of his action, as the action is not the result of an external constraint, but of a disposition whose seat is in the agent himself. But insofar as the exercise of free will includes deliberation, a good part of our actions, and in particular those which are the result of a habitus, are simply spontaneous and not strictly speaking free. But neither can it be said that they are truly constrained. On this point, it may be remarked that the reason why determinisms like those described by sociology all too easily give us the impression that they constitute a threat not simply to the freedom but also to the spontaneity of individual actions does not come from the regularity which they produce in the behavior of agents, however strict it may be. It comes rather from the fact that today, largely as a result of the progress of scientific knowledge in general and of the social sciences in particular, we experience a much greater difficulty than either Aristotle or Leibniz in attempting to draw a distinction between actions that have their principle "in" an agent and those which have their principle "outside" him, and which may take place not only without him but even against him. We can normally distinguish quite unproblematically between actions that deserve to be termed "free" and those that are "constrained". But the philosophical problem of free will soon crops up, with the idea of the unsuspected constraint and the invisible prison. If we are more or less terrified of the idea that we might not be free, it is because we have a certain idea of the appalling fate that would be our own if we were not free. As Dennett remarks, literature on this point provides us with a multitude of analogies each more worrying than the last: "not having free will would be somewhat like being in prison, or being hypnotised, or being paralysed, or being a puppet, or... (the list continues)."[6]

Dennett believes that such analogies are not simple illustrations, but that they are in a certain manner at the origin and at the foundation of the philosophical problem itself:

Are you sure you're not in some sort of prison? Here one is invited to consider a chain of transformations, taking us from the obvious prisons to unobvious (but still dreadful) prisons, to utterly invisible and undetectable (but still dreadful?) prisons. Consider a deer in Magdalene College park. Is it imprisoned? Yes, but not much. The enclosure is quite large. Suppose we moved the deer to a larger enclosure – the New Forest with a fence around it. Would the deer still be imprisoned? In the State of Maine, I am told, deer almost never travel more than five miles from their birthplace during their lives. If an enclosure were located outside the normal unimpeded limits of a deer's lifetime wanderings would the deer enclosed be imprisoned? Perhaps, but note that it makes a difference to our intuitions whether *someone* installs the enclosure. Do you feel imprisoned on Planet Earth – the way Napoleon was stuck on Elba? It is one thing to be born and live on Elba, and another to be put and kept on Elba *by someone*. A jail without a jailer is not a jail. Whether or not it is an undesirable abode depends on other features; it depends on just how (if at all) it cramps the style of its inhabitants. (Ibid., pp. 7–8)

These considerations alone serve to explain why theories which invoke social mechanisms and determinisms in order to explain our apparently most personal and free actions are often understood as being equivalent to a pure and simple negation of the realities that we call freedom and the personality. What is irksome, or even unbearable, is not the idea that our freedom of action operates within limits that are perhaps not those that we had imagined (although they might be more or less what they have to be in order for us to be able to consider ourselves what we are already, i.e. free). What irks is the idea that we might be, even in the actions which we think of as the most free, totally manipulated by invisible agents, who, as Dennett says, "vie with us for control of our bodies [or worse still our souls], who compete against us, who have interests antithetical to or at least independent of our own" (ibid., p. 7). We take it for granted, for example, that the sort of liberty that we need, and the only sort worth having, is the sort of freedom that implies that "we could just as have easily have done something else instead". But as Dennett remarks, it is precisely this supposition itself, and not the description one might attempt to give of the conditions necessary and sufficient for us to effectively have this sort of power, which demands to be examined seriously. Leibniz, for his part, saw no contradiction in the fact that an action might be completely determined (which for him was not the same as being necessary) and at the same time perfectly free.

II

In the social game, a certain number of regular patterns of behavior are the direct result of a will to conform to codified, recognized rules. In this case the regularity is the product of the rule, and obedience to the rule is an intentional act, which implies knowledge and comprehension of what the rule says in the case in question. At another extreme, one can find regularities which are explicable in a purely causal fashion with the help of underlying mechanisms, in a manner that does not seem very distant from the explanation that one normally gives of the regular behaviour of natural objects. In the human sciences as in the natural sciences, we also have a tendency to assume that wherever characteristic regularities exist, these must be due to the action of mechanisms which, if only we understood them, would allow us to explain the results. But there are equally a number of socially regular actions – possibly even the majority of behaviour patterns – which do not appear to be explicable in a satisfactory manner either by the invocation of the rules on which agents intentionally base their behaviour or in terms of brute causality. It is at this intermediary level that, for Bourdieu, the crucial notion of the *habitus* intervenes.

It should be noted in passing that if Wittgenstein is systematically critical of the tendency to conceive of the action of a rule as acting in the same fashion as that of a causal law, as though the rule acted in some way like a motor force which compelled the user to move in a certain direction. He strongly rejects the equally mythical view which consists of thinking of the laws of nature as though they were somehow the rules to which natural phenomena are obliged to conform. In a lecture recently published on free will and determinism, he underlines that a law is an expression of regularity, but it is not the cause of the existence of that regularity, which it would be if one could say that objects were constrained by the law itself to act in the way that they do. Wittgenstein concludes from this that even if human decisions presented the sort of regularity which could be expressed in the form of laws, one would be no further on in understanding how that would prevent them from being free:

There is no reason why, even if there was regularity in human decisions, I should not be free. There is nothing about regularity which makes anything free or not free. The notion of compulsion is there if you think about the regularity as compelled; as if produced by rails; if, besides the notion of regularity, you bring in the notion of: "It must move like this because the rails are laid like this."[7]

Wittgenstein maintains that the use we make of expressions like "free", "responsible", "unable to avoid" etc., "are completely independent of the question of knowing whether such things as the laws of nature exist or not". To his mind, they are also equally independent of the question of knowing if there are for example such things as laws of psychology or sociology. Consequently, the characteristic regularities that sociology and the human sciences generally succeed in demonstrating in the behavior of individual agents could not alone constitute a reason to deny that their actions are still both free and responsible. Suppose I know everything (more than physicists, biologists, psychologists, sociologists, etc.), and that this means I have the ability to calculate with certainty what someone will do at a given moment, for instance that he will steal something. Does that necessarily mean that I should no longer consider him to be responsible? "Why should I say that this makes him more analogous to machinery – except insofar as I mean that I can forecast better?" (ibid., p. 92).

Bourdieu resorts to the notion of the *habitus* in order to try and find a middle way between the objectivism with which he reproaches structuralists like Lévi-Strauss and the spontaneity that "philosophies of the subject" try to oppose to structuralism. Structuralists think of the social world "as a space of objective relations that transcends the agents and is irreducible to the interaction between individuals" (*Choses dites*, p. 18) (IOW 8). Bourdieu's intention is to re-introduce the agents that structuralism reduces to the status of "mere epiphenomena of structure" (ibid., p. 19) (IOW 9). But such agents are not conceived as the subjects of the humanist tradition, who are supposed to act only as a function of intentions that they are aware of and control, and not as a result of determining causes of which they are unaware and over which they have no influence at all. This is another point of close comparison with Wittgenstein, who is equally adamant that the solution is not simply a choice between the traditional philosophical notion of a speaking, acting subject and, on the other hand, the idea of autonomous, impersonal strategies that somehow constitute the ultimate producers of statements and actions which so-called subjects naively believe to be of their own making. These two conceptions are equally mythical, but there is, in reality, a third possible way.

For Bourdieu, one of the major disadvantages of the notion of the rule is that it allows for the masking of essential oppositions, as it can be applied with equal precision to things that are extremely different. An example he cites refers to differences between his own position and that of Lévi-Strauss:

In fact, it seems to me that the contradiction is disguised by the ambiguity of the word "rule", which enables one to spirit away the very problem that I tried to raise: it's impossible to tell exactly whether what is understood by rule is a principle of the juridical or quasi-juridical kind, more or less consciously produced and mastered by agents, or a set of objective regularities imposed on all those who join a game. When people talk of a rule of the game, it's one or other of these two meanings that they have in mind. But they may also be thinking of a third meaning, that of the model or principle constructed by the scientist to explain the game. I think that if you blur these distinctions, you risk committing one of the most disastrous errors that can be made in the human sciences, that which consists of passing off, in Marx's well-known phrase, "the things of logic as the logic of things" [Wittgenstein would term this the danger of taking as a predicate something that is merely a mode of representation]. To avoid this, you have to include in the theory the real principle behind strategies, namely the practical sense, or, if you prefer, what sports players call a feel for the game (*le sens du jeu*), as the practical mastery of the logic or of the immanent necessity of the game – a mastery acquired through experience of the game, and one which works outside conscious control and discourse (in the way that, for instance, techniques of the body do). Notions like that of habitus (or a system of dispositions), practical sense, and strategy, are linked to my effort to escape from structuralist objectivism without relapsing into subjectivism. (ibid., pp. 76–7) (IOW 60–1)

As Wittgenstein often remarked, the learning of a game can quite easily involve the explicit formulation and acquisition of the rules which govern it. But one can equally acquire the sort of regular behavior equivalent to a practical mastery of the game without the explicit statement of the rules ever intervening in the process at all. I might know how to correctly continue series of numbers because the necessary algebraic formula (perhaps I should say "a relevant formula") pops into my head. But I can also be sure that I know how to continue it correctly and do it effectively without any particular rule ever entering my mind, i.e. by only making use of the examples that I have been given. The case of learning a language obviously tends more towards the second type of example here. There is also the situation of the external observer who is trying to understand the game, and in order to do this, is formulating hypotheses about the rules that players might and perhaps do follow; i.e. he is trying to formulate a system of rules, tacit or explicit knowledge of which would constitute a sufficient (but perhaps not necessary) condition for the production of the characteristic regularities in the behavior of the players of the game.

In most cases, what Bourdieu terms "practical sense" (*le sens pratique*) or the feel for the game (*le sens du jeu*) is in fact something that is added on later to a "theoretical" knowledge of the rules, if in fact there are any, and can only be acquired by the practice of the game. An irreducibly practical knowledge can only be obtained by practice, and can only be expressed in practice. But in the case of the social game, where regularity without rules is very much (so to speak) the rule rather than the exception, it is tempting to tell oneself that it is perhaps vain to try and go beyond notions like that of a practical sense or feel for the game in search of something like a system of rules of the game. There is no proof that all practical knowledge can be reconstructed in the form of an implicit knowledge of a corresponding theory. Putnam and others are of the opinion that certain practical aptitudes, like for example an aptitude for speaking a language, might simply be too complex for one to even consider reconstructing them in such fashion. In such examples, a description of the practical knowledge that makes possible the practice in question risks being in the final analysis not very different from an appropriate description of the practice itself.

The theoretical services that Bourdieu demands of the *habitus* and its related notions are evidently quite considerable. *Habitus* is the thing that explains how "types of behaviour can be directed towards certain ends without being consciously directed to these ends, or determined by them" (ibid., p. 20) (IOW 9–10). "The habitus," he notes elsewhere, "entertains with the social world that has produced it a real ontological complicity, the source of cognition without consciousness, intentionality without intention, and a practical mastery of the world's regularities which allows one to anticipate the future, without even needing to posit it as such" (ibid., p. 22) (IOW 11–12).

It is a cause of regret to Bourdieu that "the very alternatives that the notion of habitus attempts to bypass, those of the conscious and the unconscious, or explanation by determining causes or final causes" (ibid., p. 20) are applied to his analyses. The notion of the habitus allows one to explain how the subject of practice can be determined and yet be acting too. As the *habitus* is not necessarily of a mental nature (there are forms of *habitus* which are simply corporeal), it is independent of any distinction between the conscious or unconscious, and it is no less independent of distinctions like that between the product of a simple causal constraint and an action that is "free", in that it escapes any constraints of this nature. On this point, Bourdieu is particularly insistent on the "creative" aspect of practices directed by a *habitus*:

I wanted to react against the mechanistic tendencies of Saussure (who, as I showed in *Le Sens pratique*,[8] thinks of practice as simple execution) and those of structuralism. In that respect I was quite close to Chomsky, in whom I found the same concern to give to practice an active, inventive intention (he has appeared to certain defenders of personalism as a bulwark of liberty against structuralist determinism): I wanted to stress the generative capacities of dispositions, it being understood that these are acquired, socially constituted dispositions. It is easy to see how absurd is the cataloguing which leads people to subsume under structuralism, which destroys the subject, a body of work which has been guided by the desire to reintroduce the agent's practice, his or her capacity for invention and improvisation. I should recall that this active, creative, inventive capacity is not that of the transcendental subject of the idealist tradition, but that of an acting agent. (Ibid., p. 23) (IOW 13)

Bourdieu has expressed the same sentiments elsewhere, sometimes going so far as to say that in very complex games like matrimonial exchanges or ritual practices, a system of dispositions intervenes that one can think of by analogy with Chomsky's generative grammar, "with this difference: I am talking about dispositions which are *acquired through experience*, thus variable according from place to place and time to time. This 'feel for the game' (*sens du jeu*) as we call it is what enables an infinite number of moves to be made, adapted to the infinite number of possible situations which no rule, however complex, can foresee. And so, I replaced the rules of kinship with matrimonial strategies" (ibid., p. 19) (IOW 9).

Reference to Chomsky in this sort of context is at first view somewhat surprising, above all because Chomsky is a typical representative of the idea of language as calculus, whose model is normally attributed to Frege, a model to which Wittgenstein gave some critical attention before he abandoned it altogether. In itself, the capacity to generate an infinite number of grammatically correct phrases and assign semantic interpretations to them by means of purely formal rules involves nothing which would intrinsically surpass the possibilities of a mechanism.

Moreover, as Katz and Fodor have insisted, the question of knowing which particular semantic interpretation is to be assigned to a sentence is one that must be decidable by means of formal calculus, without there being any need for recourse to any linguistic intuition: "The need to have a formal semantic theory derives from the necessity of avoiding vacuity; for a semantic theory is vacuous to the extent that the speaker's intuitions or insights about semantic relations are essentially relied on in order that the rules of the theory apply correctly."[9] Whether it is a question of the semantic aspect or the syntactic aspect of competence, in both cases the rules in question must be formally represented and their operations entirely mechanical. Nothing in Chomsky's conception of the nature of linguistic competence implies that its possessor should be either a conscious being or a person. The question to be asked is rather what must be the nature of the abstract automation that could render some physical system capable of constructing and interpreting (as we humans do) a potentially unlimited number of sentences in a natural language.

Creativity, properly speaking, as distinct from the formal generativity which results from the simple recursiveness of the rules, is situated somewhere quite different, at the level of what Chomsky calls "the creativity of usage", i.e. the capacity to use in a pertinent manner an infinity of different sentences, which for the most part are new, in situations which are themselves new. It is only at this sort of level that ideas like Bourdieu's feel for the game or the intuitions of a practical sense actually come into play. But generative linguistics has nothing to say about this sort of thing, for the simple reason that it is a theory of competence, not a theory of usage; or perhaps more precisely because the aspect of competence (if we can still speak of competence) involved in a knowledge or practical sense that cannot be explained in terms of rules does not concern generative linguistics at all. If, as Bourdieu says, some people have claimed to find in Chomsky arguments in favor of a personalist conception of the creative subject, it is only through a fundamental misunderstanding which Chomsky himself systematically perpetuated.

Neither should it be imagined that the rules of Chomskyan linguistics are closer than the theoretical models of the structuralists to what

Bourdieu terms "the principle of agents' practice", as opposed to a theory constructed to take account of that practice. Their status is that of explanatory hypotheses and essentially remains so, even if one speaks of them as rules that speakers are supposed to know and tacitly apply. Wittgenstein scholars like Baker and Hacker have suggested that Wittgenstein had discredited in advance Chomsky-like enterprises and more generally any attempt to construct a systematic theory of meaning along the lines of Frege's model of language as calculus, principally by pointing out that it is difficult to imagine how rules which we do not know, and about which we are forced (like linguists attempting to explain our behavior) to formulate hypotheses, could possibly exert a normative function: "There is no normative behaviour as long as the norms await discovery."[10]

I think that Baker and Hacker go too far on this point, if only for the reason that while Wittgenstein insists on important differences which tend to be passed over, he rarely rules out anything categorically, be it a notion like that of "tacit rule", "unconscious rule" or any other. It is perhaps quite likely that it may be impossible to use such notions in a coherent manner. But what matters most to Wittgenstein is only the question of knowing what one is doing when one uses a particular word or expression, i.e. in this particular case not forgetting that a rule that one knows and which is regularly used in the game cannot simply be opposed to a rule invoked as an explanatory hypothesis, "in the manner that the expression 'a chair which I see' is opposed to the expression 'a chair which I don't see because it's behind me'".[11]

Notions which Bourdieu attempts to restore to their rightful place, like those of innovation, invention, improvisation, etc., come into play in two quite different ways in the practice of obedience to a rule. Invention may be necessary, if the relevant rule has left a reasonably large margin of indeterminacy, or because the application of the rule in a particular case may raise a problem of interpretation which one cannot hope to resolve by invoking a supplementary rule to cover the correct fashion in which the rule is to be interpreted. Most of the rules that we use are of this type, and require for their application a certain measure of judgement or discernment. In many cases, knowing how to apply a rule correctly means, amongst other things, having the ability to interpret it in the light of certain circumstances, and even in certain cases knowing how to ignore it or break it intelligently. Musil's remark about moral rules springs to mind here, where he compares them to a sieve, where the holes are at least as important as the solid part. Certain rules give the impression of acting in the manner of a mechanism, because they determine their application in a way that leaves no room for any sort of initiative. Others limit the user's freedom to maneuver in a significant fashion, but do not determine irrevocably the movement that is to be carried out at each stage of the process. In terms of the metaphor that Wittgenstein uses, one might say that if the first type resembles rails, the second type merely determines the general direction, and not the exact path to be travelled.

In a quite general way, Wittgenstein constantly disputes the idea that rules, even of the first type, act in the manner of a causal constraint. He notes for example that we should regard demonstration not as a process which constrains us, but rather as a process that directs us (*führt*). This, amongst other things, is a manner of saying that a rule guides action, but that it does not produce it in the same way that a force produces an effect. A rule applies to a series of actions; and actions, regardless of whether they are subject to rules or not, belong to a quite different realm, and are governed by a logic which is not that of natural events.

If one follows the skeptical paradox that Wittgenstein is supposed to have formulated regarding the idea of "following a rule", one is tempted to conclude that no rule, no matter how explicit and unambivalent, can ever really determine its own application. The paradox seems to imply that regardless of which way one chooses to apply a rule at a given moment, this can be made compatible with the way in which the rule has been understood and thus far applied. The series of past applications is apparently quite incapable of imposing any restrictions on future applications, which means that at each stage of the application of a rule, an act of creativity or invention is necessary in a more or less literal sense, in order to determine what is to be done. Contrary to what certain interpreters believe, this paradox is by no means a fair representation of Wittgenstein's position. The author of *Philosophical Investigations* constantly attempts to find a middle way between the Scylla of an objectivist (i.e. Platonic) conception of the meaning of a rule, which would contain within it all possible applications, without there being any need for the user of the rule to make any contribution, and the Charybdis of creative anarchy, where everything, by contrast, is to be found in the contribution that the user makes each time.

McDowell speaks in this context of a sort of naturalized Platonism, which is to be substituted for what he terms "rampant Platonism". Wittgenstein does not reject the idea (which might well be termed Platonic) that the meaning of a rule does indeed contain in some fashion the totality of future applications of the rule, but he attempts to eliminate the mysterious, worrying elements that rampant

Platonism adds to this, which suggest that meaning can only execute this tour de force by virtue of powers which are quite unnatural and should rightly be termed magical.[12]

What one terms "doing the same thing as before" or "correctly applying the rule" does not in fact have a prior determination, independently of any regular practice of application, and has no meaning outside of this sort of practice. As Wittgenstein himself says, it is a mistake to assume that a rule by itself leads somewhere, regardless of whether people follow it or not. And it is also a mistake to assume that the rule itself can select one single possibility in an abstract space which is not structured and limited in advance by the propensities, aptitudes and reactions which constitute the links between the subject and the human world, or the universe of human practices in general.

The concept of "doing the same thing" is not pre-constituted in a Platonic world of meanings, but constituted in a practice. It is in consequence well and truly determined, even if it does not appear to be such from the point of view which is completely exterior to practice adopted by the "bad" Platonic position. If it were the case that we needed both the rule and a particular intuition in order to determine what the rule commanded us to do each time we wished to apply it, that would imply that the rule was itself impotent and inoperative, and ultimately quite useless. Wittgenstein, at times, is quite scathing about those intuitionists who believe, or seem to believe, that we need a certain intuition to know that we must write 3 after 2 in the series of natural numbers. Instead of saying that intuition is necessary at each stage of the intuition of the rule, we would be better off, he concludes, to speak of a *decision*. But he immediately adds that this would be equally deceptive, as it is quite obvious that we actually decide nothing at all. In the normal case, the correct application is no more a result of a choice between several possibilities than it is an intuition of a single, unique possibility. But to speak of a decision is the lesser of two evils, as it cuts short any temptation to search for a justification or a reason where there is none.

Wittgenstein therefore is not pleading for a decisionist conception of application, but rather attempting to discredit an intellectualist conception of the action of a rule, in virtue of which application results each time from an act of special knowledge. The idea of a decision intervenes to displace the problem from the domain of knowledge to the domain of action. The important point is that the normal consequence of the process of learning the rule is that at a certain stage of application we unhesitatingly do something for which we have no particular reason, outside of the rule itself. It is not true to say that acting in accordance with a rule always means acting according to a certain interpretation of the rule. And the consensus in application that can be detected between users is not a consensus of interpretations or intuitions, but quite simply one of actions.

Sociologists could understandably be troubled by the extremely wide usage that Wittgenstein gives to terms like those of "rule" or "convention". Although he is particularly concerned with the distinction that must be drawn between a rule that really enters into the action of a game and a rule that simply explains the action to an external observer, the rules to which Wittgenstein refers are obviously not always explicit rules, nor even the rules which players might admit to playing by when confronted with them. Wittgenstein is quite clear that the propositions which express what he calls "grammatical rules" are generally unformulated, and only rarely form part of a learning process. We absorb them along with everything else, without realising what we are doing, when we learn the language. To say that someone uses a word in a manner that conforms to a certain convention quite obviously does not imply that this convention ever really took place. In his lectures from 1932 to 1935, Wittgenstein has the following to say on the matter:

The question has been raised as to what a convention is. It is one of two things, a rule or a training. A convention is established by saying something in words, for example, "Whenever I clap once please go to the door, and if twice, please go away from the door"; . . . By a convention I mean that the use of a sign is in accordance with language habits or training. There can be a chain of conventions at the bottom of which is a language habit or training to react in certain ways. These latter we do not usually call conventions but rather those which are given by signs. One can say these signs play the role they do because of certain habitual ways of acting.[13]

There are therefore cases in which convention is the first and the linguistic *habitus* the second, and other cases, probably more numerous, where convention is only a manner of designating the linguistic *habitus* itself.

III

Bourdieu characterizes the *habitus*, in the sense in which he uses the word, as being "the product of the incorporation of objective necessity":

Since the habitus, the virtue made of necessity, produces strategies which, even if they are not produced by consciously aiming at explicitly formulated goals on the basis of adequate knowledge of objective conditions, nor by the mechanical determination exercised by causes, turn out to be objectively adjusted to the situation. Action guided by a "feel for the game" has all the appearances of the rational action that an impartial observer, endowed with all the necessary information capable of mastering it rationally, would deduce. And yet it is not based on reason. You need only think of the impulsive decision made by the tennis player who runs up to the net, to understand that it has nothing in common with the learned construction that the coach, after analysis, draws up in order to explain it and deduce communicable lessons from it. (*Choses dites*, p. 21) (IOW 11)

"The game," he adds elsewhere, "is the locus of an immanent necessity, which is at the same time an immanent logic . . . and the feel for the game, which contributes to this necessity and this logic, is a way of knowing this necessity and this logic." (ibid., p. 81) (IOW 64).

But it is quite unlikely that the sense in which the *habitus* that Bourdieu refers to here constitutes the incorporation of an objective necessity can be applied directly to the linguistic *habitus* itself. What are generally termed the rules of the social game are, in Bourdieu's view, very close to what the *habitus* or social strategies actually are. As he remarks (quite rightly, in my opinion), "in the social sciences, talking in terms of rules is often a way of hiding your own ignorance" (ibid., p. 90) (IOW 72). But in the case of language, the rules are apparently one thing, and the strategies and *habitus* where the necessities of linguistic interaction are incarnated are another thing altogether. For Wittgenstein, there is no way in which one could say of the rules of grammar, in the manner in which he understands the word, that they constitute the product of the incorporation of any sort of objective necessity. The idea of the autonomy of grammar means precisely that the rules, or if one prefers the linguistic *habitus* that corresponds to them, do not record any pre-existent necessity, but are themselves at the origin of necessity, at least insofar as what he terms "logical" or "grammatical" necessities are concerned.

Obviously this is not the place to tackle the problem of the degree of independence that the sociologist would accord to this type of necessity; for obvious reasons, the sort of necessity which is of interest to him must above all be the expression of eminently factual constraints of a social nature. It is more interesting to ask oneself instead exactly what Bourdieu really hopes to explain with the notion of the *habitus*. In the passage quoted above, he tells us that the *habitus* has the capacity to engender modes of behavior, which, while learnt, have all the characteristics of instinctive behavior. Moreover, though these modes of behavior apparently imply no form of reflection or calculation, they produce results which coincide remarkably, in a great number of cases, with what one would obtain by rational calculation. It is a fact that an appropriate training is apt to develop a series of automatic mechanisms in any normal subject, and these, so far as the result is concerned, have all the appearance of reflective, intelligent action, and dictate "the right thing to do" in cases where reflective intelligent action is quite impossible. But it is not clear that Bourdieu is adding something important to the simple recording of this fact when he speaks of "the intuitions of a 'logic of practice' which is the product of a lasting exposure to conditions similar to those in which agents find themselves" (ibid., p. 21) (IOW 11). As Wittgenstein remarks (and he finds it quite surprising), we have an almost irresistible propensity to believe that whenever someone acquires a habit or a new regular mode of behavior, a significant modification must have taken place in his mind or in his brain. And we think that the real explanation for this can only be given by a hypothetical state, a mental or cerebral mechanism that we will perhaps one day discover. It is quite possible that on this point we are perhaps rather like Lord Kelvin, who declared himself unable to understand a phenomenon until he had built a mechanical model of it.

Bourdieu is quite insistent on the predictive power of the habitus. It can, he tells us, "act as the basis of a forecast, (the specialized equivalent of the practical anticipations of ordinary experience)" (ibid., p. 96) (IOW 77), despite the fact that "it is not based on any rule or explicit law". Wittgenstein says of the word "understand", which serves at once to designate a mental event that happens at the time of hearing or uttering of the word, and something quite different, more like an aptitude or capacity: "The use of the word . . . is based on the fact that in an enormous majority of cases when we have applied certain tests, we are able to predict that a man will use the word in question in certain ways. If this were not the case, there would be no point in our using the word 'understand' at all."[14] But of course Wittgenstein does not pretend to explain this, and I doubt whether there actually exists, at present, a satisfactory means of explaining how a learning process can result in the sort of consequences, quite obviously well beyond the tiny number of examples and situations that have been explicitly envisaged, which we characterize as falling into the category of behavior we term "understanding".

We might well suspect that explanations in terms of "dispositions" or "habitus", when these terms are not characterized independently of the simple description of the sort of regular behaviour which they purport to give rise to, are purely linguistic. As Quine remarks, a dispositional explanation resembles the recognition of debt that one hopes to be able to pay off one day, by producing (like a chemist does when he comes up with a dispositional predicate like "soluble in water") a description of a corresponding structural property. But it is equally clear that the legitimacy of the use of a dispositional term cannot be subordinated in all cases to the hope or promise of some sort of reduction along these lines, and that a particular disposition might be irreducible without this necessarily having any implications for any other disposition. The debt might be unpayable only in this particular case, and the comparison with other dispositions like "soluble in water" might not hold any water at all.

In one of the rare lengthy developments of the idea of disposition to be found in his work, Wittgenstein writes:

A disposition is thought of as something always there from which behaviour follows. It is analogous to the structure of a machine and its behaviour. There are three different statements which seem to give the meaning of "A loves B": (1) a non-dispositional statement about a conscious state, i.e., feelings, (2) a statement that under certain conditions A will behave in such and such a way, (3) a dispositional statement that if some process is going on in his mind it will have the consequences that he will behave in such and such a way. This parallels the description of an idea, which stands either for a mental state, a set of reactions, or a state of a mechanism which has as its consequences both the behaviour and certain feelings. We seem to have distinguished here three meanings for "A loves B", but this is not the case. (1), to the effect that A loves B when he has certain feelings, and (2), that he loves him when he behaves in such and such a way, both give meanings of the word "love". But the dispositional statement (3), referring to a mechanism, is not genuine. It gives no new meaning. Dispositional statements are always at bottom statements about a mechanism, and have the grammar of statements about a mechanism. Language uses the analogy of a machine, which constantly misleads us. In an enormous number of cases our words have the form of dispositional statements referring to a mechanism whether there is a mechanism or not. In the example about love, nobody has the slightest idea what sort of mechanism is being referred to. The dispositional statement does not tell us anything about the nature of love; it is only a way we describe it. Of the three meanings the dispositional one is the only one that is not genuine. It is actually a statement about the grammar of the word "love".[15]

One important point about the grammar of the word "understanding" is precisely that it too is of a dispositional form, and implies in a deceptive fashion an almost inevitable reference to some underlying machinery: "But the statement 'he understands' is of the dispositional form. Although it does not refer to machinery as it seems to, what is behind the grammar of that statement is the picture of a mechanism set to react in different ways. We think that if only we saw the machinery we should know what understanding is" (ibid., p. 92).

One of the reasons Bourdieu distrusts the idea of the underlying mechanism is precisely because the behavior that it seems to explain does not have the sort of strict regularity that a mechanism would produce: "the modes of behaviour created by the *habitus* do not have the fine regularity of modes of behavior deduced from a legislative principle: the *habitus* goes hand in glove with vagueness and indeterminacy. As a generative spontaneity which asserts itself with an improvised confrontation with ever renewed situations, it obeys a practical, inexact, fuzzy sort of logic, which defines one's normal relation to the world" (*Choses dites*, p. 96) (IOW 77–8, translation altered). The notion of the *habitus*, or any other notion of a similar sort, seems effectively indispensable for a satisfactory account of regularities of a certain type: regularities which have as part of their essence a certain amount of variability, plasticity, indetermination, and imply all sorts of adaptations, innovations and exceptions of many different varieties, the sort of regularity in short which characterizes the domain of the practical, of practical reason and the logic of practice.

But the difficulty, as Wittgenstein points out, is that we have a tendency to look for a mechanism where there is none, and to believe that an adequate explanation can only be found at that level. What seems obvious in the case of the word "understanding" should equally apply to the majority of terms we employ to designate the various psychological or social forms of *habitus*: We should resist the temptation to continue looking for a mechanical explanation for something which plainly is not mechanical in nature. A good part of the resistance to Bourdieu's ideas comes not, as one would instinctively believe, from hostility to the mechanism, but on the contrary, from that tendency to believe that we would understand society better if only we could really find a way of seeing the social machinery in action.

Notes

1   Ludwig Wittgenstein, *Philosophical Investigations*, trans. G. E. M. Anscombe (Oxford: Basil Blackwell, 1958), § 82.
2   See S. A. Kripke, *Wittgenstein on Rules and Private Language* (Oxford: Blackwell, 1982).
3   P. Bourdieu, *Choses dites* (Paris: Minuit, 1987) p. 76. English translation by Matthew Adamson, *In Other Words: Essays towards a Reflexive Sociology* (Cambridge: Polity Press, 1990), p. 60.
4   Ibid., pp. 81–2 (IOW 64–5).

5 cf. *Opuscules et Fragments inédits*, published by L. Couturat, Georg Olms, Hildesheim, 1966, p. 474.
6 Daniel C. Dennett, *Elbow Room. The Varieties of Free Will Worth Wanting* (Oxford: Clarendon Press, 1984), p. 5.
7 "Lecture on Freedom of the Will", *Philosophical Investigations*, vol. 12, no. 2 (April 1989), p. 87.
8 Translated as *The Logic of Practice* (trans. R. Nice) (Cambridge, 1989).
9 Jerrold J. Katz and Jerry A. Fodor, "The Structure of a Semantic Theory", in J. A. Fodor and J. J. Katz, *The Structure of Language, Readings in the Philosophy of Language* (Englewood Cliffs, New Jersey: Prentice-Hall Inc., 1964), p. 501.
10 G. P. Baker and P. M. S. Hacker, *Language, Sense and Nonsense, A Critical Investigation into Modern Theories of Language* (Oxford: Basil Blackwell, 1984), p. 313.
11 Ludwig Wittgenstein, *Philosophical Grammar*, ed. Rush Rheesm, trans. Anthony Kenny (Oxford: Blackwell, 1974), p. 49.
12 See John McDowell, *Mind and World* (Cambridge, Harvard University Press, Mass., London, England, 1994), pp. 176–7.
13 *Wittgenstein's Lectures, Cambridge, 1932–35* (Oxford: Basil Blackwell, 1979) pp. 89–90.
14 *Wittgenstein's Lectures on the Foundations of Mathematics, Cambridge, 1939*. From the notes of R. G. Bosanquet, Norman Malcolm, Rush Rhees, and Yorick Smithies, ed. Cora Diamond (Hassocks, Sussex: Harvester Press, 1976), p. 23. See also *Wittgenstein's Lectures, Cambridge, 1932–5*, pp. 77–8.
15 *Wittgenstein's Lectures, Cambridge, 1932–35*, pp. 91–2.

4

Pierre Bourdieu: *Habitus* and the Logic of Practice

Joseph Margolis

I

There are too many convergences and specific differences between Pierre Bourdieu's account of societal life and my own to permit me to address his theory without providing a sense of how to approach the issues we share. In the interests of candor risking good manners, however, I must mention, briefly, certain initial convictions we seem to share but construe differently, and then turn at once to Bourdieu's views.

I find the following three intuitions particularly apt in the analysis of "the human condition": first, that the observers and the observeds of the human world are one and the same; second, that neither is altogether what it seems to be in spontaneous individual reflection; third, that the relationship between our perceiving the natural world and the world's being correctly perceived is an analogue of (human) self-knowledge. I see no reason to resist replacing these naive intuitions in good time. Still, in their crudity – perhaps more clearly thus than otherwise – unacceptable alternatives are instantly exposed as unpromising. Certain very strong styles of analysis go contrary to their implied instruction.

If we confine ourselves to Anglo-American and French philosophical practices, then, among the first, we should have to discount all versions of positivism and the unity of science program; and, among the second, all versions of Sartrean existentialism and Saussurean structuralism. Bourdieu is clearly attracted to such economies. My sense is that the options that remain cleave to two principal themes: one, that human thinking and action are, inherently, manifestations of history; the other, that, as historied processes, however individuated in the lives of particular selves, they are effective because their powers are structured by, and incorporate, the enabling collective powers of the forms of life of which they are manifestations.

The economy of beginning thus is too cryptic to be entirely trusted. I think Bourdieu is generally hospitable to these five themes, that is, including the two corollaries just mentioned.[1] I am committed to them.

Bourdieu departs from them, somewhat, in a certain characteristic way. When we espy the telltale signs in what he writes, we begin to grasp the force and limitation of his investigations and explanatory practices. Bourdieu finally adheres, I think, to a certain foundational view of how the oppositional role of the sexes generates – universally – the historically variable structures of different societies. I take that line of speculation to be doubtful – much thinner than any we should rely on and contrary in spirit to a strong historicism.

Bourdieu says, quite characteristically: "A vision of the world is a division of the world, based on a fundamental principle of division which distributes all the things of the world into two complementary classes. To bring order is to bring division, to divide the universe into opposing entities, those that the primitive speculation of the Pythagoreans presented in the form of 'columns of contraries' (*sustoichiai*).... The cultural act *par excellence* is the one that traces the line that produces a separated delimited space."[2] To oversimplify for the moment, I suggest that Bourdieu escapes both structuralism (Lévi-Strauss's, since his own empirical work has been in the ethnology or anthropology of Algeria and southeastern France) and existentialism (Sartre's, given his own personal history) – by way of insisting on three essential themes: (*a*) that human *agents* are not mere *subjects* (automatically following *rules* or autonomously exercising existential freedom); (*b*) that actions are not to be understood in terms of "obedience to a rule" but rather in terms of exploiting real possibilities and realistic *strategies*;[3] and a third theme (*c*) that needs still to be defined.

Already in *Outline of a Theory of Practice*, Bourdieu brings together his parallel objections to Lévi-Strauss and Sartre. Against Lévi-Strauss, he says:

In order to escape the *realism of the structure*, which hypostatizes systems of objective relations by converting them into totalities already constituted outside of individual history and group history, it is necessary to pass from the *opus operatum* to the *modus operandi*, from statistical regularity or algebraic structure to the principle of the production of this observed order,[4]

and, against Sartre, just two pages on, he adds:

If the world of action is nothing other than his [Sartre's] universe of inter-
changeable possibles, entirely dependent on the decrees of the consciousness
which creates it and hence totally devoid of *objectivity*, if it is moving because
the subject chooses to be moved, revolting because he chooses to be revolted,
then emotions, passions, and actions are merely games of bad faith, sad
farces in which one is both bad actor and good audience.[5]

These remarks fix the last theme wanted, namely, (*c*) that an *objective*
human science must address the *real* practices of the members of a
society – in which there cannot be a disjunction between the powers
of individual agents and the empowering processes of the social world
in which they live and act, and which do not take the form of
instantiating constitutive rules.

I take (*a*) – (*c*) to be as clear and straightforward a set of clues
about Bourdieu's sociology-*cum*-philosophy as any that may be given,
and I support them. They explicate Bourdieu's sense of the false
"objectivity" of the hidden structures the structuralists insisted on,
as well as the false "reality" of a Sartrean consciousness detached
from the world it practices on. They place Bourdieu correctly, if I may
speak thus. But what their explication shows is that, although
Bourdieu finally rejects the fictions of structuralism, he does not
adopt the same stance against binarism (which, of course, structuralism insists on).

The truth is, Bourdieu allows himself (I believe) to be tricked by an
equivocation symptomatic of his entire *oeuvre*. For, although it is true
that *predication is oppositional*, it is (and should be) an empirical
matter as to whether *the ordered predicates that best serve explanation in the human sciences are binary*. I hardly think they are, and
Bourdieu's own studies, for example regarding the marriage practices
among the Berbers, tend to show that the binary "rules" of kinship
plainly give way to the diverse "strategies" of marriage.[6]

Still, Bourdieu appears (to me) to insist on binarism. It is the
explicit inflexibility of the structuralist's use, not the supposed validity, of a foundational binarism that Bourdieu opposes. He does not
really oppose the latter. Let me offer this as a provisional finding. If it
requires adjustment, I shall certainly allow whatever qualifications
will be needed. But there cannot be any serious doubt about
Bourdieu's inclination to favor binarism in a way that generates
structuralist societies. This is surely what he means in remarking
that "non-literate societies seem to have a particular bent for the
structural games which fascinate the anthropologist" – he has
the Kabyle and related peoples in mind.[7] But he is also tempted –
the term may be too weak – to apply binarism to modern societies,
where there is an "overlay" of variable and labile structures that

obscure the would-be underlying binarism and misleadingly put its proper foundational function in considerable doubt. Thus he says: "Psychoanalysis, a disenchanting product of the disenchantment of the world, which tends to constitute *as such* a mythically overdetermined area of signification, too easily obscures the fact that one's own body and other people's bodies are always perceived through categories of perception which it would be naive to treat as sexual, even if... these categories always relate back, sometimes very concretely, to the opposition between the biological defined properties of the two sexes."[8] I think this is meant to be a binarism that constrains the contingencies of cultural history.

Let me leave it at that for the moment. My reason for pressing the point is that the *habitus* is never really segregated (in Bourdieu's mind) from this universal generative structuralism, and that the linkage helps to explain Bourdieu's sense of the microprocesses of social functioning. I, on the other hand, claim that the binarism cannot be convincingly sustained in its universal (or modal) form; that it applies, empirically, only piecemeal, to strongly traditionalist and preliterate cultures; and, most important, that it violates the deeper historicity of the human condition itself (which Bourdieu seems very often to favor). The issue is as ancient as Presocratic philosophy – which Bourdieu himself signals.

Bourdieu risks his entire sociology on the adequacy of "gender" oppositions, which he intends at least metonymically. But neither gender nor sex – the one, for social and ideological reasons, the other, for biological reasons[9] – can be convincingly so construed. His own studies should have made this plain. The insistence is not so much a return to an old structuralism as it is a weakness regarding historicity, determinism, the requirements of objectivity and realism, and, ultimately, the relationship between body and mind. My concern is this: one cannot displace structuralist rules by improvisational strategies (within the practice of effective action) without also replacing a binarism of descriptive and explanatory categories by an open-ended diversity of evolving social strategies. To endorse the one and resist the other is profoundly inconsistent. The "'Fieldwork in Philosophy'" interview seems to be congruent with these notions, but other strands of Bourdieu's thought are more difficult to reconcile with what *he* says (in the interview) and (frankly) with what I would favor for quite different reasons. I'm certain that part of the convergences between our views is due to our having been equally impressed with Wittgenstein's notion of the *Lebensform* and Marx's "Theses on Feuerbach." The difference between us lies with the treatment of history and the flux.

II

Bourdieu's binarism merely alerts us to deeper difficulties – those in particular that have to do with the meaning of the *habitus* and, ultimately, with the treatment of the relationship between mind and body. There is a certain slackness in Bourdieu's analysis of the *habitus*, though it is very good as a general schema. Where it goes wrong, or begins to lose its surefootedness, may be guessed from his own explicative images. (If I am mistaken in this, I should be happy to recant.)

Let me cite two carefully phrased passages about the *habitus* that I find at once marvelously suggestive and distinctly worrisome. In one, Bourdieu says:

> Practical belief is not a "state of mind," still less a kind of arbitrary adherence to a set of instituted dogmas and doctrines ("beliefs"), but rather a state of the body. Doxa is the relationship of immediate adherence that is established in practice between a *habitus* and the field to which it is attuned, the pre-verbal taking-for-granted of the world that flows from practical sense.

The second remark, only a few lines away, goes on to say:

> Practical sense, social necessity turned into nature, converted into motor schemes and body automatisms, is what causes practices, in and through what makes them obscure to the eyes of their producers, to be *sensible*, that is informed by a common sense. It is because agents never know completely what they are doing that what they do has more sense than they know.
>
> Every social order systematically takes advantage of the disposition of the body and language to function as depositories of deferred thoughts that can be triggered off at a distance in space and time by the simple effect of replacing the body in an overall posture which *recalls* the associated thoughts and feelings, in one of the inductive states of the body which, as actors know, give rise to states of mind.[10]

My diagnosis runs as follows. What Bourdieu says conveys a sense of the spontaneous activity of speech and behavior in ordinary human life. This is perhaps what "motor schemes" and "body automatisms" mean. But the image cannot be right if we are supposed to understand the particular utterances and acts *that* instantiate the *habitus* "by a common sense" (as Bourdieu puts it). Either it does not address the right issue or it is the wrong image.

These are provocative charges: I must show them to be fair complaints. The passages cited remind us, of course, of the remarkable fluency of the improvisational play of ordinary human life. Bourdieu is fond of reminding us of that: it's essential to the theme of the *habitus.* Partly, I believe, it confirms the intrinsic failure of Lévi-Strauss's and Sartre's alternative visions of a human science; and, partly, it confirms the need to insist that a valid theory must center on the features of the *habitus* itself. So much is reasonable and well worth emphasizing. But if we ask *what* the *habitus is,* what the telling features of its functioning structures are, what we get from Bourdieu is a kind of holist characterization that never comes to terms with its operative substructures. For, consider that the spontaneous play of ordinary life is *not* like an actor's performance: the actor's skilled "inductions" (in Bourdieu's image) are triggered *by a finished and familiar script*; whereas (to continue the image) the ordinary human agent (in "acting his part") creates a fresh script nearly always and continually.

The nagging impression I have is that the image of the actor *is* the one Bourdieu wants. It's the key to his brand of structuralism. Recall, for instance, that, in his critique of Lévi-Strauss's absurd account of the exchange of gifts, Bourdieu astutely remarks: "the [structuralist] model which shows the interdependence of gift and counter-gift destroys the practical logic of exchange, which can only function if the objective model (every gift requires a counter-gift) is not experienced as such. And this misconstrual of the model is possible [he says] because the temporal structure of exchange (the counter-gift is not only different, but *deferred*) masks or contradicts the objective structure of exchange."[11]

What Bourdieu is very good at providing are *non*-structuralist (non-algorithmic) analyses of *structuralist puzzle-cases*. To use his own idiom: he supplies a *modus operandi for an opus operatum*; whereas what he needs (pursuing his example) is an open process in which the gift that will be given is *not yet*, in the very process, telically obliged – "doomed" – to be a gift! I fear that when he treats the *habitus* globally, he treats it in a genuinely openended way but does not then identify its microstructure; and when he gives us a clue about its substructure, he reverts to the structuralist orientation but not to its failed theory. (He appeals to "strategies" but not to "rules," to binarism but not to formalism.) That is what I gather from his having remarked that the counter-gift is "deferred." Of course it is, but that's why it cannot capture the work of the *habitus* – *if*, that is, the *habitus* is meant to be the ubiquitous feature of ordinary life. It may be that, here and there, there are highly ritualized forms of life – life around the Kabyle house, for instance[12] – that are best construed as a continually re-enacted script, but that cannot possibly be the exemplar of post-traditional modern society.[13] Or, so I claim.

If you grant the force of saying this, you should begin to worry about Bourdieu's treatment of body and mind. I agree that it is the *bodily* aspect of an act that makes it "sensible," robust enough to be perceived at all. But I cannot agree with Bourdieu's pointed comment that "practical belief is not a 'state of mind' . . . but rather a state of the body." Doubtless, he says this in part to distance himself rhetorically from Lévi-Strauss and Sartre. But the fact is, the *habitus* is meant *to overcome the disjunction* between mind and body – within the dynamics of a public culture. That now generates a puzzle we have not yet acknowledged. *How*, we may ask, do "body automatisms" work? Either Bourdieu fails to say, or, if he does explain, his clue cannot serve.

It's true he adds the following – against Lévi-Strauss and Althusser:

I wanted . . . to reintroduce agents that Lévi-Strauss and the structuralists, among others, Althusser, tended to abolish, making them into simple epiphe-nomena of structure. . . . I am talking about dispositions *acquired through experience*, thus variable from place to place and time to time. [Bourdieu means that he is attracted to Chomsky's universalism but is not talking about innate dispositions.] This "feel for the game," as we call it, is what enables an infinite number of "moves" to be made, adapted to the infinite number of possible situations which no rule, however complex, can foresee. And, I replaced the rules of kinship [in the example given] with matrimonial strategies.[14]

But, if what I've said is reasonably correct, then the "feel for the game" *can't* capture the (full range of the) *habitus*. Bourdieu never questions the notion of a "move"; he questions only the adequacy of *structuralistic rules* for explaining the infinite variety of "moves" or (as with the counter-gift) why we should hold to "rules" and not to "strategies." I agree that "strategies" are better than rules, but they won't do either.

At the risk of insisting too pointedly then, let me show you why. I want to say that Bourdieu is entirely right in his global use of *habitus* or *hexis*, and entirely wrong in his detailed reading of his own model. "Adopting a phrase of Proust's," he says, "one might say that arms and legs are full of numb imperatives. One could endlessly enumerate the values given body, *made* body, by the hidden persuasion of an implicit pedagogy which can make a whole cosmology, through injunctions as insignificant as 'sit up straight' or 'don't hold your knife in your left hand'." This is exactly right and beautifully put. But it goes wrong at once: "The logic of scheme transfer [Bourdieu goes on] which makes each technique of the body a kind of *pars totalis*, predisposed to function in accordance with the fallacy of *pars pro toto*, and hence to recall the whole system to which it belongs, gives a general scope to the apparently most circumscribed and circumstantial observances. The cunning of pedagogic reason lies precisely in the fact that it manages to extort what is essential while seeming to demand the insignificant. . . . Bodily hexis is political mythology realized, *em-bodied*, turned into a permanent disposition, a durable way of standing, speaking, walking, and thereby of feeling and thinking."[15]

There are two weaknesses lurking here, neither entirely explicit, sometimes even opposed: one, the presumption that there *is* a totality (a system) of some kind (open or closed) that each act or disposition to act "recalls," subtends, perhaps in some way signifies; the other, the presumption that that alone accounts for the fluency of our acts and dispositions and, therefore, the privilege assigned the body.

I say that there is no evidence at all that ordinary life *is* a system of any kind. It is true that Wittgenstein speaks of a form of life as a "system," but Wittgenstein means to emphasize the improvisational continuity of an openended practice in which neither "rules" nor "strategies" could yield sufficient closure.[16] (Bourdieu *is* drawn to Wittgenstein.) Perhaps the Zuñi once approximated a closed society devoted to the magical repetition of their particular form of life (as described by Ruth Benedict);[17] but, as I say, it is a model that cannot possibly be convincing in the modern world.

I think it is just Bourdieu's adherence to this subtler structuralism that explains both his attraction to the importance of the supposed binarism of gender and to the faulty metaphor of mind and body. "The opposition between male and female is realized in posture, [he says,] in the gestures and movements of the body, in the form of the opposition between the straight and the bent, between firmness, uprightness and directness . . . and restraint, reserve and flexibility . . . these two relations to the body are charged with two relations to other people, time and the world, and through these, to two systems of value."[18] I realize that Bourdieu has the Kabyle in mind; but does he mean that binarism works in their world but not in ours; or does he mean that ours, like theirs, *is* a "system" for which, though structuralist "rules" will not do, more flexible "strategies" will? The latter reading seems more likely.

If the "Belief and the Body" paper is a reliable clue, then Bourdieu cannot be but read as a subtler advocate of structuralism and binarism. Keep that in mind as a possibility: the binary division of labor between the sexes in the Kabyle world is not in any sense a

confirmation of binarism in that or any other world; and the validity
of binarism in the Kabyle world poses a puzzle that cannot be dis-
joined from the fate of any would-be objective account of the life of
any society.

III

Let me come at this from an altogether different direction. Consider
two very large philosophical questions that any model of Bourdieu's
sort must ultimately address: (a) that of the ontic relation between
culture and physical nature and the distinctive properties of the
cultural world; (b) that of the epistemic problem of predication, of
"real generality," of the spontaneous extension of general predicates
to instances that are not first learned as the exemplars of their acceptable use. For brevity's sake, let me say that my own resolution of (a)
accords with the items of my original tally (which Bourdieu would
probably not oppose); and, regarding (b), the resolution I offer rejects
all versions of the theory of "universals" (as utterly hopeless and
beside the point) and locates the solution *in* the consensual (but not
criterial) practices of historicized *Lebensformen*.[19] I don't believe
Bourdieu would agree to this.

My complaint amounts to this: regarding (a), the rhetorical disjunction between mind and body, which bears on the generative
binarism of the sexes, *cannot*, on my view, possibly accommodate
the distinction between the natural and the cultural or Bourdieu's own
insistence on overcoming "dualism";[20] and, regarding (b), there *is* no
structured or algorithmic way to ensure a resolution, among the apt
members of any historicized society, of the problem of objective
predication that would entrench (cognitively or "practically") the
generative binarism of the sexes or any substitute, whether biological
or cultural. The resolution of (a) admits the importance of the physical embodiment of cultural life and behavior, but *not* anything like the
semiotics of the *body* – except metonymically, assigned in a subaltern
way *from* the vantage of the emergent (*em*-bodied) culture. And the
resolution of (b) requires, *everywhere*, the reidentification of predicative similarities – *a fortiori*, structural similarities – *within* the consensual practices of a particular *Lebensform* (within some society's
form of life, or, more accurately, within some society's form of life *as*
observed by us observing our doing just that).

There is no way of overcoming the dualism of mind and body or of
nature and culture except by construing the "mental" and the
"cultural" predicatively; and, there is no way of doing that except

by construing the entities to which the relevant predicables are ascribed as suitably emergent with respect to physical nature and indissolubly "embodied" as the complex entities they are.[21] This affords the only viable strategy for resolving (a), short of embracing some form of physicalism. Bourdieu has no interest in supporting physicalism. But if one proceeds thus, it is at least problematic – impossible, I should say, for reasons that will soon appear – that the categorization or description of any culture should privilege the movements or dispositions of the *body*. The body is implicated, of course, in every socially significant act or disposition but not separably from the significative. Otherwise, only a version of what has come to be called "supervenience" (or "nonreductive physicalism") could possibly vindicate Bourdieu's metaphor. As I see matters, this is precisely what is risked in structuralism and what is resolved (if indeed it is resolved), however inchoately, in Hegelian, Marxist, Foucauldian, and feminist accounts. Once you admit culture and history and the encultured competence of human selves, you cannot deny that, ultimately, "materiality" and "signification" are inseparable.[22]

I insist that Bourdieu's intention must have been metaphoric (when he declared that "practical belief is not a 'state of mind' . . . but rather a state of the body"): if he had meant it literally, his entire theory would have collapsed at once, on the assumption (which he evidently shares) that the cultural cannot be reduced to the physical or treated as "supervenient";[23] and if he meant it figuratively, then the formula could not but be profoundly incomplete. There is no conceptual reason why supervenience should not be false, and there is no empirical reason to believe it is true.[24]

If you grant the argument, a graver difficulty begins to surface. There *is*, first of all, something of a suggestion of extensional equivalence between the cultural and the physical, in Bourdieu, in addition to the standard structuralist equivalences he wishes to construe in terms of "strategies" rather than "rules." For he explicitly says:

When the properties and movements of the body are socially qualified, the most fundamental social choices are naturalized and the body, within its properties and its movements, is constituted as an analogical operator establishing all kinds of practical equivalences among the different divisions of the social world – divisions between the sexes, between the age groups and between the social classes – or, more precisely, among the meanings and values associated with the individuals occupying practically equivalent positions in the spaces defined by these divisions.[25]

There is certainly no way to support this thesis either in a modal or contingently universal sense. There *may* be societies that exhibit such extraordinary correspondences, but they could not behave in any significantly historicized way.

What Bourdieu adds leads to the quite remarkable thesis that he puts this way: "The relation [of social distinctions] to the body is a fundamental dimension of the *habitus* that is inseparable from a relation to language and to time... Social psychology is mistaken when it locates the dialectic of incorporation at the level of *representation*, with body image.... What is 'learned by body' is not something that one has, like knowledge that can be brandished, but something that one is."[26] Perhaps; but this touches only on the fluency of naturally acquired habits of life. It has nothing to do with binarism or correspondence or supervenience or structuralist systems or "practical belief." It makes a mystery of the enculturing process, and it enlists us ingeniously into supporting Bourdieu's own structuralism. What *is* the "analogical operator" after all? In the "'Fieldwork in Philosophy'" paper, Bourdieu warns us to pay attention to "the historicization of [our] concepts," warning against premature fixities that "hinder and imprison thought."[27] Why should we not turn the warning against Bourdieu's own binarism?

Furthermore, "*what* is 'learned by body'" is confirmed, shaped and endorsed, legitimated, *by* the collective consensual practices of an encompassing *Lebensform*: it cannot be shown to be valid simply as the spontaneous responsiveness of an individual "body." The "knowledge" assigned the body lies in its spontaneity and fluency all right; but its fluency *is what is consensually so judged, and what is so judged is the cultural aptness of the relevant properties of what we do and make and judge relative to an evolving Lebensform*. The fluency belongs to the individual agent or "body"; but its cognitive aptness is a function of the way an agent *shares* the practices of an encompassing society. There *are* no predicative rules *or* strategies *for* individual agents *to* internalize, or what rules or strategies there are are parasitic on these deeper enabling powers. There *is* nothing fundamental *in being culturally apt* that *could be* governed by an internal "analogical operator." The "operation" in question is inseparable from the ongoing consensual coherence of the aggregated behavior of the members of a viable society. Bourdieu's formula does not define the "logic" of predication – it therefore fails to define the "logic of practice." Predication is not an "analytical operator" internal to any or all of us. There is no such thing. I take this to be the principal distinction between Bourdieu and Wittgenstein on the matter of *Lebensform* and *habitus*.

This brings me to problem (b) and its connection with (a). Two themes are needed. For one thing, the "cultural" is a blunderbuss notion. I call the mark of the cultural the "Intentional" and collect under it an endlessly varied assortment of predicables concerned with meaning, significance, signification, symbolic import, semiotic import, language, representationality, expressivity, referentiality, truth, metaphor, rhetoric, style, genre, purpose, historicity, institutions, practices, habits, traditions, rules, and the like.[28] The Intentional incorporates the "intentional" (of Brentano and Husserl) and the "intensional" (the non-extensional), but it goes beyond those notions in being ascribed primarily to instantiations of *the collective life of a society* (as the other notions are not) – to whatever rightly falls within a *Lebensform*. The slightest reflection on the "Intentional" pretty clearly shows that the human sciences must treat it as *sui generis*.

Now then, the second theme affects the methodological fortunes of the Intentional as well as the natural or physical. For, *if*, as I have suggested, the valid predication of general attributes is a function of the consensual practices of a historical society, *if* the Intentional is *sui generis*, *if* the consensual use of general terms affects discourse about the physical world as well as the cultural, then there can be very little reason to suppose that there *is* an "analogical operator" (interior to the "body") that functions to ensure binarism or, more specifically, the generative function of the "opposed" sexes and a sense of the infinitely many "moves" of the social "game" *in accord with some such generative binarism.*

Bourdieu has very little to say about classificatory practices, except to fall back to some version of the "logic of practice" of the sort already mentioned.[29] More than that, there *is* no principled distinction between the "folk" competence of basic predicative discourse and its professionalization; there is only a difference between the various societies whose *Lebensformen* are invoked.[30]

IV

I have been contesting Bourdieu's theory of practice, primarily because I agree with his general sense of the dynamics of social life. I draw back at two points. For one thing, I detect in his own discourse the vestiges of canonical structuralism and an existential phenomenology, despite his effective escape. At any rate, I cannot be sure how strongly entrenched his binarism is, or ultimately how different his "strategies" are from structuralist "rules." For a second, I cannot find in Bourdieu a sustained and frontal account of the cognitive aspect of the "logic of practice." My sense is that he abandons the first, though, if he does, I cannot see that he could then hold on for long to the universalism that seemed to surface in his admitted attraction to Chomsky's views (with the qualification already acknowledged). On the other hand, I find that Bourdieu admits the point in a forthright way – correctly, if I may intrude my assessment. For, in answering the interviewer's question about a comparison with Habermas's insistence on "universal norms," Bourdieu explicitly says: "I have a tendency to ask the problem of reason or of norms in a reasonably historicist way. Instead of wondering about the existence of 'universal interests', I will ask: who has an interest in the universal? . . . I think historicism must be pushed to its limit, by a sort of radical doubt, to see what can really be saved."[31] Clearly, a strict binarism would be incompatible with this concession. My own formulation is very similar to Bourdieu's: historicism and universalism, I claim, are incompatible.[32] (I have put the thesis to Habermas in person, but he has never answered.) Furthermore, Bourdieu perceives that the argument leads to the dictum: "To say that there are social conditions for the production of truth is to say that there is a politics of truth."[33]

It is the relative neglect of an analysis of the conditions of "knowledge" operative in practice that concerns me most. I cannot see how to ensure the theoretical contribution of the *habitus* without a reasonably detailed account of the *cognizing* process of social life. That is what I meant by the problem of predication and the irrelevance of the "body's" fluent and spontaneous aptitude. I have myself witnessed the skill of the Greek peasant equivalent of the Yugoslav *guslar* in combining the formulaic and the improvisational in songs about immediate events.[34] But that is merely a site of the paradigmatic exercise of encultured aptitudes: it cannot replace their analysis.

I am inclined to believe that it is because he conflates the two issues that Bourdieu is drawn to binarism in the explication of "practical taxonomies."[35] This is the only way to read the careful phrasing: "The habitus continuously generates practical metaphors, that is to say, transfer (of which the transfer of motor habits is only one example) or, more precisely, systematic transpositions required by the particular conditions in which the habitus is 'put into practice'."[36] First of all, Bourdieu assigns to the *habitus* an *active* role, which can only be a metaphor for the processes of the knowledge that belongs to "practice" (not otherwise explained). Secondly, it leans in the direction of the old structuralism. Thirdly, it is ultimately incompatible with Bourdieu's insistence that the *habitus* is variably constituted and reconstituted by the aggregated behavior of the apt members of a society. "The habitus," he says, "is not only a structuring structure, which organizes practices and the perception of practices, but also a structured structure: the principle of division into logical classes which organizes the perception of the social world is itself the product of internalization of the division into social classes."[37]

Clearly, the historicizing theme and the reflexive and reciprocal process of structuring and being structured cannot support anything like Lévi-Strauss's structuralism; *but there is no evidence that Bourdieu's adjustment does not support binarism*. On the contrary, there is every evidence that Bourdieu is himself a binarist:

inevitably inscribed within the dispositions of the habitus [Bourdieu says,] is the whole structure of the system of conditions, as it presents itself in the experience of a life-condition occupying a particular position within that structure. The most fundamental oppositions in the structure (high/low, rich/poor etc.) tend to establish themselves as the fundamental structuring principles of practices and the perception of practices.[38]

Binarism constitutes Bourdieu's most pointed approach to the logic of predication and (therefore) to the "logic of practice." But binarism does not explain the first logic, it presupposes it; and binary distinctions neither confirm binarism nor are more perspicuous, predicatively, than other categorical schemes.

Bourdieu explicitly says (as he must, on his own thesis): "the conditions associated with a particular class of conditions of existence produce *habitus*, systems of durable, transposable dispositions, structured, that is, as principles which generate and organize practices and representations that can be objectively adapted to their outcomes without presupposing a conscious aiming at ends or an express mastery of the operations necessary in order to attain them."[39] This confirms the sense in which Bourdieu regularly favors the theme of fluency over the cognizing "logic" of the *habitus* – and the possibility that he believes binarism relieves him of the need to go further.

The critical point is that the *extension* of general predicates, whether Intentional or physical, whether in accord with binarism or not, can (so I am arguing) only be explained in terms of the collective, consensual, and historicized drift of the *lebensformlich* practices of particular societies. There may be some biologically favored "disposition" toward *certain* classifications. Short of innatism, however, there is no way to understand the matter in terms of the internalized aptitude of individual "bodies" (or agents). The "aptitude" is itself a function of the consensual validation of the diverse acts and dispositions of the aggregated members of a society. The *habitus*, I should say, cannot be the cognizing aptitude of practice: there is no such aptitude; it is rather the running abstraction of the collective thread of the converging fluencies (and their "correction") of aggregated individual life. It has no criterial function of any sort. Alternatively put, the analysis of the *habitus* must accord with the analysis of the "knowledge" of "real generals." No one like Bourdieu, who favors *Lebensformen* and historicity, could come to any other finding. So the resolution of this puzzle – remarked in an earlier tally – is one that can accommodate the theme of "strategies" replacing "rules," but it need not restrict itself in this way any more than in the structuralist's way.

Perhaps the point may be put thus: practice is a logical space, not a cognizing faculty of any sort. Similarly, *habitus* is not the work of any agency, but rather the abstracted chronicle of the fluent processes by which whatever work is done is done. What specifically belongs to cognition and intelligence in cultural space is not clarified by the "logic of practice": it is presupposed by it. If I am right, there is nothing in Bourdieu that comes to terms with the microprocesses of cognition in the world of practice. I frankly believe Bourdieu misconstrues the matter. He thinks of "practical knowledge" almost facultatively, as providing an alternative to Aristotle's well-known contrast (between the theoretical and the practical) and *as arising as such* as a result of the cultural embodiment that *habitus* signifies. I accept the notion of cultural embodiment; I deny that that gives us a sense of the nature of the perception, judgment, or effective action that the fluency of cultural life endlessly confirms. You may think I misread Bourdieu, but here is his own statement:

This relation of practical knowledge is not that between a subject and an object constituted as such and perceived as problem. Habitus being the social embodied, it is "at home" in the field it inhabits, it perceives it immediately as endowed with meaning and interest. The practical knowledge it procures may be described by analogy with Aristotle's *phronesis* or, better, with *orthe doxa* of which Plato talks in Meno: just as the "right opinion" "falls right," in a sense, without knowing how or why, likewise the coincidence between dispositions and position, between the "sense of the game" and the game, explains that the agent does what he or she "has to do" without posing it explicitly as a goal, below the level of calculation and even consciousness, beneath discourse and representation.[40]

Again, I say this captures beautifully the sense of the fluency of cultural life; but it has nothing to do with the analysis of the cognizing process that fluency is meant to qualify.

The point at stake is this: the cognizing powers of theoretical knowledge, as in the sciences, *is similarly marked by the fluency of habitus*. Theorizing discourse *is* a form of "practice." There's the reversal of Aristotle and the common discovery of Marx and Wittgenstein. Bourdieu speaks as if there were a certain new competence that we manifest in specifically cultural life; whereas the truth is, there is nothing that is paradigmatically human (that is, manifest in thought and knowledge and practice and technology) that is not a form of cultural life. Since it would not be responsive to account for the cognizing power of the sciences in terms said to function "below the level of calculation and even consciousness," it cannot be responsive to appeal to it in addressing the "logic of practice." The reason is plain: even *at* "the level of calculation and . . . consciousness," *fluency* functions "beneath discourse and representation" – or, better, discourse and representation function fluently "beneath" the level at which whatever *they* single out they single out.

We have no idea how, effectively, we *are* or become fluent; but our fluency is not a distinct cognitive power. It cannot be admitted without analysis. It is only the site of an extraordinary competence. There is, in Bourdieu, no account of referential and predicative competence. That cannot be different in theoretical and "practical" life. But Bourdieu speaks as if it is. It is because of that that he is attracted to binarism. Binarism suggests that there is a certain subterraneous cognizing competence – perhaps akin to an instinct (I admit I am tempted to read Bourdieu thus) – that sees in the relative fixity of the binarism of the sexes a competence to generate through that tacit power (interacting with its environment) whatever further binary articulations may be wanted for the form of life of this or that society.[41] I am inclined to think that Bourdieu means what he says here – literally. He speaks of a competence that has directly absorbed (internalized, learned) the structural or structuring powers of one's society's *habitus*. That competence is not fixed by rules, it is true; it proceeds by strategies (which are very much in accord with Wittgenstein's notion of knowing "how to go on"). But this itself may be construed as rejecting an inflexible model of animal instinct and as (merely) preferring the somewhat more flexible (but ultimately inflexible) models of theorists like Tinbergen and Edward Wilson. In any case, I cannot see that Bourdieu has gone beyond this.

If that is so, then Bourdieu has been gravely misled; first, because binarism is a purely formal, not a cognitively active, principle; second, because there are neither *a priori* nor empirical reasons for thinking that binarism is true; third, because the cognizing competence of acting in accord with rules or by way of strategies is ultimately the same; fourth, because the fluency of practical life would show the same apparent autonomy, whether it proceeded by rules or by strategies; and finally, because there is no way to equate the reporting of the fluency of our cognitive powers and their analysis, or to infer convincingly that the admission of the first obviates the need for the second.

The essential clue is this. Cognitive competence of any kind is assignable only to individual agents. *Habitus* signifies the collective fluency of a form of life. For conceptual reasons, therefore, *habitus* cannot be a cognitive power. Q.E.D. Nevertheless, the cognizing powers of humans entail internalizing the forms of life of which *habitus* is the abstract thread: the cognizing powers of aggregated agents is collective; that is, it is, in every individuated token, an exercise of an ability that cannot be characterized except in collective terms. For instance, only individual agents speak a language, but a language is a collective possession. To speak is to utter, as an individual, tokens of language that manifest (in an individual) the enabling power of the *habitus* of a particular form of life; it is also the "effect" (in collective life) of the thus-enabling power of speech to alter the continuing *habitus* by which others (including ourselves) are able to speak aptly at a later moment. At no point will there be a collective agent, however. Fluency addresses the congruity between aggregated agency and the abstracted *habitus* of a viable society: it presupposes but does not explore the cognizing process by which it works. The process can only be fathomed in the way in which perception and understanding and reference and predication actually function. The reason the matter is important is simply that the clues that the *habitus* provides are regularly ignored by epistemologies that take as their paradigm our knowledge of the physical world. In a curious way, that *was* the fault of structuralism *and* existentialism. Bourdieu should (I suggest) have gone on, therefore, to account for our cognizing powers in terms of the way the internalized culture functions *in* perception and reference and predication and the like. That is missing in nearly all epistemologies. I confess I find it missing in Bourdieu.

Notes

1   See, for instance, Pierre Bourdieu, "'Fieldwork in Philosophy'" (an interview with A. Honneth, H. Kocyba, and B. Schwibe, Paris, April, 1985: Originally "Der Kampf um die sybolische Ordnung," *Ästhetik und Kommunikation* XVI, 1986), *In Other Words: Essays towards a Reflexive Sociology*, trans. Matthew Adamson (Stanford, 1990). The interview has appeared also as "The Struggle for Symbolic Order," trans. J. Bleicher, *Theory, Culture, and Society*, III (1968).

2   Pierre Bourdieu, "Irresistible Analogy," *The Logic of Practice*, trans. Richard Nice (Cambridge: Polity Press, 1990), p. 210. I regard the references to the Presocratics as confirming an important part of my own analysis.

3   This is the sense, for instance, of "'Fieldwork in Philosophy'," p. 9.
4   Pierre Bourdieu, *Outline of a Theory of Practice*, trans. Richard Nice (Cambridge University Press, 1977), p. 72.
5   *Outline of a Theory of Practice*, p. 74.
6   Bourdieu reports his findings in just this vein, in "'Fieldwork in Philosophy'," p. 8. See, also, *The Logic of Practice*, Introduction.
7   "Belief and the Body," *The Logic of Practice* p. 293n9.
8   Ibid., pp. 77–8.
9   See John Money and Anke A. Ehrdhardt, *Man & Woman, Boy & Girl; The Differentiation and Dimorphism of Gender Identity from Conception to Maturity* (Baltimore: Johns Hopkins University Press, 1972).
10 Pierre Bourdieu, "Belief and the Body," *The Logic of Practice*, pp. 68–69.
11 "'Fieldwork in Philosophy'," p. 23, also, Pierre Bourdieu, "The Work of Time," *The Logic of Practice*.
12 See Pierre Bourdieu, "The Kabyle House or the World Reversed," *The Logic of Practice*.
13 See Alvin W. Gouldner, *The Dialectic of Ideology and Technology; The Origins, Grammar, and Future of Ideology* (New York: Oxford University Press, 1976), chs 1–2.
14 "'Fieldwork in Philosophy'," p. 9.
15 "Belief and the Body," pp. 69–70.
16 See Joseph Margolis, "Wittgenstein's 'Form of Life': A Cultural Template for Psychology," in Michael Chapman and Roger A. Dixon (eds), *Meaning and the Growth of Understanding; Wittgenstein's Significance for Developmental Psychology* (Berlin: Springer-Verlag, 1987).
17 See Ruth Benedict, *Patterns of Culture* (Boston: Houghton Mifflin, 1934), ch. 4.
18 "Belief and the Body," p. 70.
19 My own resolution of (a) appears in *Texts without Referents; Reconciling Science and Narrative* (Oxford: Basil Blackwell, 1989), ch. 6. My resolution of (b) appears in "The Passing of Peirce's Realism," *The Transactions of the Charles S. Peirce Society*, XXIX (1993).
20 Bourdieu himself says that the "notion of habitus" is related to "an attempt to break with Kantian dualism and [for instance] to reintroduce the permanent dispositions that are constitutive of realized morality (*Sittlichkeit*), as opposed to the moralism of duty," "'Fieldwork in Philosophy'," p. 12. The only point I would reserve judgment on concerns the interpretation of "permanent dispositions."
21 A summary of the argument is given in *Texts without Referents*, ch. 6.
22 You may find it instructive to compare the contest regarding the "priority" of body or sign, in the recent feminist discussions of the distinction between the male and female. See, for instance, Judith Butler, *Bodies That Matter* (New York: Routledge, 1993), particularly p. 31. I have benefited, here, from Dorothea Olkowski, "Materiality and Language: Butler's Interrogation of the History of Philosophy," *Philosophy & Social Criticism*, XXIII (1997).

23   The supervenience theory has been championed by Donald Davidson, "Mental Events," "The Material Mind," *Essays on Events and Actions* (Oxford: Clarendon, 1980). The supervenience theory holds that "there cannot be two events alike in all physical respects but differing in some mental respect, or that an object cannot alter in some mental respect without altering in some physical respect," p. 214 ("Mental Events"). For a rigorous critique, see Simon Blackburn, "Supervenience Revisited," in Ian Hacking (ed.), *Exercises in Analysis: Essays by Students of Casimir Lewy* (Cambridge: Cambridge University Press, 1985). See also, Jaegwon Kim, *Supervenience and Mind: Selected Essays* (Cambridge: Cambridge University Press, 1991).

24   Herbert Feigl had, some years ago, formulated a pertinent worry of his regarding (what he called) the "many–many" problem: that is, that, for any significant action (signaling, making a chess move), there are indefinitely many physical movements that might embody that action; that, for any particular movement, indefinitely many different actions may be embodied in it; and that there is no rule or algorithm that could legitimate reliable inferences in either direction. Pertinent judgments depend on context, intention, history, form of life. Feigl never developed the account needed. I may add that I have heard him mention the "many – many" problem several times, but I have not found it in his published papers.

25   "Belief and the Body," p. 71.

26   "Belief and the Body," pp. 72–3.

27   "'Fieldwork in Philosophy'," p. 16; see also, p. 17.

28   I give an account of this range in *Texts without Referents*, ch. 6; in *The Flux of History and the Flux of Science* (Berkeley: University of California Press, 1993); and in *Interpretation Radical But Not Unruly: The New Puzzle of the Arts and History* (Berkeley: University of California Press, 1995).

29   See, for instance, Bourdieu, "Social Space and Symbolic Power," *In Other Words*, particularly pp. 130–1; and "Irresistable Analogies."

30   Compare Pierre Bourdieu, "The Practices of Reflexive Sociology" (The Paris Workshop), in Pierre Bourdieu and Loic J. D. Wacquant, *An Invitation to Reflexive Sociology* (Chicago: University of Chicago Press, 1992), for instance pp. 241–3; and *Homo Academicus*, trans. Peter Collier (Stanford: Stanford University 1984), Postscript.

31   "'Fieldwork in Philosophy'," p. 31.

32   See Joseph Margolis, *Pragmatism without Foundations: Reconciling Realism and Relativism* (Oxford: Basil Blackwell, 1986), ch. 2.

33   "'Fieldwork in Philosophy'," p. 32.

34   See "Belief and the Body," pp. 74–5.

35   See "Irresistible Analogy."

36   Pierre Bourdieu, *Distinction: A Social Critique of the Judgement of Taste*, trans. Richard Nice (Cambridge, Mass.: Harvard University Press, 1984), p. 173.

37 *Distinction*, p. 170.
38 *Distinction*, p. 172.
39 Bourdieu, "Structures, *Habitus*, Practices," *The Logic of Practice*, p. 53.
40 Pierre Bourdieu and Loic J. D. Wacquant, "The Purpose of Reflexive Sociology" (The Chicago Workshop), *An Invitation to Reflexive Sociology*, p. 128.
41 For a sense of the aptness of this analogy, see N. Tinbergen, *The Study of Instinct* (New York: Oxford University Press, 1969).

5

Can there be a Science of Existential Structure and Social Meaning?

Hubert Dreyfus and Paul Rabinow

Pierre Bourdieu has developed one of the most analytically powerful and heuristically promising approaches to human reality on the current scene. As opposed to the other two plausible living contenders, Jürgen Habermas and Jacques Derrida, Bourdieu has continued and enriched the line of modern thought that runs from Durkheim and Weber through Heidegger to Merleau-Ponty and Foucault. Unlike Habermas, who is seeking universal, rational, procedural norms based on speech acts which, though empty, would ground evaluations of all human action, and unlike Derrida, who, also prioritizing language, sees all human reality as ungrounded and pushes us towards the recognition and furthering of multiplicity and instability for their own sake, Bourdieu, through an analysis of the prelinguistic, embodied structures that give stability and intelligibility of human action, provides an account both of the universal structures of human being and of the contingent practices that sustain, perpetuate, and modify these structures.

   Bourdieu's theory of the *sens pratique* allows him to use phenomenological insights from early Heidegger and Merleau-Ponty to give a highly satisfactory account of the essential social character of human reality. We want, however, to distinguish two components in Bourdieu's work: an ontologically informed research program, which we call "empirical existential analytics", and the scientific theory of social meaning – Bourdieu's theory of symbolic capital – which we argue is a specific and contestable interpretation of who we are and

From *Bourdieu: Critical Perspectives*, ed. C. Calhoun, E. LiPuma and M. Postone, University of Chicago Press, Chicago, and Polity Press, Cambridge, 1993.

what we are always up to. We think that these two components are analytically separable and that objective description is the appropriate way to approach what human beings *are* and how their social practices cohere. We hold, however, that the *meaning* of human action is not accessible to a scientific theory; to understand the significance of human action requires an interpretive approach (for an elaboration and defense of our view, see Dreyfus and Rabinow 1983).

The apparent coherence of Bourdieu's objective account of the general and specific structures of the habitus and of the struggle for symbolic capital that the habitus seems to embody obscures from both Bourdieu and his critics another distinction. Without arguments to the contrary, it would seem that one has no right to conclude from the universal *ontological structure* of human being that the many ways that this structure gets filled out in the everyday life of societies covers up a specific truth, universal or otherwise, about the *meaning* of human being. Bourdieu would seem to owe us an argument as to why we should not take seriously the distinction between coping skills and their alleged unifying meaning, and, if we do, how the same methodology could be expected to be applicable to both domains. In our view, if one were to address these issues, then the debate over the importance of Bourdieu's work would be clarified and raised out of the current polemical stalemate.

We would like to show here: (1) that Bourdieu implicitly operates with two different methods and two different vocabularies when dealing with one or the other of the domains we have distinguished; (2) that as soon as the distinction of domains is made explicit, we can see the appropriateness of Bourdieu's objective approach to the study of everyday realities, but without further argument there is as yet no reason to believe that the same method can be fruitfully applied to the study of the meaning of human being – if there is any; (3) that the attempt to give a scientific account of the truth of human being leads to what seem to be serious methodological problems; and (4) that methodological caution would suggest we stick to the phenomenological evidence that different societies have had different cultural understandings of what human life is all about, that our culture has had a whole series of such understandings, and that we are situated in the latest one.

An Empirical Analytics of Social Existence

Husserl, Heidegger, and Merleau-Ponty, in spite of their disagreement, all held that in order to guide empirical studies, one needs to have an adequate ontology of the domain to be investigated. As we are using the term, ontology gives us the *general* structures of human being. Phenomenological ontology studies the structures of skills (perception and motility) and the way in which they give us access to various modes of being and constitute us as the kinds of being we are.

Bourdieu's notion of habitus, which guides his study of social human being, demonstrates the importance of having a solid ontological basis for one's research. Habitus, as Bourdieu uses the term (1979a: vii), refers to "a system of durable, transposable dispositions which functions as the generative basis of structured, objectively unified practices." Human beings are socialized into this system of dispositions that enables them to produce on the appropriate occasion skillful social activity that embodies, sustains, and reproduces the social field that in turn governs this very activity. Bourdieu remarks: "Merleau-Ponty, and also Heidegger, opened the way for a non-intellectualist, non-mechanistic analysis of the relations between agent and world" (1990d: 10).

The general form of this existential ontology is already fully worked out in *Being and Time*. Everyday coping (primordial understanding as projecting) is taken over by each individual by socialization into the public norms (the one) and thus forms a clearing that "governs" people by determining what possibilities show up as making sense. Heidegger moves beyond Husserl and the Cartesian tradition when he points out that:

The one (*Das Man*) as that which forms everyday being-with-one-another... constitutes what we call *the public* in the strict sense of the word. It implies that the world is always already primarily given as the common world. It is not the case that on the one hand there are first individual subjects which at any given time have their own world; and that the task would then arise of putting together, by virtue of some sort of an arrangement, the various particular worlds of the individuals and of agreeing how one would have a common world. This is how philosophers imagine these things when they ask about the constitution of the intersubjective world. We say instead that the first thing that is given is the common world – the one. (1985:246)

Bourdieu makes this point forcibly from the side of the human sciences, in introducing his notion of habitus:

[H]abitus is the product of the work of inculcation and appropriation necessary in order for those products of collective history, the objective structures (e.g., of language, economy, etc.), to succeed in reproducing themselves more or less completely, in the form of durable dispositions, in the organisms (which one can, if one wishes, call individuals) lastingly subjected to the same conditionings. (1977c: 85)

Bourdieu also sees the sense in which, thanks to the habitus, *the* world is prior to *my* world. "Since the history of the individual is never anything other than a certain specification of the collective history of his group or class, *each individual system of dispositions* may be seen as a *structural variant* of all the other group or class habitus" (p. 86).

Heidegger's existential ontology is the best description of human social being that philosophers have yet offered, but it is totally abstract. Heidegger is not interested in how the clearing – the understanding of being – is instantiated and how it is picked up by individuals and passed along from one generation to the next. Wittgenstein (1973), with his emphasis on forms of life, and Merleau-Ponty (1962), with his descriptions of the lived body, help us to see that Heidegger's ontology can be extended to the ontic realm – that is, to the domain of social and historical analysis. To fill in being-in-the-world one must see that what Heidegger is talking about are social *practices* (Wittgenstein) and that these practices are *embodied skills* that have a common style and are transposed to various domains (Merleau-Ponty); that is, that social skills have a unity and form a social field (Bourdieu). This makes possible an account of how durable and transposable bodily dispositions are appropriated and "projected" back into the situation without appeal to conscious or unconscious representations. Such is Merleau-Ponty's account of embodiment, relating action and the perceptual field by way of an intentional arc: "[T]he life of consciousness – cognitive life, the life of desire or perceptual life – is subtended by an 'intentional arc' which projects round about us our past, our future, our human setting, our physical, ideological and moral situation, or rather which results in our being situated in all these respects" (1962:136).

Merleau-Ponty, however, deals only with the general structure of perception and action. It is Bourdieu's notion of habitus that finally makes these ideas concrete. His use of phenomenological ontology allows us to see the way in which the bodily habitus anchors the homologies and analogies of the social field, how the ability to respond appropriately to events in the world arises from skills without recourse to rules and representations, and how what it is to be something in the social world is determined by and reciprocally determines practice. As Bourdieu nicely says (1990d: 194), there is an "ontological complicity between the habitus and the social field." Our socially inculcated dispositions to act make the world solicit action, and our actions are a response to this solicitation. Bourdieu, like Merleau-Ponty, exploits the richness of the word *sens* to capture the directedness of comportment; he also thinks of each practice as getting its significance from its place in the whole.

Such an ontology sets up the possibility of three kinds of research:

1   One can refine, extend, and unify the ontology. (For example,
    Bourdieu extends phenomenological ontology to the social field.)
2   One can give an objective description of how the general onto-
    logical structure works and show ethnographically how it gets
    worked out in specific societies at specific times (for example, an
    account of how the Berbers' habitus produces and is produced by
    the structure of the Berber house), thereby offering a "radical
    critique of theoretical reason" that accounts for the failure of
    other theories by showing that they are based on a mistaken
    ontology that privileges theory (for example, that Lévi-Strauss's
    structuralist theory of gift exchange cannot account for what it is
    to be a gift).
3   One can give an account of the meaning of the organized practices
    that relates comportment to an implicit understanding of what
    human beings are up to – an understanding that it is the job of the
    social scientist to make explicit.

These three dimensions of investigation comprise what we mean by
an ontologically informed research program whose results – and this
is Bourdieu's outstanding achievement – give us the categories in
which to see what social reality is, through a specific and general
description of how social practices work, and in the process demonstrates the scope and limits of human science.

An Empirical Metaphysics of Cultural Meaning

In order to launch his *science* of human being, Bourdieu needs an
explanatory principle that would account for the significance of *all*
practices beyond their local sense. We call "metaphysical" any such
account that claims to know objectively what it is to be a human
being. For example, the meaning of human being might be that man is
created by God to serve and praise him, or that man is the highest
manifestation of the will to power, or that human being is "a null
basis of a nullity" called to face up to its nothingness. A science of
human behavior for Bourdieu cannot just catalog these interpretations but must produce a single account of what human life is all
about. In Bourdieu's account, "social life ... is a race of all against
all": "The competition for a social life that will be known and recognized, which will free you from insignificance, is a struggle to the
death for symbolic life and death" (1990d: 196).

Bourdieu's originality consists in seeing that this is not a Hobbesian psychological claim. It is not a statement of a "naive finality," but an ontological claim about how "the principle of competition" in the social field is "the principle of all truly social energy" and is "productive of agents who act" (1983b: 2). Or more precisely:

> The motor – what is sometimes called motivation – resides neither in the material or symbolic purpose of action, as naive finalists imagine, nor in the constraints of the field, as the mechanistic thinkers suppose. It resides in the relation between the habitus and the field, which means that the habitus contributes to determining what determines it. (p. 194)

Bourdieu offers a specific account of how the social field works. It is a competition, not just for life and security as in Hobbes, but for advantage, and not just material advantage as in Marx, but more general symbolic advantage.

> [T]he science of economic practices is a particular case of a *general science of the economy of practices* capable of treating all practices, including those purporting to be disinterested or gratuitous, and hence noneconomic, as economic practices directed towards the maximizing of material or symbolic profit. (1977c: 183)

We think Bourdieu's project shows that he has correctly understood that for there to be a normal science, there must be specific, falsifiable, universal claims. In a human science, then, such a claim sets up a field of research in which the claim can be tested and in which any anomalies that arise can be seen as puzzles motivating further research. Such a program would establish sociology as a normal science.

Although Bourdieu does not thematize the distinction between *objective description* (point two in the ontological research program mentioned above) and *scientific theory* (which we are arguing goes beyond that program), his writings contain ample examples of both methods at work. Recognizing such a distinction would pose no serious problems for Bourdieu. For example, his analysis shows that one can describe the working of habitus (the Berber house) without recourse to the notion of symbolic capital. Indeed, Bourdieu's writings show that not only is objective description a convincing method for describing structures such as the Berber house, but that the method can be successfully extended to descriptions of the various social ways of making sense of what Merleau-Ponty calls "facticities", such as the seasons, fertility, death, eating, and so forth.

Bourdieu's attempt to formulate a scientific theory of social meaning has a radically different structure, however, from his objective description of social practices, and it raises many problems. Like the

scientific revolution in the physical sciences, Bourdieu's unified
science necessarily denies the validity of the manifold significance of
the practices to the practitioners. Behind these appearances he finds
the explanatory reality – the meaning of human being (maximizing
symbolic capital) – which structures the social field embodied in the
habitus. But in a theory of human being, unlike a theory of nature, the
theory must account for why the practitioners are deluded and why
the scientist is not. One way to account for the apparent anomalies,
the disparity between appearance and reality, is to claim that the
practices only work because their true meaning is repressed, denied,
disguised, concealed, and so on. Thus the logic of such a scientific
theory of human being leads Bourdieu, as it did Marx and Freud, to
postulate a repressed truth and to claim to be able to liberate human-
ity by revealing it.

Like Heidegger in Division Two of *Being and Time*, one could look
for an explanation of this ontological complicity: namely, that the
interestedness of everyday life – that is, the illusion that there are
intrinsic meaningful differences – is a motivated cover-up of the basic
arbitrariness of human purposes, sedimented in the social field, which
Heidegger calls "fallenness". Bourdieu opts for the cover-up story.
Illusio is his name for the self-deception necessary to keep players
involved in the game: "*Illusio* in the sense of investment in the game
doesn't become illusion, in the originary sense of the art of deceiving
myself... until the game is apprehended from the outside, from the
point of view of the impartial spectator, who invests nothing in the
game or in its stakes" (1990d: 195).

Such a structure, which has been called a "hermeneutics of suspicion", may well be inevitable in scientific theories of human being. If
there *were* an invariant, contentful human nature underlying and
explaining appearances, this Galilean strategy would be the one to
follow, but if there is no invariant human nature, then we would
expect serious methodological difficulties to emerge. Such a theory
must be able to answer objections, such as Popper's, that its redescrip-
tion of the phenomenon cannot be falsified and, consequently, that it
is not a science. The more common sense denies that *all* action is
motivated *solely* by the attempt to use the structure of the social field
to increase symbolic capital, the more the scientist sees evidence of the
necessity of preserving the *illusio* in order for the system to work. But
if the theorist, in the name of science, denies the surface meaning of
the phenomenon – that is, uses the objections of the actors that they
are being misinterpreted as further evidence for the universal principle
being affirmed – then either the theory must have independent evidence, such as successful prediction and control, to justify this move,

or else its claims to scientificity remain questionable. The theory will be able to take care of all anomalies, but only by making it impossible for there to be true anomalies.

An even stronger objection to Bourdieu's particular version of this demystifying methodology would be that symbolic capital is circularly defined so that whatever one acquires by one's social behavior can be tautologically re-encoded in terms of symbolic capital:

> Everyone knows by experience that what gets the senior civil servant going may leave the research scientist cold and that the artist's investments remain unintelligible to the banker. This means that a field can function only if it can find individuals who are socially predisposed to behave as responsible agents, to risk their money, their time, and sometimes their honor or their life, to pursue the objectives and obtain the profits which the field offers and which, seen from another point of view, may appear illusory. (1990d: 194)

Everything from accumulating monetary capital to praise for being burned at the stake automatically counts as symbolic capital. To say that whatever people do they do for social profit does not tell us anything if profit is defined as whatever people pursue in a given society.

These two problems arise because, in order to have a science, Bourdieu needs to claim that there is an analog to human nature and use it as a universal, explanatory principle. If, however, in response to the methodological problems it raises, one gives up this universal claim, as well as the science that it makes possible and that it is in turn supposed to justify, none of Bourdieu's objective descriptive contributions to our understanding of specific societies and society in general need be sacrificed. Bourdieu's powerful analyses have revealed to us a world permeated by strategies and strategists of symbolic capital and a social field that motivates and produces such strategies and strategists. All that needs to be abandoned is the empty claim that the struggle for symbolic capital alone constitutes human beings and the social field. Bourdieu's own metaphysics of meaning can still be retained as a hermeneutic strategy for opening up socially important areas of investigation that have so far been neglected by the human sciences. But the principle that is revealing as a heuristic principle becomes concealing if it is understood as totalizing; for then (1) it conceals what does not fit, or else (2) it requires a repression account of exceptions, and (3) the resulting demystifying methodology can never take actors' self-understanding at face value. (Not that they are always right, but the idea that a specific illusion is required to make the system work demands that the actors can *never* be right about their specific motivations.)

In order to preserve the revealing power of Bourdieu's insight, while avoiding its concealing effects, one must abandon the claim to have a scientific sociology. But all that is abandoned ultimately is the illusion that one is doing real science and all the symbolic (and material) capital that accompanies this privileged position.

The most telling objection, however, comes from the critique of metaphysics built into the ontology of Heidegger and Merleau-Ponty, which Bourdieu uses to such great advantage in his analyses of social reality. The very phenomenon of the ontological complicity of social space and habitus leads these thinkers to the thesis that one is inevitably situated within one's culture's understanding of reality. This ontology was developed to criticize the will to truth in the Platonic metaphysical tradition. But the Platonic view that truth can be arrived at by a completely detached unsituated thinker is the metaphysics that makes possible modern science.

Bourdieu's attempt to combine these two, antithetical ontologies seems to us a dubious undertaking. The strain shows when Bourdieu, on the one hand, points out the dangers of the unselfconscious projection of our science onto the understanding of reality implicit in the practices of other cultures, as when anthropologists try to understand native navigation as the application of an unconscious theory, and, on the other hand, demystifies the Algerian peasant who "maintain[s] a magical relationship with the land [that] make[s] it impossible for him to see his toil as labour" (1977c: 174). Thus Bourdieu's ontology enables him to avoid the mistake of reading the sociologist's theoretical approach to reality into the practices of other societies, whereas scientific theory requires him to impose our Western demystifying understanding of reality on other societies as the condition for arriving at a scientific understanding of their culture.

It follows from the Heideggerian/Merleau-Pontian understanding of human finitude as our inevitable involvement in a particular understanding of reality that constitutes us, that, as Bourdieu recognizes and demonstrates, you cannot get out of your own *sens pratique* just by recognizing that you have one. But this would seem to leave Bourdieu with a dilemma. If we are stuck in our embodied habitus, as Merleau-Ponty holds, then there is no position from which to do an objective, detached study of one's own sense of reality. If, however, in the interests of liberation, one claims, as Bourdieu does in *Leçon sur la leçon* (1982b), that doing objective social science enables one to stand outside the habitus and its *illusio* and demonstrate the working of social injustice, there is no convincing way of accounting for this new motivation. Bourdieu's answer appears to be that when the scientist gets outside the social habitus, he or she is simply open to a new motivation: namely, to expose social injustice. Heidegger held a similar view: both that anxiety is the experience that human life is ungrounded and that nothing is worth doing and that authentic action unproblematically consists in simply doing what shows up as needing to be done. But Heidegger abandoned this unconvincing solution, as well as the problem, when he abandoned Division Two of *Being and Time* as still too metaphysical. Bourdieu's fruitful research program based on the ontology of Merleau-Ponty would in no way be compromised if he, like Heidegger, abandoned the claim to be speaking from a uniquely authentic position. But he would then be obliged to admit that his *Wissenschaft* belongs not among the natural sciences but among the human ones.

References

Dreyfus, Hubert and Rabinow, Paul 1983: *Michel Foucault: beyond structuralism and hermeneutics*, 2nd edn. Chicago: University of Chicago Press.

Heidegger, Martin 1985: *The History of the Concept of Time*, trans. T. Kisiel. Bloomington: Indiana University Press.

Merleau-Ponty, M. 1962: *Phenomenology of Perception*. London: Routledge & Kegan Paul.

Wittgenstein, Ludwig 1973: *Philosophical Investigations*, trans. G. E. M. Anscombe. New York: Macmillan.

6

Theory in Practice

Louis Pinto

Is it possible to speak of the theoretical gains in Bourdieu's work, and of its contribution to philosophical analysis, without by this very action betraying or contradicting the principles that it contains, whose apparent purpose is to demonstrate the impossibility of separating the sense of a theory from its concrete use in the acquisition of knowledge?[1] There is undoubtedly a genuine risk, when one is using the language of the university thesis, of failing to recognize the almost imperceptible presuppositions of the position which both engenders and justifies it: the context, both genetic and referential, tends to be considered of relatively secondary importance, or merely accessory to the more essential content of the discourse. But however formalized it may be, the content is never transparent or unambiguous, as any number of mistakes and misunderstandings can demonstrate. What must be remembered is the extent to which any theoretical discourse, and more particularly any philosophical discourse, can generate specific illusions as soon as it becomes separated from a certain predetermined situation, which determines the conditions under which it functions effectively, and it begins to spin out of control, or as Wittgenstein put it, starts to go off the rails. Intellectual discussions would often be a lot more intelligible if theses were treated as a function of the intellectual habitus which gives them unity and coherence, and even more so if this habitus were then to be related to the problem areas and projects in the contemporary space against which the habitus is defined (by means of reaction, reformulation etc.).

Among Bourdieu's texts there is at least one that clearly reveals a theoretical intention in the practical state: the beginning ("Preface" and "Introduction") of *The Logic of Practice*.[2] This text is doubly instructive, explicitly defining the two great intellectual traditions against which but also in relation to which Bourdieu elaborated his theories, and thus clarifying the nature of his relation to the philosophical field.[3] It also provides a few transposable schemes which can be generalized and applied for the reflexive treatment of theoretical alternatives that become apparent in the practice of research. In *The Logic of Practice* (and in several other texts, notably those which look at the opposition between traditions which privilege knowledge, communication, and meaning, and traditions which privilege power relations between groups[4]), what is at issue is the opposition between objectivism and subjectivism. And Bourdieu's refusal of the binary oppositions is accompanied by an almost Leibnizian mode of understanding (rather than reconciling) opposites, which consists in unveiling the rational presuppositions hidden by each point of view, and showing how the conflict between apparently opposing visions originates, and is supported, not by pure logic, but by social constraints, whose importance is not perceived.

The Refusal of Theoretical Alternatives

For young philosophers of the post-war generation, who arrived on the scene after the great explosion of existentialist thought, the intellectual field was structured by the contrasting poles of existentialism (as incarnated by Sartre and above all Merleau-Ponty) and the opposing pole of rationalist, scientific culture represented initially by Brunschvicg, and then Bachelard, Canguilhem and Koyré. One way of understanding the different trajectories followed by apprentice philosophers at the beginning of the 1960s is in terms of the different composition of symbolic capital they possessed, and in particular the relative weight of scientific culture. Those closest to scientific culture were opposed to the exponents of a culture founded essentially on the humanities, and were dedicated to a radical subversion of the history of philosophy. The movement, however, was not without its pitfalls: there was a genuine risk of exclusion from the ranks of philosophers altogether, by seeming to push their scientific orientation too far toward "positivism".

Compared to the almost respectful subversions performed by individuals from the same generation more mindful of the proprieties (notably where academic success was concerned), Pierre Bourdieu's enterprise seemed to strike right at the heart of philosophy itself. It not only implied a confrontation with a concrete "terrain" at a time when writers at the forefront of philosophy were either proposing other sorts of texts for examination, or were simply looking at

canonical texts in a different manner, but it also adjourned *sine die* the
philosophical discourse of transcendence by means of which any
product which was labelled a theoretical text would normally have
been received. In the introduction to *Un art moyen* one can see the
beginnings of the ideas that would become so important in *Outline of
a Theory of Practice*[5] and *The Logic of Practice*: "It is time that the
human sciences abandoned to philosophy the fictitious alternative
between a subjectivism which persists in attempting to find the
place of pure origin of a creative action which cannot be reduced to
structural determinisms, and an objectivist pan-structuralism which
hopes to generate structures directly by a sort of theoretical parthe-
nogenesis.... To recall that objective conditions exist, and are realized
only in and as a product of the interiorization of the object conditions
that make up the system of dispositions is not to fall back into the
naïvetiés of subjectivism or personalism".[6]

Bourdieu's reaction against the structuralist style, contained in the
"theory of practice", found some of its resources in the opposing
tradition of phenomenology and existentialism. Merleau-Ponty was
one of the people who went furthest in demonstrating the specificity
of practical experience. Fighting simultaneously on two fronts,
against a materialist sort of naturalism and an intellectual brand of
spiritualism,[7] he proposed a mode of description where the fundamental elements were not closed substances but dynamic systems.
Using totalizing notions like that of the Gestalt, and "relation of the
world", he attempted to show that most of the questions and aporias
of traditional philosophy were the result of a point of view of knowledge which tried to undo and take apart something which actually
presented itself to spontaneous consciousness as an indivisible unity.
Perception, like gesture and expression, located as it is in a place
which is prior to the objective and the subjective, causes the world
to exist not as a totality of existing things, laid out in some fashion as
though to divine understanding, but as the horizon of everything
which is given as yet-to-be-done: "The football pitch, to a player
who is in the game, isn't an 'object'.... The pitch isn't given to him,
but is present as the immanent term of his practical intentions: the
pitch is more like a part of the player's body".[8]

To say that consciousness, before being a Cogito, is an "I can",[9] is
to note the pre-eminence of practical experience in the "foyer" that
makes up the Ego, but only through the possible experiences that
define it. Evoking what he calls the "general attitude towards the
world", Merleau-Ponty elsewhere proposes that "every individual
possesses a general structure of behavior which is expressed through
certain constants, regarding courses of action, sensitivity and motor

thresholds, affectivity, body temperature, breathing, pulse rate, blood pressure ... ".[10] One can easily imagine that statements along such lines (as well as notions like the general scheme, the opposition between intellectual comprehension and motor or practical comprehension, etc.) stimulated young philosophers wanting to escape the sovereign pretensions of philosophy without falling into any empiricist renunciation of philosophy.

The Self-Limitation of Scholarly Knowledge

The theory of practice also includes the imposition of form upon experience in a manner that one would hesitate to call "theoretical". To discover practice is most importantly to lose the assurance that theory is thought to bring, or rather it is to lose the belief in the omnipotence of the cognitive capital which is supposed to define the scholar-theorist. The academic establishment of which the scholar is the product does not merely procure legitimate knowledge, it also guarantees the legitimacy of those who are licensed to legislate the legitimate interpretations of the world. The establishment guarantees, at least ideally, the presumption of validity which is based on the idea that things are being represented "the way they really are", and this is the belief that is in question. The authority which is invested in qualified individuals excludes as unthinkable even the possibility of challenging their activity by a comparison with the singular properties of their own individual point of view: strictly speaking, they seem not to have a point of view, because, by definition, it is impossible to see from what other place that point of view might be determined.[11]

In turning to ethnology at the end of the 1950s, the young philosopher Bourdieu could have easily kept up the illusion of scholarly universalism, while accumulating the external trappings of academic excellence. His work on Kabylian society would have allowed him to expect scientific recognition, above all from the ruling authorities in the world of anthropology. Here his study of the idea of the "home" (examining the homologies between different regions of space, domestic space and the body) might be considered exemplary as it both made use of recent structuralist theory, and drew up a coherent program for further investigation.[12] Its constant oscillation between ethnology and sociology, the alternating between the view of the Kabylian peasant as part of the structure of a traditional village, and as a victim of the crisis in the means of peasant reproduction (which was also seen to affect the Algerian under-proletariat and peasants in the Béarn) were all clear indicators that the theoretical capital of structuralism could not simply be blindly applied in such cases and needed to be reviewed.

One way to conserve this capital was to transpose it from its original domain by attributing structuralism's intellectual structures to native peoples in some imperfect, approximative form, as a sort of sense of practice. The idea of the "rule" was superceded by the idea of the "strategy":[13] a social agent adjusts to situations with the results of a process of learning which spare him from a constant process of calculation and reflection. We still have equivalent, oppositional terms (such as high and low, right and left, sacred and profane, masculine and feminine etc.), but their status has become rather more profane, and, as simple schemes, the structures function in a more supple, conditional and limited fashion. Their space is not that of pure thought and formal combinations, of which a society, in Lévi-Strauss's view, is merely the empirical expression. Their place is instead the human body, as the ultimate condition of possibility of automatisms and their organization. Linked to the proprieties of agents and therefore to their interests, these structures have a social role to fulfil. Finally, mental structures, rather than being turned into absolutes as though they were transcendent structures, must rather be related to objective structures that constitute social formation, above all because they are the result of constraints which are not simply grounded in "human understanding" alone.

Bourdieu offers many exemplary descriptions of lived experience. But from the outset, he has insisted that sociology must be the subject's reappropriation of the meaning of experience originally (and socially) placed under the sign of alienation. The "subject", far from being that radical transcendence of which certain philosophers speak, is engaged and enveloped in a world which cannot be kept at a distance, and which imposes a horizon of various possibilities (responsibilities to be taken on, things to be accomplished, deferred, or annihilated). Subjects are constituted in and through this process of "pre-occupation" [pré-occupation].

The truth of experience which a sociologist hopes to catalogue presents itself initially, when seen from the inside, in the form of disenchantment and disillusion,[14] which is the practical equivalent of phenomenological reduction. After the act, it becomes clear that one has been caught up in the game. The very sense of urgency which the game seems to impart (where the possibilities to be accomplished appear to be indicated in a commanding, imperative manner) projects belief and engagement. The game of course is a metaphor, borrowed from the tradition of moralists and philosophers, but one which takes on a special meaning in sociology, as it demonstrates in the "pour soi" mode that same intricate and recursive network of expectation and probability, structure and planning as previous academic analyses attempted to build into theory in an "en soi" mode. Thinking through the game implies detachment and distance, not only with respect to the childish games that bring a smile to the face of the intellectual, but also when we think of the games that intellectuals themselves are playing. But to the person who attempts to think through all games, there still remains the game that he himself is playing, in which he is himself caught up; an unusual game, as the belief that it presupposes is realized in the study of all beliefs.

Of course, the sociologist's "subject", situated in the social world, does not in fact busy himself with all those slightly nebulous tasks that are the traditional concerns of philosophers of subjectivity (like hoping, loving, hating). He is more concerned with possibilities and properties of advancement that derive largely from "objective" distributional mechanisms of society, such as income or academic degrees. Because all the individuals in any given set (class, sex etc.) can be situated at a given moment in a given space of properties corresponding quite narrowly to a series of objective probabilities, the relation to the social world is inevitably characterized by certain fundamental modalities, which will indicate a space somewhere between a possession of all the attributes guaranteeing access to the various socially valorized possibilities, and a total lack of those attributes. Self-confidence belongs to the dominant parties whose excellence is a result of uniting "is" and "ought", being from the outset capable of being what one should be and what others cannot actually attain since those others' very efforts to achieve such excellence works against their achieving it.[15] This social "reality principle" which ensures that everyone goes to the limits of his or her possibilities is nothing other than the *habitus* itself, as an interiorization of external determining factors. Interiorization in the sense that it becomes something mental, and hence something profound involving a relation to the self; interiorization too in the sense that one takes on, or makes one's own, the thing that one feels somehow destined for.

By using his notion of the *habitus* to bring together the possible and probable, subjective hope and objective probability, the scientific path proposed by Bourdieu effects a reversal on phenomenology and existentialism. One can either valorize the remaining continuity of his work with these philosophical traditions in terms of its theorizing of lived experience. Or one can valorize Bourdieu's advances towards new theoretical objectives and towards an explanatory framework that philosophy itself seemed incapable of providing, a theory that could link the intelligibility of lived experience to the search for some sort of general unity in the subject, not that of an intentional aim, but rather a web of operations whose origin is the private trajectory of a given individual.

The *habitus* is a unifying principle, which makes possible a unitary, non-objectivist conception of social science. It strives to avoid drab uniformity, and goes beyond the fragmenting of experience into the various domains of practice like the spheres of the private and the public, the family, professional, cultural, economic heritage, etc. Its aim is to discern the links and parallels that exist between the practices of the same agent in different domains and to understand the relative weight or contribution that any defined practice (whether cultural, economic, domestic or whatever) makes to the production and reproduction of the identity of the social agent.

The alienation of the subject from himself is to a large extent the result of the fragmentation of the experience of the social world which is reproduced by positivist science and by phenomenology. The reversal performed by Bourdieu's sociology consists largely in abandoning the illusion of the subject without ever abandoning the totalizing project that was always discernible beneath that idea, giving it a more powerful formulation instead, so that identity is no longer a substance, but something that regulates the individual's transformations.

Defining identity by invariance, Bourdieu proposed an analysis of reproduction (both individual and collective) which included a study of the system of strategies of reproduction beyond phenomenal experience, as well as the study of that limit case of reproduction which he termed "reconversion" (understood as a change in properties for the purpose of maintaning one's relative position in the social space). This progress of abstraction that his opponents so much attacked constituted paradoxically a big gain in the understanding of the general meaning of agents' experience, as it negated the rather arbitrary boundaries of academic discourse, which all too often did little more than reproduce the oppositions of common sense.

Presuppositions and Predispositions

The purely intellectual needs for going beyond structuralism could never have inspired Bourdieu's new theoretical strategy, if (as Bourdieu himself has often recognized[16]), it had not been backed up by the desire to break with a particular experience of the intellectual world, "an almost visceral refusal of the ethical position implied by structuralist anthropology, and of the superior, distant relation that it created between the observer and the object, i.e. its ignorant subjects...".[17] Science's distance from the social world, which is nowhere more apparent than in structuralist ethnology, seems to gain in acceptability the more the social distance between the scientist and native grows. Proximity, on the other hand, engenders an unsustainable tension between identities which can only exist through separation: that of the researcher and that of the native, the researcher forgetting that he too is a native. The "double game" "double I" is stretched to breaking point.[18] For if one is to privilege the oppositional pairs of one universe, it is necessarily at the price of denying those of the other.

Thus in order to maintain a scientific façade, one must privilege above all else the objective language of rules, and thus, paradoxically, forget all that one knows as a native, i.e. as a person who has "a less abstract idea than home people of what it is to be a mountain peasant".[19] One must assume that typically intellectual form of arrogance which assigns the native person the status of an object of thought, incapable of many things: incapable of improvising new patterns of behavior, of playing with the rules through interpretation or even criticism, and incapable of possessing an even partial understanding of what is being done.

Such arrogance leads to naivety. In giving the scholar a monopoly on legitimate interpretation, it negates the extent to which the scholar's point of view might already have been anticipated by the native and integrated into his own point of view. To speak of the social world should properly involve an acceptance of two different forms of humility. Besides the traditional admission that scientific knowledge implies a complex and meticulous work of objectification, one should also make room for a more specific confession of the genuine limitations of theoretical knowledge and acknowledge that there are always two modes of being. Beyond the theoretical relation, there is always the practical relation to the world.

The theory of practice can be seen as the theorized expression of the attempt to overcome the contradictions of a "double I" caught between theory and practice, between the noble, unreal atmosphere of the academia and the brute, original universe. It is a question of inventing a theoretical, expressive form which escapes the effects of theoretical domination through theory, and develops the only kind of theoretical practice that can redeploy the tools used by the academy to new uses previously inconceivable in the "scholastic" tradition: In short, to wager that it is possible to have a science that does not derive its authority from escaping the real, or even, to turn science against its customary uses. As Bourdieu once said, "What I have done in sociology and ethnology has been as much a reaction to my education as it has been a result of it".[20]

Thus the refusal to choose between opposites, between subjectivism and objectivism, phenomenology and structuralism, finalism and mechanism and other couplings has not been a purely intellectual exercise. It is the refusal of someone who experiences an almost existential malaise when forced to engage totally in one of the innumerable social and intellectual games which have two inverse and symmetrical positions, or when asked to rejoin his socially granted place and share the illusions of all those complicitous adversaries who perpetuate the game by their disagreement, and their identity by their difference.

Transposed into the pure field of theory, the resistance to intellectualism took on a shape which was both socially legitimate and intellectually profitable. Against the scholar's traditional disinterested understanding, sociology proved itself by valorizing indigenous "common sense", action, interest, pleasure, the body, and much else besides. These are the legitimate resources of philosophical culture, but are present only in the practical state, where they must be brought into action to countermand the state of unreality which is one of the major effects of the traditional scientific treatment of experience.

A Copernican Sociology: The Objectification of the Scholar as Subject

For the sociologist, a theory of practice is first and foremost a theory of his own practice as knowing subject. To simply recognize native peoples in all their alterity would inevitably prove to be insufficient, if this was not accompanied by a complementary movement of self-examination. This introspection is a sort of solidarity from several points of view. First of all, it is a question of apprehending the limitations imposed on academic knowledge by the fact that native peoples are not simply defined by their status as objects of thought. By virtue of an experience which is socially quite improbable, the sociologist must renounce the traditional instruments of the cultivated, intellectual observer if he wishes to recognize the logic and necessity[21] of others, or even simply acquire the practical intelligibility behind their thoughts and words. As Wittgenstein demonstrated, what passes for the mythology of the native person might well be nothing less than a clever artifice that serves to camouflage the myths that are made explicit in the language and vision of the observer.[22]

The practice of others is neither an expression of "ignorance" as the intellectualist tradition incarnated by Frazer would have it, nor a more or less transparent game of transcendent rules as the structuralists would prefer, but rather a rule-governed, conditioned series of improvisations which has both objective and subjective limits and invariants in many forms: anticipations, compromises, challenges, and renunciations, to list but a few. A truly intelligent process of understanding the other can only come about through objective knowledge of causes, because the knowledge that facilitates an understanding of the native's logic is the only real manner in which the illusory temptations of condescension and well-meaning exoticism can be avoided.

The condition which allows the other to appear is the objectification of objectification, i.e. a process of self-objectification, and as such, a means of taking account of all the passions, even the purely intellectual ones, which the knowing subject experiences due to his specific position. In order to characterize the paradoxical position that this comprehending objectification occupies, Bourdieu has recently taken to using terminology from other intellectual horizons, quite distant from the positivist one of sociology, like "intellectual love" and "spiritual exercises".[23]

Once the false distance of objectivism has been destroyed, the other can be recognised as another "I": as an I, because it manifests generic traits and shared experiences, like honor, generosity, shame and confusion, and as an Other, because no matter how well founded in reason or necessity the practice of the other might be, it still belongs to a universe which is foreign, and which can only be appropriated through thought. Right up to the final act of writing, the sociologist should reflect on the obligations that are created for him by the status of this other objectified "I".

Secondly, reflexive sociology assumes the possibility of objectifying the scholar's point of view through that most essential instrument, the science of symbolic products. Setting up the idea of a "sociology of culture" doesn't simply imply being interested in a specific category of goods, but is above all an understanding of the inseparably transcendent and historical conditions of possibility of the scholar's representation and knowledge of the social world. At the outset, Bourdieu did not attack head on the fields philosophy designated as noble. Instead, he concentrated on the necessary preliminaries for his sociology of the scholar-subject through modest empirical inquiries on students and culture. To describe students was to map out the conditions and modalities of the academic and cultural excellence of his masters or peers while apparently talking only of apprentices, and thus to draw

up, or at least sketch out, a program for a sort of socio-analysis. The
rupture with academic ethnocentricity which had begun with the
work on Algeria, on the "illiterate" of the third world, found its
quite logical continuation in this later work on the regulators of
literary culture, and culminated in *Homo Academicus*.[24]

The central question of inheritance provides the connection
between these different studies. In whichever part of the social
world one chooses to examine, the heir is not simply the receiver of
some profit or privilege, but also the one who achieves the optimal
adjustment between two different orders. One order is external and
concerned with the distribution of the chances of appropriating the
inherited goods, and the other is internal, and concerned with
the aspiration to the destiny to which one is designated. The heir is
the person somehow disposed to receive whatever he has the right to
pretend to, that which is made for him. In effect, goods are only
constituted as goods in a relation of appropriation which presupposes
potential owners, who consider themselves to be worthy inheritors
and are acknowledged as such.

The sociology of culture also reveals its own heirs, products of a
social world marked by the comfortable familiarity of the insider and
the distress of the excluded outsider. The heir exists in opposition to
excluded nonmembers, newcomers and parvenus. To its improbable
elect, who for the most part come from popular backgrounds, the
academia proposes new fathers of its own kind, i.e. it offers them a
new filiation, and the destiny of an oblate. All this can only really be
escaped by challenging science and turning it from its natural course.
Such an enterprise presents enormous difficulties, because it tends to
become (as a mere science of such symbolic challenging) legitimate
and mild.

The different possibilities of inheritance have been Bourdieu's constant concern, from the most disinherited of the colonial world to the
most favored heirs, like the bourgeois boss or homo academicus, or
even those inheritors of deserted lands that have no future, and the
luckless heirs who sometimes push audacity to its limits and father
"symbolic revolutions".[25] The study of the French university system
allowed him to examine the relations between the hierarchy of scholarly values and the social hierarchy of the different kinds of habitus,
and thus to illuminate the mechanisms of scholarly selection. But this
study also allowed him to discern and examine that idea of greatness
which is handed down (and grows, diminishes or disappears) rather
like capital but exists in the still untheorized form of *cultural capital*,
a form of greatness that can never be totally objectified and that
marks those who appropriate it for themselves in a legitimate and

natural fashion, from interlopers whose pretensions to claim it are
discouraged.

The manner of being that defines the *habitus* is a sort of possession
and use, an acquired possession marked with time, whether it may be
the mark of ancient time or the time of effort and apprenticeship, and
where future time is also promised, as an assurance, an obligation, or
whatever. In his own way, in his own domain, the sociologist redis-
covers the Leibnizian critique of Cartesian mechanism, above all in
the refusal to admit the pure exteriority of movement; because behind
the fleeting positions and punctual realities available for empirical
observation, he attempts to discern the invisible influence of previous
movements and the presentiment of states to come, to see the dynamic
unity of effort or energy. The pertinent reality can only be that of
"trajectories,"[26] for the individuals who are examined only reveal
their full identity if one manages to unravel in time their law of variation, their particular "formula". Capital is that which is unequally
distributed and unequally available, which cannot be acquired instantaneously, and which presupposes the instruments of its appropriation. And none can escape its measure,[27] as no one is a pure subject,
nor an original source of choice or rationality. The social world is
peopled with heirs, even if it is often the case that all that is inherited
is the absence of an inheritance.

If the book *Les Héritiers*[28] was innovative, this was because it
invented a way of speaking of culture which took account of assumptions behind the practices being instilled in the student population and
beyond. While the dominant discourses of culture are often intimately
linked to the "internal" consideration of content (opus operatum), the
scientific view, by contrast, sets out to examine the general relation to
culture (modus operandi) in its all different modalities and models of
excellence. What is considered pertinent, in such a context, is often
remarkably different. No longer protected by indigenous proprieties,
the cultural content can then be thought through with reference to
universes very different in their social definition, linked to them by an
identical organizing principle in the form of the habitus, which is at
work equally in the spirit of the institution and in its body, marking
every gesture and pose, and regulating its likes and dislikes.

As the major invariant which required further definition and elaboration, the dominant habitus was already characterized, to different extents in different domains, by traits such as ease, naturalness,
and grace, which indicated an apparently timeless familiarity with
supreme values, and an assurance which authorized a distance from
rules, constraints and necessities. This vision called into question
some of the tacit presuppositions of the point of view normally

adopted by intellectuals when talking of the "bourgeois", and revealed a certain underlying complicity and similarity which united these two dominant groups beyond their most apparent differences.

The pre-eminence accorded to practical sense in the form of a "relation to culture" involved, or rather illustrated, a revolution in the scientific representation of the social world which might rightly be described as Copernican, in the sense that objective knowledge must include knowledge of the conditions of objectification. To think through the condition of the heir was not simply to take an object amongst others, but to allow oneself the means of an intellectual liberty regarding inheritance of any sort. It was to demonstrate the form of the yet unthought, not, like other theorists, in the shape of clandestine theories of some nebulous idea of what constituted "the West", but rather in the tacit (apparently anodyne yet extremely effective) schemes which determine and place limits on legitimate thought. And there was a considerable risk that all of those who had become theorists through their possession of specific capital would be rather disappointed here, and discover that while they had assumed that science would allow them to take up a theoretical position in debates, with a recognizable and accepted point of view, it would instead become apparent that the theory of practice also applies to the practice of theory, and even to philosophy too.

Theory as Knowledge and Power

A practical genealogy of the theory of practice ought to demonstrate at least that these Copernican renunciations, while depriving us of an inheritance of happy certitude, more than compensate for this in another manner. We would do well to remember that given the dominant presence of the idea of "theory" that was strongly and durably marked by the culture of philosophy, sociology (and particularly empirical sociology) was inevitably destined for rejection and would soon have found itself placed outside the boundaries of the field of theory. While the dominant structuralism seemed to incarnate intellectualism in its most accomplished forms, in order to challenge this domination *and* philosophy's there was need for a more powerful theory, i.e. one capable of assimilating the gains of structuralism while also demonstrating its limits.

What was required was a theory that went further than its predecessors (which Bourdieu thought were guilty of a "massive renunciation"[29]), and would actually take account of what seemed most foreign to scholarly understanding, i.e. the lived experience of native peoples. This was not to be considered residual, but as an integral part of reality. The "objective reality" revealed by the researcher's observation is always to be found at some level (conscious or unconscious) of an agent's mind. It might be said to condition him, but only in the form of dissimulation or denial, like the man of honor in a traditional society who "gives without counting"[30] as well as that of the contemporary student who hopes to prolong indefinitely the indetermination of an existence without constraints.[31]

The knowledge of the social conditions of misunderstanding constitutes one of the fundamental aspects of science, if one understands that the social world exists also in the objectivity of representations and points of view.

In the final analysis, it is quite clear that, conceived as an alternative to structuralism, the theory proposed by Bourdieu transcends sociology's limits and points towards a general theory of anthropology, encompassing both ethnology and sociology. The intellectualist presuppositions of structuralism could initially be used to examine the very similar universe studied by ethnologists, who, although not always aware of this, work on limit cases of societies in which relations of force are as small as possible: hence the project to treat structures primarily through some sort of cognitive relation of meaning.[32]

The theory of practice, by contrast, because it foregrounded strategy, interest, and capital, appeared much more appropriate for the description of differentiated universes like modern societies. Moreover, at the heart of pre-capitalist societies, a form of capital was discernible in the idea of symbolic capital, which has equivalents in our own societies. The general anthropology suggested by Bourdieu transformed the status of structuralist theory, which had been quite dominant until then, by according it a more limited function, reducing its status to that of one particular pole. The theoretical approach exemplified by Durkheim, Cassirer and Saussure does an excellent job of providing certain logical classifications, but is quite incapable of coping with ideas like conflict, class struggle and politics, which are therefore consigned to the other pole, represented by Weber and Marx;[33] this second pole of course has its own limitations and blindspots.

One major gain in surpassing the intellectualist point of view was to oblige those possessing all the resources of theory to abandon their privilege of exteriority in relation to the social world. The point of view from which the sociologist (as subject) sees and constructs the social world must also be viewed as an object. To combat the dominant hierarchies which simply reproduce the point of view of the dominant parties, Bourdieu used the only possible device at his disposal to subvert them, that of a total objectification which embraced not simply the set of all possible "objects" (regardless of rank or social strictures) but the objectification of those objects too, and so, ultimately, of the producers of that process as well.

There is another set of dualistic alternatives that Bourdieu's theory of practice urges us to transcend: the particular versus the universal, history as against scientific rationality, the cynical vision of what are apparently the purest of intentions (e.g. the scholar's) and the good conscience of idealism. Science is a game that would be nothing without passion, but where competition elicits effects that are not simply reducible to passion. It can thus be considered either from an epistemological point of view by looking at its works, or from a sociological point of view by examining that endless movement (where memory is of such importance) towards the construction of its universal claims.

One of the functions of the notion of the field,[34] which was elaborated after the notion of the habitus, is to make possible and begin the objective analysis of competing positions, particularly, but not exclusively, in the intellectual universe. Instead of living these alternatives and conflicts on a practical, involved level (which is sometimes painful and cruel), the idea of the field is a tremendous intellectual advance that allows one to think through points of view in the relative truth that they have as points of view. By putting in question the theoretical posture that science calls "the final analysis", it implies not a profession of faith in some sort of relativism but an affirmation of immanence, i.e. the deep-rooted historicity of all cultural productions, even those apparently "final" ones of scientific logic.[35] There is neither dogmatism nor terrorism in this move towards objectification: to demonstrate to the world the manner in which knowledge is mediated is above all to de-dramatize it, showing the differences that underlie objectification. It is to demonstrate concretely that any position (as inscribed in a field) can be examined fairly, in a process of positive description which is free from any prejudicial epistemological evaluation, even when it brings considerable and occasionally decisive clarification. Such, after all, is the function of radical rationalism, provoking us to recognize as far as we possibly can the effects of historical determination, even in the genesis of universals.

Conclusion

I believe that Pierre Bourdieu's originality is not where it is usually thought to be. His "theory", if indeed this is the word that we want, is first and foremost a working method founded on reflexivity, and this perhaps is "the most significant product of [his] whole undertaking."[36] Sociology is obliged to deconstruct with its own means the reality that the social world constructs through language: to scientifically deconstruct the socially effective constructions typically held to be legitimate. It thus brings a healthy methodological nominalism, which allows one to resist the verbal icons and fetishes of generalizing theoretical discourse (the academia, the state, the class etc.).

But this critical stance, if it has obvious philosophical implications, is quite different from the one which has traditionally prevailed in philosophy. For it always starts out from the social world in order to think out the conditions of objective knowledge as well as the obstacles to this knowledge. Whereas the questions addressed by philosophers often reflect the traits of an intellectual practice dominated by "scholastic" abstraction, as the poverty of examples propped up by some rudimentary form of phenomenology seem to show, Pierre Bourdieu's sociology has the merit of always attempting to keep its "theoretical" objectives proportional to the empirically testable means implied by sociological practice.

His method tends towards the dissolution of certain questions,[37] demonstrating that they depend in part on fictitious oppositions like those evoked above (e.g. the subjective and the objective, reason and cause, explaining and understanding, economy and culture), but also demonstrating that these oppositions also have a social foundation which philosophers forget to take into account, due to their conception of what belongs within the frame of their enterprise. This omission is perhaps philosophy's last great form of naïvety.

Notes

1   On this point, see in particular the second part of *Réponses*, "La pratique de l'anthropologie réflexive. Introduction au séminaire de l'Ecole des Hautes Etudes en Sciences Sociales, Paris (October 1987)", in P. Bourdieu, with L. Wacquant, *Réponses, Pour une anthropologie réflexive* (Paris: Seuil, 1992), pp. 187–231; English translation, "The Practice of Reflexive Sociology (The Paris Workshop)", in Pierre Bourdieu and Loïc J. D. Wacquant, *An Invitation to Reflexive Sociology* (Chicago: University of Chicago Press, 1992), pp. 217–260.

2   Pierre Bourdieu, *Le Sens pratique* (Paris: Minuit, 1980); in English, *The Logic of Practice*, tr. R. Nice (Cambridge: Polity Press, 1989).

3   See also, among other texts that are at least partly autobiographical, P. Bourdieu, *Choses dites* (Paris: Minuit, 1987), in particular pp. 13–46; in English, *In Other Words: Essays Towards a Reflexive Sociology*:

trans. M. Adamson (Cambridge: Polity Press, 1990); the preface to the English edition of *Homo Academicus*, trans. P. Collier (Cambridge: Polity Press, 1988); "Aspirant philosophe. Un point de vue sur le champ universitaire dans les années cinquante", in *Les Enjeux philosophiques des années cinquante* (Paris: Centre Georges Pompidou, 1991), pp. 15–24.

4   Cf P. Bourdieu, "Genèse et structure du champ religieux", *Revue française de sociologie*, vol. 12 no. 3, 1971, pp. 295–334, and "Sur le pouvoir symbolique", in *Annales*, no. 3, 1977, pp. 405–11.

5   P. Bourdieu, *Esquisse d'une théorie de la pratique* (Geneva: Droz, 1972); translated as *Outline of a Theory of Practice*, tr. R. Nice (Cambridge: Cambridge University Press, 1977).

6   P. Bourdieu, Introduction to P. Bourdieu, L. Boltanski, R. Castel, J-C. Chamboredon, *Un art moyen, Essai sur les usages sociaux de la photographie* (Paris: Minuit, 1965), p. 22; English translation, *Photography: A Middle-brow Art*, trans. Shaun Whiteside (Cambridge: Polity Press, 1990), p. 5 (translation altered).

7   M. Merleau-Ponty, *La structure du comportement* (Paris: PUF, coll. Quadrige, 1990), p. 100 (first edition 1942); English trans. *The Structure of Behavior*, trans. Alden Fisher (London: Methuen, 1963).

8   Ibid., pp. 182–3.

9   M. Merleau-Ponty, *La Phénoménologie de la perception* (Paris: Gallimard, 1945), p. 160; *Phenomenology of Perception*, trans. Colin Smith (London: Routledge and Kegan Paul, 1962); for this part of Merleau-Ponty's thought, central to any analysis of the idea of the *habitus*, see P. Bourdieu and L. Wacquant, *An Invitation to Reflexive Sociology*, pp. 21–2.

10 M. Merleau-Ponty, *La Phénoménologie de la perception*, pp. 160–1.

11 As a study of the university field, and dedicated therefore, in a certain measure, to the objectification of those who normally objectify, *Homo Academicus* put into practice in systematic form the intellectual position which had long been discernible in the work of Pierre Bourdieu.

12 "La maison Kabyle ou le monde renversé", a text published in 1969 as part of a homage to Claude Lévi-Strauss, was reproduced first as a "study of Kabyle ethnology" in *Esquisse d'une théorie de la pratique*, then as an appendix in *Le sens pratique*, where it was preceded by a brief note intended "to evoke the limits of structuralist thought" (p. 441). In English it appears as an appendix entitled, "The Kabyle house or the world reversed", in *The Logic of Practice*, trans. Richard Nice (Cambridge: Polity Press, pp. 271–84), where Bourdieu notes in a footnote that "this interpretation of space inside the Kabyle household remains within the limits of structuralist thought" (pp. 316–17).

13 Critiques of the notion of the rule fall into one of three categories: the notion's inadequacy for describing observed reality, internal contradiction, and implied consequences regarding the general objectives of social science.

14 Bourdieu prefers the latter term, doubtless as "disenchantment" has too many Weberian overtones.

15 P. Bourdieu, *La Distinction, Critique sociale du jugement* (Paris: Minuit, 1979), p. 286; *Distinction: A Social Critique of the Judgement of Taste*, trans. Richard Nice (London: Routledge and Kegan Paul, 1986), p. 256.

16 See for this above all *Choses dites*, pp. 32–3; English translation, *In Other Words, Essays Towards a Reflexive Sociology*, tr. M. Adamson (Cambridge: Polity Press, 1990), pp. 21–2, and *Réponses*, pp. 176–7 (English translation, *An Invitation*, pp. 202–3)

17 Ibid., p. 31. *In Other Words*, p. 20 (translation amended)

18 *Le Sens pratique*, p. 30.

19 Ibid., p. 30; "double je, ou . . . double Je"; (this play on words is omitted from the English translation, p. 14); see also *Choses dites*, p. 32 (*In Other Words* p. 20), and *Réponses*, p. 138ff. (*An Invitation*, pp. 162–7). In the German edition of *Choses dites*, Bourdieu describes in greater detail the role that personal experience of Algeria has played for him (an experience above all, it should be remembered, of the war of independence). Spontaneously attracted by the generous principles of progressive French intellectuals like Sartre, and driven by a desire to bear witness, he found himself simultaneously immersed in a terrain which helped him to measure the abyss between intellectual representations of the protagonists (Algerian revolutionaries, racist "pied-noir" etc.) and his own impressions which were much closer to the lived experience of the actors in the conflict, and to their categories and their affective ties.

20 *Réponses*, p. 176; *An Invitation*, p. 204.

21 The philosophical tradition which opposes reason and nature, liberty and necessity, etc., has a tendency to make practical logic quite unintelligible, as it is not a question of some sort of abstract reason faced with a series of abstract possibilities, but rather the meeting of two different series of causes: that of objective, conditional probabilities (like getting his work into the museum, becoming a doctor, etc.) and that of subjective dispositions which, produced by the same conditions as the objective ones, favor whatever course of action has the greatest chance of success; any failure here of course is also worthy of scientific examination.

22 L. Wittgenstein, "Remarks on Frazer's *Golden Bough*", in *Philosophical Occasions*, 1912–1951 (Cambridge: Hackett, 1993); and J. Bouveresse, "L'animal cérémoniel: Wittgenstein et l'anthropologie", *Actes de recherche en sciences sociales*, 16 (1977).

23 See "Comprendre" in P. Bourdieu, *La Misère du monde* (Paris: Seuil, 1993), pp. 909 and seq.

24 "*Homo Academicus* represents the culmination, in at least a biographical sense, of a very self-conscious 'epistemological experiment' I started in the early 1960s" (*Réponses*, p. 147; *An Invitation*, p. 67).

25 One could advance the hypothesis that the formation of Bourdieu's own intellectual *habitus* was the chance product of a double crisis in means

of reproduction: the one affecting the peasant universe of his origins, the other, slightly more contemporary, calling into question the foundations of the university itself.

26 For this reason the analysis of the conditions of transmission of (symbolic) cultural capital are what best lead to an understanding of both the formation of the *habitus* and the condition of the heir.

27 This extremely general formulation should not serve to obscure the existence of a multiplicity of different forms of capital, corresponding to the multiplicity of socially differentiated universes.

28 P. Bourdieu and J.-C. Passeron, *Les Héritiers: Les étudiants et la culture* (Paris: Minuit, 1964), in English, *The Inheritors – French Students and their Relation to Culture* (1964), trans. R. Nice (Chicago: University of Chicago Press, 1979).

29 *Un art moyen*, p. 17; *Photography: A Middle-brow Art*, p. 1.

30 See the study, "Le sens de l'honneur", (reproduced in *L'Esquisse*) where one can find, particularly on p. 43, a first draft (1960) of the later analyses of the relations between honor and economy, gift and exchange, etc. See *Outline of a Theory of Practice*, trans. Richard Nice (Cambridge: Cambridge University Press, 1977), p. 48.

31 *Les Héritiers*, p. 83ff; *The Inheritors*, 54 ff.

32 There were of course also attempts to adapt structuralism to the terrain of more developed societies, but they seemed to inevitably become embroiled in the formalism and idealism which characterized semiological approaches to fashion, literary texts, etc.

33 See the article cited above, "Genèse et structure du champ religieux", (p. 295): "In order to escape from one of these magic circles without simply falling into the next one [...] one should try and situate oneself in terms of a geometrical relation, where different perspectives come into play, i.e. at a point from where one can see at the same time everything that is both visible and invisible from all the other points of view".

34 By allowing us to make explicit the question of the unity of analysis, and obliging us to revise quite comprehensively naive ideas about choice and causality in the social world, the notion is clearly indispensable to the theory of practice, which it completes and renders considerably more complicated.

35 On the historicity of reason see, for example, P. Bourdieu, *Choses dites*, p. 43 ff, as well as *Réponses*, p. 162 ff.

36 *Le Sens pratique*, p. 30; (Engl., p. 15).

37 "To 'dissolve' the big questions by applying them to objects that from a social point of view were minor or indeed insignificant, and in any case closely defined, and thus capable of being empirically apprehended such as photographic practices". P. Bourdieu, *Choses dites*, p. 30 (IOW 19).

7

Performativity's Social Magic

Judith Butler

Modalities of practices...are powerful and hard to resist precisely
because they are silent and insidious, insistent and insinuating.

Pierre Bourdieu

The work of Pierre Bourdieu has become important to a number of
intellectual inquiries across the social sciences and the humanities as
much for its interdisciplinary range as for the theorization of social
and linguistic practice that it offers. Clearly informed by a Marxian
conception of class, although reformulated in less substantializing
terms, Bourdieu's work offers a reading of social practice that reintroduces the market as the context of social power, and argues
that social power is not fully reducible to the social practices they
condition and inform.

Bourdieu will insist that a certain intellectualism, taking place
recently under the rubric of "literary semiology" or "linguistic formalism", misconstrues its own theoretical construction as a valid
description of social reality. Such an intellectual enterprise, according
to Bourdieu, not only misunderstands the positions of social power
that it occupies within the institutions of the legitimate academy, but
it also fails to discern the critical difference between *linguistic* and
social dimensions in the very textual practices that it attends.

He will also argue, however, that a certain subjectivism[1] undermines the effects of an ethnographic practice that imagines itself to
inhabit the very social practices that it reveals, and which does not
consider the problem of translation that inevitably emerges between
the taken-for-granted reality of the ethnographer and those of the
subjects he attends. In relation to this latter problem, Bourdieu
elaborates the conception of the *habitus*, those embodied rituals of

everydayness by which a given culture produces and sustains belief in its own "obviousness".[2] In this way, Bourdieu underscores the place of the body, its gestures, its stylistics, its unconscious 'knowingness' as the site for the reconstitution of a practical sense without which social reality would not be constituted as such. The practical sense is a sense of the body, where this body is not a mere positive datum, but the repository or the site of incorporated history.[3]

The *habitus* maintains a constrained but non-causal relation to the practices that it informs. Composed of a set of dispositions that incline subjects to act in certain ways, the *habitus* does not determine that action causally. These dispositions may be said to motivate certain actions and, to the extent that these actions are regularized, to compel a set of practices. But practices are not unilaterally determined by the *habitus*; they emerge at the site of conjuncture between the *habitus* and what Bourdieu will call specific social "fields" where the ultimate or ultimately determining field is "the market".[4] Practices presuppose belief, where belief is generated by the *habitus* and, specifically, the dispositions out of which the *habitus* is composed. And yet, as a necessary counter to this apparently subjectivistic account of practices, Bourdieu will argue that a set of fields and, indeed, the market as ultimate field, will inform and limit practices from an objective direction.

For the moment, I propose to consider first the generative capacity of the *habitus* on practice, and then consider the "objective" determination of practice performed by fields. I will propose that the distinction between the subjective and objective dimensions of practice is itself difficult, if not impossible, to maintain, considered from the point of view of practice and its theoretical reconstruction. The distinction between subjective and objective will be shown to operate homologously to the distinction between the linguistic and the social, and to what is claimed for the "internal" dimension of performative language over and against what is "external" to language.

Bourdieu will invoke the phenomenon of *social magic* to characterize the productive force of performative speech acts, and yet this same term might well apply to the *habitus*, his notion of "the bodily hexis", and the social effects that this embodied practice produces. The generative or productive domain of the *habitus* is not linked to the problem of performativity that Bourdieu elaborates in relation to the problem of intellectualism and linguistic formalism. In these latter contexts, Bourdieu rethinks the meaning of performative speech acts in a direction counter to Austin's in order to establish the dual and separate workings of social and linguistic elements in constituting what makes certain kinds of speech acts into "social magic", that is, what gives certain speech acts the efficacious force of authority. To what extent is the *habitus* structured by a kind of performativity, admittedly one that is less explicit and juridical than the examples drawn from the operation of state power, i.e. marriage, declarations, pronouncements of various kinds? To what extent can performativity be thought as an embodied activity for which the distinction between the social and the linguistic would not be readily thinkable?

Bourdieu's work thus gives rise to two interrelated questions which will form the focus of this essay: (1) can the "generative" dimension of the *habitus* be thought in relation to the efficaciousness of the illocutionary performative speech act, (2) can the social and linguistic dimensions of the performative speech be strictly separated if the body becomes the site of their convergence and productivity? In other words, once the body is established as a site for the working through of performative force, i.e. as the site where performative commands are received, inscribed, carried out, or resisted, can the social and linguistic dimensions that Bourdieu insists on keeping theoretically separate, be separated at all in practice?

The Body and its Belief

> The body believes in what it plays at: it weeps if it mimes grief. It does not represent what it performs, it does not memorize the past, it *enacts* the past, bringing it back to life.
>
> Bourdieu, "Belief and the Body"[5]

Following Merleau-Ponty, Bourdieu understands the body as a form of engagement with the world, where this engagement is understood as a kind of regularized activity that conforms to the "objective" demands of a given field. The body does not merely act in accordance with certain regularized or ritualized practices, but it *is* this sedimented ritual activity; its action, in this sense, is a kind of incorporated memory.[6] Here the apparent materiality of the body is recast as a kind of practical activity, undeliberate and yet to some degree improvisational. But this *habitus* that the body *is* is generated by the tacit normativity that governs the social game in which the embodied subject acts. In this sense, the body appropriates the rule-like character of the habitus through playing by those rules in the context of a given social field.[7] Its participation in the game is the precondition for a mimesis or, more precisely, a mimetic identification, that acquires the habitus precisely through a practical conformity to its conventions. "The process of acquisition," Bourdieu writes, is "a practical *mimesis* (or mimeticism) which implies an overall relation of identification and has nothing in common with an *imitation* that would presuppose a conscious effort to reproduce a gesture, an utterance or an object explicitly constituted as a model."[8] This acquisition is historical to the extent that the "rules of the game"[9] are, quite literally, *incorporated*, made into a second nature, constituted as a prevailing *doxa*. Neither the subject nor its body forms a 'representation' of this conventional activity, for the body is itself formed in the *hexis*[10] of this mimetic and acquisitive activity. The body is, thus, not a purely subjective phenomenon that houses memories of its participation in the conventional games of the social field; its participatory competence is itself dependent on the incorporation of that memory and its knowingness. In this sense, one can hear strong echoes of Merleau-Ponty on the sedimented or habituated "knowingness" of the body, indeed, on the indissociability of thought and body: "Thought and expression...are simultaneously constituted, when our cultural store is put at the service of this unknown law, as our body suddenly lends itself to some new gesture in the formation of habit."[11]

To the extent that Bourdieu acknowledges that this *habitus* is formed over time, and that its formation gives rise to a strengthened belief in the "reality" of the social field in which it operates, he understands social conventions as animating the bodies which, in turn, reproduce and ritualize those conventions as practices. In this sense, the *habitus* is formed, but it is also *formative*. The *habitus* is not only a site for the reproduction of the belief in the reality of a given social field – a belief by which that field is sustained – but it also generates *dispositions* which are credited with "inclining" the social subject to act in relative conformity with the ostensibly objective demands of the field.[12] Strictly speaking, the *habitus* produces or generates dispositions as well as their *transposability*. The problem of translating between competing or incongruent fields is potentially resolved through recourse to the habitus. Resolving the problem of translation is not simply a matter of conceptually or intellectually demarcating the conventions that govern a given social field other than one's own, but, rather, suspending the intellectualist conceit of a representational demarcation in favor of a mimetic and participatory 'knowledge' decidedly more incorporative.

What precisely is the formative capacity of the *habitus*, and how does it work to "incline" action of a given kind without fully determining that action? First of all, the *habitus* does not act alone in the generation of dispositions, for the field exercises its demands as well. The distinction between the *habitus* and the field is a tenuous one, however, since the *habitus* does not merely encounter the *field*, as a subjective phenomenon encounters a countervailing objective one; rather, it is only on the condition that a 'feeling for the game' is established, that is, a feeling for how to operate within the established norms of the social field, that the habitus is built up. Indeed, the *habitus* is the sedimented and incorporated knowingness that is the accumulated effect of playing that game, operating within those conventions. In this sense, the *habitus* presupposes the field as the condition of its own possibility.

And yet, Bourdieu will invoke the trope of an epistemological encounter or event both to separate and to render dynamic the productive convergence of the subjective domain of the *habitus* and the objective domain of the field. The dispositions generated by the *habitus* are themselves "durably inculcated by the possibilities and impossibilities, freedoms and necessities, opportunities and prohibitions inscribed in the objective conditions"; further, the *habitus* will "generate dispositions objectively compatible with these conditions and in a sense pre-adapted to their demands."[13] The dispositions are thus generated by the *habitus*, but the *habitus* is itself formed through the mimetic and participatory acting in accord with the objective field. Indeed, the rules or norms, explicit or tacit, that form that field and its grammar of action, are themselves *reproduced* at the level of the *habitus* and, hence, implicated in the *habitus* from the start.

This mutually formative relation between *habitus* and field, however, is occluded by the dramatic trope that figures their relation as an "encounter" or epistemological "event". This staging of the relation presumes that the *habitus* must be adjusted by the field and that an *external* relation between them will be traversed through the action by which a *habitus* submits to the rules of the field, thus becoming refashioned in order to become "congruent" or "compatible". Hence, the ideal of *adaptation* governs the relation between *habitus* and field, such that the field, often figured as preexisting or as a social given, does not alter by virtue of the *habitus*, but the *habitus* always and only alters by virtue of the demands put upon it by the "objectivity" of the field. Clearly an effort to avoid the pitfalls of subjectivism and idealism, the thesis of the objective field nevertheless runs the risk of enshrining the social field as an inalterable positivity.

Indeed, the question of whether or not the field itself might be altered by the *habitus* appears ruled out by virtue of the objective agency attributed to the field. Bourdieu continues the above remarks with the following: "The most improbable practices are therefore excluded, as unthinkable, by a kind of immediate submission to order that inclines agents to make a virtue of necessity, that is, to refuse what is anyway denied and to will the inevitable."[14] Bourdieu thus draws on the Althusserian formulation of 'subjection' to ideology as the mastery of a certain practice in showing how submission to an order is, paradoxically, the effect of becoming savvy in its ways.[15] For Bourdieu, however, there is an "order" which "inclines" agents to "submission", but "inclination" is also conditioned by the *habitus*, and so remains to a certain extent a site where the demands of the objective order and "regulated improvisations"[16] of the *habitus* are negotiated. If the order "inclines", but if the *habitus* is also that which produces dispositions that "incline", then whatever discrepant pressures exist between these separate sources that bear on inclination may well produce inclination itself as a site of necessary ambivalence. Indeed, the psychoanalytic argument would doubtless underscore that the mimetic acquisition of a norm is at once the condition by which a certain resistance to the norm is also produced; identification will not "work" to the extent that the norm is not fully incorporated or, indeed, incorporable. The resistance to the norm will be the effect of an incomplete acquisition of the norm, the resistance to mastering the practices by which that incorporation proceeds.[17] But because for Bourdieu practical mimeticism works almost always to produce a conformity or congruence between the field and the *habitus*, the question of ambivalence at the core of practical mimeticism – and, hence, also in the very *formation* of the subject – is left unaddressed. Indeed, where there is discrepancy or "misrecognition" in Bourdieu, it is a function of an "encounter" between an already formed subject in an epistemological confrontation with an external and countervailing field.

For Bourdieu, practical mimeticism for the most part *works*, and this achieved congruence between field and *habitus* establishes the ideal of adaptation as the presiding norm of his theory of sociality. If the *habitus* is from the start implicated in the field, then the *habitus* only disingenuously confronts or "encounters" the field as an external and objective context. On the contrary, the "inclining" produced by the *habitus* and the "inclining" produced by the field may well be the *same* inclining. Discerning the discrepant pressures of either side of this conjectured encounter would be rendered impossible.

Indeed, one might well argue that if the incorporated and mimetic participatory engagement with the world that marks the *habitus* as such is constituted by the very field that it comes to encounter, then the figuring of the "encounter" as an epistemological face-to-face is itself a belated and imposed scenario, one which occludes the formative operations of the field in the formation of the embodied subject itself. Indeed, is there a subject who pre-exists its encounter with the field, or is the subject itself *formed* as an embodied being precisely through its participation in the social game within the confines of the social field? This question is important not only to underscore that the *habitus* does not primarily "encounter" the field as an external or objective field, but to show that the field could not be reconstituted without the participatory and generative *doxa* of the *habitus*. Conversely, the *habitus* presupposes the field from the start, and is itself composed of sedimented rituals framed and impelled by the structuring force of that field. Indeed, it seems that the subject, insofar as it is necessarily embodied, and the body is itself the site of "incorporated history", is not set over and against an "objective" domain, but has that very "objectivity" incorporated as the formative condition of its very being.

When Does a Speech Act "Act"?

> The essentially performative character of naming is the precondition of all hegemony and politics.
>
> Ernesto Laclau[18]

The distinction between the subjective and objective domains of practice are offered by Bourdieu in order to illustrate both the necessary convergence of the two domains and their irreducibility to one another. This dualism, however, comes to haunt the very notion of practice that is supposed to render those disparate aims congruent or compatible. The presumptions of an objective field or the "market" as a preexisting context, on the one hand, and a subject spatially positioned in that context, on the other hand, are sustained in the very notion of practice, constituting an intellectualist dualism at the core of a practical activity that may well enact the refutation of that very dualism.

The distinction between social and linguistic practice that emerges in the context of Bourdieu's various remarks on performative speech acts suggests not only that this distinction is a tenuous one, but that it holds significantly restrictive consequences for his understanding of performativity as political discourse. Further, it seems that, apart from the "official" use of the speech act on the part of state authorities, there is a more tacit or covert operation of the performative that produces prevailing *doxa* in much the same way that Bourdieu describes the *doxa*-generating capacity of the *habitus*.

In particular, there is the question of interpellations that might be said to "hail" a subject into being, that is, social performatives, ritualized and sedimented through time, that are central to the very process of subject-formation as well as the embodied, participatory *habitus*. To be hailed or addressed by a social interpellation is to be constituted discursively and socially at once. Being called a "girl" from the inception of existence is a way in which the girl becomes transitively "girled" over time. This interpellation need not take on an explicit or official form in order to be socially efficacious and form-ative in the gendering of the subject. Considered in this way, the interpellation as performative establishes the discursive constitution of the subject as inextricable from the social constitution of the subject. Further, it offers an account of the social as formative of the subject where the dramatic scenario of the "encounter" between *habitus* and the social reduces that relation to that of a naive and disingenuious epistemological exteriority. Although Althusser's own account of interpellation does not suffice to account for the discursive constitution of the subject, it sets the scene for the misappropriation of interpellating performatives that is central to any project of the subversive territorialization and resignification of dominant social orders. Before elaborating this latter point, however, I would like to turn to Bourdieu's intervention in the debate on performative speech acts, and consider the extent to which the dualism he maintains between the linguistic and social dimensions of performative acts produces a set of conceptual difficulties that undermine the political promise of his own analysis.

Linguistic utterances are forms of practice and are, as such, the result or consequence of a linguistic *habitus* and a linguistic market, where the market is understood as the ultimate field or, equivalently, the field in which a practice receives its final determination.[19] The linguistic *habitus* of the performative is, for Bourdieu, the *habitus* of official state speech or official discourse in general. Thus he argues that "politics is the arena *par excellence* of officialization strategies" and further, "the principle of the magical efficacy of this performative language which makes what it states, magically instituting what it says in constituent statements, does not lie, as some people think, in the language itself, but in the group that authorizes and recognizes it and, with it, authorizes and recognizes itself."[20]

Bourdieu's references here to the "some people [who] think" that the principle of the performative is to be found in language itself appears to be a reference to "literary semiology", the tradition of structuralism and poststructuralism:

bracketing out the social, which allows language or any other symbolic object to be treated like an end in itself, contributed considerably to the success of structuralist linguistics, for it endowed the "pure" exercises that characterize a purely internal and formal analysis with the charm of a game devoid of circumstances.

It was therefore necessary to draw out all the consequences of the fact, so powerfully repressed by linguists and their imitators, that the "social nature of language is one of its internal characteristics", as the *Course in General Linguistics* asserted, and that social heterogeneity is inherent in language.[21]

This last phrase is, I think, rich in ambiguity, for if this "social heterogeneity" is "inherent in language", then what is the status of its "heterogeneity"? Indeed, the two terms appear to war against one another, producing the question of whether the social that is internal to the linguistic is self-identically social or whether it does not, by virtue of its instrumentality, become a specific dimension of the linguistic itself. This problem reemerges for Bourdieu when he tries to account for the problem of performativity, itself a linguistic practice, in terms that recall his discussion above of *habitus* and field in their convergent and productive relation to practice more generally:

Every speech act and, more generally, every action, is a conjuncture, an encounter between independent causal series. On the one hand, there are the socially constructed dispositions of the linguistic habitus, which imply a certain propensity to speak and to say determinate things (the expressive interest) and a certain capacity to speak, which involves both the linguistic capacity to generate an infinite number of grammatically correct discourses, and the social capacity to use this competence adequately in a determinate situation. On the other hand, there are the structures of the linguistic market, which impose themselves as a system of specific sanctions and censorships.[22]

It seems that the "action" which is the speech act is the conjuncture not merely between *any* causal series, but between the *habitus* and the field, as Bourdieu defined them. Further, there are two "hands" here, which appear to be divided as the linguistic and the social. Here the question is precisely how to read Saussure's claim that "the social nature of language is one of its internal characteristics"; what does it mean for the social to be "internal" to the linguistic? In the above, Bourdieu refers to "socially constructed dispositions of the linguistic *habitus*," but is there a linguistic *habitus* that is distinguishable from a social *habitus*?[23] There is a linguistic capacity, considered as an abstract and infinite potential, that is then subjected to a *social* capacity to use this competence adequately in a determinate situation.

But to what extent does the distinction between the social and the linguistic in this instance presuppose the linguistic agent as a language *user*, that is, one who uses or deploys language in an instrumental way? Can the rich sense of the "practical" offered elsewhere by Bourdieu, related as it is to the non-deliberate and ritualistic production of belief in the social order's claim to ontological weight, be reckoned against this notion of linguistic practice as the instrumentalized use of language? If the subject only comes "to be" within the *habitus* that renders that subject intelligible and possible, what does it mean to position that subject in an exterior and instrumental relation to the language without which it could not be?

This becomes a problem for Bourdieu's account of performative speech acts because he tends to assume that the subject who utters the performative is positioned on a map of social power in a fairly fixed way, and that this performative will or will not work depending on whether the subject who performs the utterance is already authorized to make it work by the position of social power it occupies. In other words, a speaker who declares a war or performs a wedding ceremony, and pronounces into being that which he declares to be true, will be able to animate the "social magic" of the performative *to the extent* that that subject is already authorized or, in Bourdieu's terms, *delegated* to perform such binding speech acts.[24] Although Bourdieu is clearly right that not all performatives "work" and that not all speakers can participate in the apparently divine authorization by which the performative works its social magic and compels collective recognition of its authority, he fails to take account of the way in which social positions are themselves constructed through a more tacit operation of performativity. Indeed, not only is the act of "delegation" a performative, that is, a naming which is at once the action of entitlement, but authorization more generally is to a strong degree a matter of being addressed or interpellated by prevailing forms of social power. Moreover, this tacit and performative operation of authorization and entitlement is not always initiated by a subject or by a representative of a state apparatus. For example, the racialization of the subject or its gendering or, indeed, its social abjection more generally is performatively induced from various and diffuse quarters that do not always operate as "official" discourse.

What happens in linguistic practices reflects or mirrors what happens in social orders conceived as external to discourse itself. Hence, in Bourdieu's effort to elaborate the paradox of a "social heterogeneity inherent in language", he construes a mimetic relation between the linguistic and the social, rehabilitating the base/superstructure model whereby the linguistic becomes epiphenomenal:

the social uses of language owe their specifically social value to the fact that they tend to be organized in systems of difference...which reproduce...the system of social difference...To speak is to appropriate one or other of the expressive styles already constituted in and through usage and objectively marked by their position in a hierarchy of styles which expresses the hierarchy of corresponding social groups.[25]

Referring to the "generative capacities of language [to] produce statements that are *formally* impeccable but semantically empty," he proceeds to claim that "rituals are the limiting case of situations of *imposition* in which, through the exercise of a technical competence which may be very imperfect, a social competence is exercised – namely, that of the legitimate speaker, authorized to speak, and to speak with authority."[26] Of interest here is the equivalence posited between "being authorized to speak" and "speaking with authority", for it is clearly possible to speak with authority *without* being authorized to speak. Indeed, I would argue that it is precisely the *expropriability* of the dominant, 'authorized' discourse that constitutes one potential site of its subversive resignification. For what happens when those who have been denied the social power to claim "freedom" or "democracy" appropriate those terms from the dominant discourse and rework or resignify those highly cathected terms to rally a political movement?[27]

If the performative must compel collective recognition in order to work, must it compel only those kinds of recognition that are already institutionalized, or can it also compel a critical perspective on existing institutions? What is the performative power of claiming an entitlement to those terms – "justice", "democracy" – that have been articulated to exclude the ones who now claim that entitlement? What is the performative power of calling for freedom or the end to racism precisely when the one or the "we" who calls has been radically *dis*enfranchised from making such a call, when the "we" who makes the call reterritorializes the term from its operation within dominant discourse precisely in order to counter the workings of dominant discourse? Or, equally important, what is the performative power of appropriating the very terms by which one has been abused in order to deplete the term of its degradation or to derive an affirmation from that degradation, rallying under the sign of "queer" or revaluing affirmatively the categories of "blacks" or "women"?

The question here is whether the improper use of the performative can succeed in producing the effect of authority where there is no recourse to a prior authorization; indeed, whether the misappropriation or expropriation of the performative might not be the very occasion for the exposure of prevailing forms of authority and the exclusions by which they proceed?

Would such strategies work, though, if we were to accept Bourdieu's description of the constraints on who can wield the "social magic" of the performative?

Most of the conditions that have to be fulfilled in order for a performative to succeed come down to the question of the appropriateness of the speaker – or, better still, his social function – and of the discourse he utters. A performative utterance is destined to fail each time that it is not pronounced by a person who has the "power" to pronounce it, or more generally, each time that the "particular persons and circumstances in a given case" are not "appropriate for the invocation of the particular procedure invoked".[28]

Bourdieu's larger point is that the efficacy of performative speech acts (he refers to illocutionary acts in Austin's account) is based not in language, but in the institutional conditions that produce and receive given linguistic practices. The "social magic" of the performative is thus extra-linguistic, and this extra-linguistic domain – marked as "institutional conditions" – is figured in a productive and mimetic relation to the linguistic practices that its authorizes. Here one would want to know whether this "productive and mimetic" relation is not itself one of signification, broadly construed, and whether the relationship of "reflection" figured as existing between language and its institutional conditions is not itself a theory of representation and, hence, a theory of language as well. For if "language" will signify "institutions", then surely an account of this notion of signification is in order given that it appears to condition – and, hence, to refute – the very claim of a set of institutions outside language.[29]

One might well return to the fields of "linguistic semiology" in order to ask a set of questions about how, in fact, institutions do come to operate their specific forms of social magic. If a performative brings about what it names, does it do this by itself, or does it proceed through a kind of citation or appropriation of "authority" that effectively produces the *effect* of authority at deauthorized sites on the social map? What happens when this authority-producing effect takes place at "sites" that the social map fails to include as authorized "positions"?[30] If institutions "position" subjects, what are the means by which that positioning takes place? The domain of the social cannot be reduced to a spatialized context "in which" a temporalized *habitus* in general or the linguistic *habitus* in particular effects its rituals. For the question of how social positions are produced and reproduced will raise the question of the "temporality" of positions themselves.

Although Bourdieu understands himself to reject the Marxian notion of class in its substantializing form through embracing a notion of "class position," is it not the case that the spatial metaphorics of "positions" can be as equally reifying as the monolithic conception of class itself?[31] For "positions" are not mere spatial locations, but temporally reproduced effects and, hence, as subject to a logic of iteration, dependent on unstable forms of rearticulation.[32] Although Bourdieu underscores the temporal dimension of the *habitus* and of social practice as *ritual*, it seems that the focus on temporality disappears when he shifts into the "objective" domain of the social field, a field described almost exclusively in spatialized terms. Left unaccounted for within this topography is the critical question of how "positions" achieve their spatial status within the current political imaginary, and how this achievement might constitute precisely an erasure of the historical formation of "positions" as a theoretical foundation?

If a "social position" is produced in part through a repeated process of interpellation, and such interpellations do not take place exclusively through "official" means, could this reiterated "being hailed into social existence" not become the very occasion for a reappropriation of discursive power, a further articulation of the *habitus*, a "regulated improvisation", to use Bourdieu's terms. Further, if this "unofficial" operation of the social performative does become repeated and ritualized as a *habitus*, how would such a notion of performativity recast Bourdieu's notion of a corporeal history, the embodied history of *having been called a name*. One need only to consider how racial or gendered slurs live and thrive in and as the flesh of the addressee, and how these slurs accumulate over time, dissimulating their history, taking on the semblance of the natural, configuring and restricting the *doxa* that counts as "reality".

It is in this sense that the performative calls to be rethought not only as an act that an official language-user wields in order to implement already authorized effects, but precisely as social ritual, as one of the very "modalities of practices [that] are powerful and hard to resist precisely because they are silent and insidious, insistent and insinuating." The performative is not merely an act used by a pregiven subject, but is one of the powerful and insidious ways in which subjects are called into social being, inaugurated into sociality by a variety of diffuse and powerful interpellations. In this sense the social performative is a crucial part not only of subject *formation*, but of the ongoing political contestation and reformulation of the subject as well. In this sense, the performative is not only a ritual practice: it is one of the influential rituals by which subjects are formed and reformulated.

How would one distinguish – in practice – between the social and the linguistic on the occasion of that ritual of social inauguration and maintenance by which a subject is alerted to its "place" through the name it is called or a subject is formed through the name that it understands itself to be called without there having been an official call? If the *habitus* is both formed and forming, and if such interpell-ations are central to both that formation and its formative effects, then social interpellations will be performatives on the order of the *habitus,* and their effects will be neither linguistic nor social, but indistinguishably – and forcefully – both.

Notes

1 Bourdieu's work conducts a critique of intellectualism and subjectivism that draws on the kind of critical work of exposing false antinomies that Merleau-Ponty initiated in relation to the discipline of psychology in *The Phenomenology of Perception* (New York: Routledge, 1962).

2 Bourdieu's notion of the *habitus* might well be read as a reformulation of Althusser's notion of ideology. Whereas Althusser will write that ideology constitutes the "obviousness" of the subject, but that this obviousness is the effect of a *dispositif.* That same term re-emerges in Bourdieu to describe the way in which a *habitus* generates certain beliefs. Dispositions are generative and transposable. Note in Althusser's "Ideology and Ideo-logical State Apparatuses" the inception of this latter reappropriation: "An individual believes in God, or Duty, or Justice, etc. This belief derives (for everyone, i.e. for all those who live in an ideological representation of ideology, which reduces ideology to ideas endowed by definition with a spiritual existence) from the ideas of the individual concerned, i.e. from him as a subject with a consciousness which contains the ideas of his belief. In this way, i.e. by means of the absolutely ideological 'conceptual' device (*dispositif*) thus set up (a subject endowed with a consciousness in which he freely forms or freely recognizes ideas in which he believes), the (material) attitude of the subject concerned naturally follows". See Louis Althusser, "Ideology and Ideological State Apparatuses," *Lenin and Philosophy* (New York: Monthly Review Press, 1971).

3 See J. Thompson's editor's introduction, in P. Bourdieu, *Language and Symbolic Action* (Cambridge, Mass.: Harvard University Press, 1991), p. 13.

4 Bourdieu argues that this conjuncture between *habitus* and field is for the most part congruent or compatible.

5 *The Logic of Practice* (Stanford: Stanford University Press, 1990), p. 73.

6 Bourdieu argues in a vein highly reminiscent of Henri Bergson's argument in *Matter and Memory* that the body acts as a repository for the entirety of its history. Bourdieu writes, "the *habitus* – embodied history,

internalized as a second nature and so forgotten as history – is the active presence of the whole past of which it is the product" (The Logic of Practice p. 56). The metaphorics of the body as "depository" or "repository" recalls Bergson (and Plato's discussion of the *chora*, that famous receptacle in the *Timaeus*). But the presumption that the entirety of memory is preserved or "acted" in the present characterizes the temporal dimension of the body's materiality for Bergson: "...memory itself, with the totality of our past, is continually pressing forward, so as to insert the largest possible part of itself into our present action". Earlier in *Matter and Memory*, he writes, "Habit rather than memory, it acts our past experience but does not call up its image". See Henri Bergson, *Matter and Memory* (New York: Zone, 1988), 151, 108.

7   To participate in a social game is not the same as acting according to a rule, for the rules that condition and frame actions are not fully explicit, and the "following of the rule" is not fully deliberate. For an interesting and helpful discussion of this Wittgensteinian problem as it emerges in Bourdieu's social theory, see Charles Taylor, "To Follow a Rule...", reprinted in this volume.

8   *The Logic of Practice*, p. 73.

9   Ibid., p. 66.

10 Ibid., p. 69.

11 Maurice Merleau-Ponty, *The Phenomenology of Perception*, p. 183.

12 For an interesting and thoughtful consideration of the paradoxes produced by Bourdieu's theory of "inclination" and "motivation", see Theodore Richard Schatzki, "Overdue Analysis of Bourdieu's Theory of Practice", *Inquiry*, 30 (March 1987), pp. 113–35.

13 *The Logic of Practice*, p. 54.

14 Ibid.

15 Note the equivalence implied by the disjunctive "or" in the following passage from Althusser: "The school teaches 'know how'...in forms which ensure subjection to the ruling ideology or the mastery of its 'practice'." "Ideology and Ideological State Apparatuses", p. 133.

16 *The Logic of Practice*, p. 57.

17 See Jacquelyn Rose on the failure of identification in *Sexuality and the Field of Vision* (London: Verso, 1986), p. 91.

18 Ernesto Laclau, "Preface" to Slavoj Žižek, *The Sublime Object of Ideology*, p. xiv.

19 "It is in relation to the market that the complete signification of discourse occurs", *Language and Symbolic Power*, p. 38. Bourdieu appears to presume the unitary or systematic workings of something called "the market" without questioning whether there are not competing market forces that are not contained by a unitary notion of the market (i.e. the thesis that capitalism produces excess market phenomenon that it cannot control and that undermines its own hypostatization as a unity). Nor does he consider that there might be a genealogy of "the market" that would undermine the thesis of its unitary and ultimately determining character. Further, he appears to codify the distinction between the

economic and the cultural which Karl Polanyi has argued is the symptomatic conceptual effect of capitalism itself. See Karl Polanyi, *The Great
Transformation.*
20 *The Logic of Practice*, pp. 109–10.
21 Bourdieu, Introduction, in *Language and Symbolic Power*, p. 34.
22 *Language and Symbolic Power*, p. 37.
23 For an excellent discussion of this problem, see William F. Hanks,
    "Notes on Semantics in Linguistic Practice", in *Bourdieu: Critical Per-
    spectives*, ed. C. Calhoun, E. Lipuma, and M. Postone (Chicago: Uni-
    versity of Chicago Press, 1993) pp. 139–55.
24 Bourdieu also argues that this magic is to be understood as the power to
    produce collective recognition of the authority of the performative, and
    that the performative cannot succeed without this collective recognition:
    "One should never forget that language, by virtue of the infinite gen-
    erative but also originative capacity – in the Kantian sense – which it
    derives from its power to produce existence by producing the collect-
    ively recognized, and thus realized, representation of existence, is no
    doubt the principal support of the dream of absolute power." *Language
    and Symbolic Power*, p. 42.
25 Ibid., p. 54.
26 Ibid., p. 41.
27 For a relevant discussion of the phantasmatic promise of the performa-
    tive, see Slavoj Žižek, *The Sublime Object of Ideology* (London: Verso,
    1989), pp. 94–120.
28 "Authorized Language" in *Language and Symbolic Power*, p. 111.
29 One might consider the usefulness of transposing Baudrillard's critique
    of Marx to a critique of the social and linguistic distinction in Bourdieu.
    Working within a very different tradition, one might consider the task
    that William Hanks holds out for rethinking the relation between lin-
    guistic formalism and semantics: "...the challenge is to see the literal
    core of language as already permeated by context and subject to recon-
    figuration and novel production in activity." See William F. Hanks,
    "Semantics in Linguistic Practice", in *Bourdieu: Critical Perspectives*,
    p. 155.
30 Derrida remarks that no performative can work without the force of
    iterability, that every appearance of a subject who works the perform-
    ative is the effect of a "citation" that both offers the performative an
    accumulated force and belatedly positions "the subject" as the fictive
    and intentional originator of the speech act itself. See Jacques Derrida,
    "Signature, Event, Context", *Limited Inc.*, ed. Gerald Graff (North-
    western University Press, 1986), p. 18.
31 "Concluding Remarks: For a Sociogenetic Understanding of Intellectual
    Works," *Bourdieu: Critical Perspectives*, p. 264.
32 See the appropriation of the Gramscian notion of rearticulation in
    Ernesto Laclau and Chantal Mouffe, *Hegemony and Socialist Strategy*
    (London: Verso, 1986).

8

Practical Reason and Cultural Constraint: Agency in Bourdieu's Theory of Practice

James Bohman

Most explanations of rational action in the social sciences regard practical reason as both individualist and instrumental. On this view, social actions are in the first instance to be explained intentionally. In such explanations, what explains an action is the particular agent's beliefs and desires. Sometimes a collective agent's intentions may be invoked, but, more often than not, only as an individual agent "writ large." Such explanations are also generally instrumental, since what makes actions rational is the relation of consistency between means and ends, no matter what they happen to be. This idealized picture of the rational actor is perhaps best captured by Carl Hempel's description of the well-informed engineer, who masterfully and fully consciously chooses among all the available alternatives. A competent engineer is one who chooses the optimal solution to a problem of design, since "the range of permissible solutions is clearly delimited, the relevant probabilities and utilities are precisely specified, and even the criteria of rationality to be employed (e.g., maximization of expected utilities) is explicitly stated."[1] But short of these improbably well-defined and ideal conditions, it is hard to see how such standards of rationality, more accustomed to rarified air of theoretical reason, are supposed to apply in actual social settings.

In contrast to these idealized accounts, both philosophers and social scientists have developed other, more contextual, accounts of practical rationality, building on Aristotle's phronesis or practical judgement and on Wittgenstein's rule-following. In *The Logic of*

Practice and other writings, Pierre Bourdieu develops a new and insightful formulation of an explanatory account of practical reason in the social sciences. Whatever its positive features, he argues that it must avoid the past mistakes and antinomies of social theory: the "subjectivism" of intentionalist explanations, the "intellectualism" of rule-following accounts, and the "objectivism" of structuralism and Durkheimian social structure.

The problem with Hempel's engineer is that he is not social, but an unconstrained chooser limited only by his natural environment. Are the social and cultural constraints on agency analogous with such natural ones, as Durkheim sometimes thought for social facts? Durkheim never fully clarified how such facts constrain action, appealing to many diverse mechanisms, such as sanctions or structural limits.[2] But perhaps his clearest and most influential description of such constraints is that they are *norms* which "regulate" social action. In contrast, Wittgenstein provides an alternative account of such constraints in his notion of "following a rule," indeed one that has had an equally important influence in sociology and anthropology. For Neo-Wittgensteinian social science, rules are *constitutive* of practices and not merely regulative constraints. Bourdieu's culturally embodied notion of practical reason, and indeed the purpose of his concept of *habitus*, is to provide just such a constitutive account of cultural constraint without the traditional conception of regulative rules or internalized norms. In this respect, his notion of practical reason bears a strong resemblance to ethnomethodology.[3] But Bourdieu does not share the ethnomethodological emphasis on social order as enacted in punctual and episodic situations of social action. Rather, actors are socialized into a *habitus*, into a set of dispositions and orientations that do not simply "regulate" their actions, but define just who and what they are. It is in virtue of being socialized into a common background of pre-reflective assumptions and orientations that agents have goals at all.

In this essay, I want to explore the explanatory power of this alternative account of practical agency under cultural constraints. Most of all, I want to consider the adequacy of Bourdieu's attempt to replace regulative norms and rules with such constitutive conditions of agency. In the first section, I will consider his general account of socialization into a *habitus* and then consider his paradigm, or core, case for its explanatory power: being a person who can be verbally intimidated by authority. Next, I shall consider whether or not this paradigm case can be generalized as Bourdieu thinks it can, by considering Bourdieu's general explanation of successful communication and speech. Here Bourdieu's alternative account of performative speech and criticism of illocutionary force is crucial. In the third section, I shall argue that his explanation of speech depends on an entirely too strong and constitutive role for power, needed in order to replace the constraining role of regulative rules. Bourdieu's strong claims for this sort of explanation are simply not consistent with the main mechanism of "symbolic power": what he calls "the imposition of form." Finally, I shall propose a different account of culturally constrained agency, one which permits a greater role for reflection and innovation by which actors are able to transform the conditions of social action themselves.

Practical Reason Without Rules: Some Paradigm Cases

The search for a general theory of social action usually begins by referring to a set of phenomena that constitute its successful core, from which it gradually generalizes to other instances.[4] The core cases for rational choice theory, for instance, are cases of maximizing economic behavior. Normative explanations, by contrast, refer to cases of conscious compliance to rules, such as the behavior of a judge in court. Bourdieu has another core case in mind, from which he thinks that he can then generalize to a comprehensive account of practical reason. In his first major theoretical work, *An Outline of a Theory of Practice*, Bourdieu identifies the core phenomenon of a "logic of practice." He disputes the common Mausian explanation of gift exchange in terms of a norm of reciprocity, here in the Kabyle society of Algeria. Bourdieu also shows that much more is involved than simply following a rule. The norm of reciprocity does not get at what is most important in returning the gift, including the timing of the gift and its size. Such exchanges are hardly utility maximizing, nor are they strictly speaking reciprocal: what is established is a certain sort of social relationship, one that Bourdieu describes as "symbolic violence." For a better endowed giver, an exchange can be a means to impose a strict relation of hierarchy and debt upon the receiver.[5]

Bourdieu's analysis of speech provides a similar sort of core phenomenon. He disputes Comte's description of language as the "common wealth" of a culture as an idealized fiction which Bourdieu derides as "linguistic communism."[6] By contrast, language-in-use is always the official language authorized by some group, a language which speakers and hearers commonly recognize as legitimate without deliberate intention or the acceptance of a norm. "The distinctiveness of symbolic domination," Bourdieu claims, "lies precisely in the fact that it assumes, of those who submit to it, an attitude which challenges the usual dichotomy of freedom and constraint," between deliberate choice and normative restriction.[7] A social and historical account of practical reason must avoid appealing either to speaker's intention or to linguistic rules as explanatory terms, if it is to see how power is "imposed" on others in the symbolic realm. I argue that Bourdieu does not escape the objectivist antinomies which he finds in much previous social science, falling clearly in the objective side of the dichotomy in his description of power.

Consider the phenomena of verbal intimidation. It is one of the many acts of speech whose success depends on the social position of the speaker in relation to the hearers. Such an act will succeed only in virtue of *who* is speaking, not what is said or how. Indeed, what is important for Bourdieu is not the act of intimidation itself. Intimidation succeeds "only on a person predisposed to feel it, whereas others will ignore it."[8] We search for false causes if we look to features in the act of intimidation itself or to some intention behind it. What explains its symbolic violence is the *habitus* in which this action takes place, in the dispositions inculcated in the agent by insignificant aspects of everyday life, in bodily comportment, or in myriad ways of seeing things or talking about them. Such dispositions are not internalized norms or rules. Rather than regulate what one does, they tell one who one is, i.e., whether one is the kind of person who is intimidated in this particular situation by this particular person. This explanation lies outside of language or linguistic competence, in the *habitus* in which speakers are socialized into their particular identity and social relations with others.

How does the inculcation of dispositions explain such phenomena? Bourdieu clearly demarcates his explanations and their explanatory power from alternative explanations of the same phenomena in terms of intentions or rules, in alternative explanations offered by Jürgen Habermas and Jon Elster. Even if Bourdieu shows the inadequacy of some forms of explanations employing rules or intentions, he has not shown that explanations in terms of dispositions and *habitus* can successfully replace them or the theories that support them. Indeed, the concept of *habitus* makes it more difficult for Bourdieu to explain many of the phenomena that these other theories explain very well, such as theoretical reflection, cultural conflict, and social change. Bourdieu does identify a set of core phenomena that *habitus* may well explain, such as the imposition of form, style and taste, but does not succeed in expanding the core set and its explanatory assumption to other phenomena that rules and intentions already explain.

Habitus is supposed to explain how it is that agents come to share a culture and its practices, even when there are asymmetrical social positions and relations of domination. Bourdieu solves the Parsonian problem of social order not through the internalization of norms, but through the "inculcation" of dispositions that come not only from being socialized into a culture generally, but into a particular subordinate or dominant position within it. It operates through the agent's own dispositions rather than coercion, through "generative and implicit schemata" rather than sanctioned rules.[9] Even if sanctions or rules were present, it would still have to be explained why it is that agents are predisposed to accept them. This is the role of *habitus*.

As in any functionalist explanation, *habitus* is indirectly reconstructed through its effects upon actions. Through these effects, Bourdieu tries to show that the actions of persons are coordinated in regular and reproducible patterns, "without in any way being the product of rules... and without presupposing a conscious aim or express mastery to attain them."[10] For example, what we find when looking at rules such as "preferred marriages" is a wide discrepancy between "official" and "practical" kinship, between what people collectively endorse and what they actually do. In practical kinship, we find what is really operating is not official belief systems but "generative schemata" and "second-order strategies" that regulate improvization within the set of possible marriages, where the chosen one is designed to achieve the greatest accumulated advantage, including power, resources and recognition. *Habitus* is thus a "pre-strategic basis of strategy," and as such it tends to reproduce the same conditions that make the strategic moves possible in the first place. Other goals or cognitive abilities need to be referred to only if such explanations fail. *Habitus* cuts across both: it is both the shared "cognitive and volitional structure" and the "socially structured situation" in which the agents' goals, interests and positions are defined. Even when agents are trying to achieve their own strategic aims, the desires which they have and the situation in which they find themselves are simply "a variant" of this shared *habitus*.

The explanatory power of *habitus* can be contrasted to an explicitly cognitivist one offered by Elster for the phenomena of "sour grapes." As Hume describes it: "We are no more acquainted with the impossibility of satisfying any desire than the desire itself disappears."[11] How do we explain how such preferences are formed? Elster appeals to a specific cognitive mechanism, by which agents adjust their desires to what is attainable, as does the fox in Aesop's fable. Elster's explanation works by showing how such irrational preferences are extinguised as the result of this mechanism of "adaptive preference formation," a mechanism for reducing the cognitive dissonance between beliefs (about what is attainable) and desires (about what we want to attain). How is Bourdieu's explanation different from Elster's intentionalist one?

Bourdieu's explanation appeals to already inculcated dispositions and ways of thinking and perceiving that constitute the agent's identity. I do not have the extinguished desires, because I am the sort of person who does not want such things; as the son of an English worker, I simply do not wish to go to Oxford or have the dispositions of a don as part of my *habitus* (unless, of course, what it means to be an Oxford don changes). Elster's explanation refers to a mechanism which may or may not be at work in any particular case of unattainable goals; it is indeterminate whether or not every case of such phenomena could be explained by precisely this mechanism. Moreover, it is indeterminate in a further way: if I am under the sway of some false beliefs, such as that "the grapes are sour anyway," by becoming aware of their falsehood the force of the particular mechanism of dissonance reduction may disappear. But, in explanation in terms of a *habitus*, it is more difficult to change my dispositions. If they constitute the sort of person who I am, then I cannot change them like I could change my beliefs. It is difficult not to see how such dispositions provide a useful link between the motivation of an agent and his action in a socially structured situation, but only in a one-sided, causal-like way, as terms like "inculcation" and "conditioning" suggest. The fact that such dispositions still leave room for agents to be better or worse at achieving their strategic goals does not alter the fact that they take their own identity and the definition of the situation as limits within which to act. Just as a player cannot stop playing one game and suddenly play another, agents can become good at their social role, but not adopt some other role or identity.

If this is the case, cultural constraints on agency turn out, because they constitute the very identity of social agents, to be stronger than those imposed through regulative norms or sanctions. The problem is that such holistic, cultural conditioning into an entire set of dispositions is too under-determining to provide an exhaustive explanation of such phenomena as sour grapes. For this reason, Elster rightly criticizes Bourdieu for committing a typical functionalist fallacy in explaining this phenomenon in terms of social effects, without providing any specific mechanisms for how these effects are produced.

But the problem with the explanatory role of *habitus* is not just methodological. Rather, it is a problem with the type of explanation being offered, as can be seen in the same sort of explanation of verbal intimidation which Bourdieu thinks that the concept of *habitus* can provide. Intimidation either works or it doesn't. If it works, then I am predisposed to feel it; if it doesn't work, then I am predisposed to ignore it. There is no independent way of determining the fact of the matter. No cognitive or linguistic mechanism needs to be invoked at all: "the features that are most influential in forming a *habitus* are transmitted without passing through language or consciousness," but "inscribed" in our bodies, in things, in situations and everyday life.[12] It is in virtue of being a particular agent with a particular identity and of having a particular position in one's habitus that I have dispositions that permit the speaker to succeed; conversely, the speaker succeeds in virtue of being the particular agent who he is in relation to me. But this is not enough. Even if this is true, it would still be necessary to show how such an action succeeds in any particular case, since surely intimidation is sometimes contested and sometimes not. Indeed, sometimes this very contestation may help reproduce the original relations of power and habitus; but, sometimes it may not, as I will show below.

The deeper problem is that such constraints are as much hidden from agents as they are obvious to the social scientific observer. Actors are, in effect, "cultural dupes" to their habitus as they were "judgmental dopes" to Parsonian norms. Thus, Bourdieu does not dispute the explanatory force of rules or norms for the same reason as other theorists, such as in Garfinkel's more radical critique.[13] Explanations involving constitutive identities or dispositions are not all that different from those involving regulative rules, since both involve the same holistic descriptions of the constraints on social action. A more consistent critique of norms would abandon the vocabulary of "laws," "markets," and "determinations" that Bourdieu still maintains and go fully interpretive. Bourdieu needs to be clearer that even shared means are subject to constant interpretation and reinterpretations, often in ways that contest current identities and practices. But Bourdieu does not want to go that route, since he thinks that one of the great contributions of his conception of *habitus* is how it describes the operations of "symbolic" power. He even claims that such an account could provide the powerless with "weapons of defence against symbolic domination," but it is hard to see how this could be true, especially since there are no "mechanisms" which produce such domination to simply undo.[14] Such a supposedly critical purpose underlying Bourdieu's explanations puts him back on the horns of another dilemma. If an agent is already dominated, then symbolic violence works by definition; if symbolic violence does not work, then the agent already is not dominated.

In our context, the most crucial failing of these explanations of phenomena such as intimidation is that in the end they do not offer an alternative account of practical reasoning. For Bourdieu, practical reasoning is still strategic and goal-directed, in that its purpose is to describe how agents achieve their predisposed goals in light of the actions of others and the constraints in which they operate. It is manifested in making the appropriate gift, giving a speech in the right style, and so on. But the rationality of such "second-order strategies," strategies within given goals and constraints, should suggest a deeper revision of instrumental notions of reason. Such second-order strategies need not be confined to perfecting the practice of gift giving for greater effect; rather, it suggests a reflective and interpretive capacity in agents that extends to second-order desires, to having the capacity to have desires for certain desires. Such a capacity is necessary in order that we do not construe agents as "rational fools," in Sen's apt phrase.[15]

Bourdieu's strategic, market-oriented actors will be no less "symbolic" fools, unless they can begin to reflect upon and thus to transform the dispositions that they have been socialized into, at least one at a time. Such reflective and interpretive agency loosens the ties between action and *habitus*, and makes possible a self-interpreting form of identity for at least some aspects of everyday life, as well as for practices such as character planning typical of many religious traditions. Bourdieu does indeed use the term "reflexivity" to describe the self-referential character of his own analyses as theorist, or "cultural producer." However, such Wittgensteinian self-referentiality refers to sociologists and their theories, and not to the second-order, critical and transformative capacities of social agents themselves.[16] By contrast, reflexivity in the critical sense refers to a constitutive property of agency and thus of practical reason, and not to the self-referential, epistemological conditions of sociological theory.[17] Reflexivity is not primarily an "effect" of theory, as Bourdieu often argues, but a component of public, practical reason.

Agents equipped with a different set of skills and wider reflective practices could become aware of such practical constraints, as much as be influenced by them cognitively, and in so doing alter the way in which they operate. But this capacity requires a different sort of practical reason than an instrumental one, a capacity most often related to language use. Bourdieu cannot extend agents' capacities to broader interpretive and cognitive activities, since this would undermine his account of the effects of social and cultural power. In the next section, I shall explore what sort of conception of social power is at stake here, especially as it is developed in the criticism of

Austin and Habermas' notion of illocutionary force. Bourdieu claims that there is no such force inherent in language; the cultural background which determines the "success" of speech is not just a set of shared dispositions but socially structured and authorized power relations, or a "market," to use another of Bourdieu's favorite explanatory metaphors for cultural inequalities. To be dominated is to be socialized into such relations of asymmetric power.

Illocutionary Force, Social Power and the Imposition of Form

If habitus by itself is under-determining simply as a pre-reflective cultural background into which we are socialized, then how is it supposed to explain social phenomena such as intimidation? Bourdieu does not appeal, as he might, to the force of inculcated dispositions as the way in which a *habitus* imposes itself upon the identity of the members of a culture. What characterizes socialization into a *habitus* is what Bourdieu calls "the imposition of form," the imposition primarily of dominant modes of expression and ways of seeing the world. Bourdieu applies this analysis of symbolic power above all to the language use of dominated speakers, whose speech lacks the legitimacy and authority to accomplish their goals and to acquire cultural advantage and wealth. Dominant speakers, conversely, can effectively accomplish what they want in speech and impose their form, styles and modes of expression upon others with their authority. No matter how linguistically competent, speakers are neither equally situated nor socially authorized to use the same speech acts.

It is precisely the analysis of power that Bourdieu thinks is lacking from philosophical and linguistic analysis from Saussure to Chomsky and Austin to Habermas. Explanations employing a notion of illocutionary force do not capture the social conditions of success or felicity for different speakers. More importantly, Bourdieu explains such success externally. Such success can be explained entirely through reference to social conditions and context, and these conditions are themselves to be explained in terms of asymmetrical relations of power. First of all, any specific language use in a context is not just the result of the universal linguistic competence which enables the production of an infinite number of well-formed sentences. Rather, the "form" of language use is always specific, and it is by virtue of such form that a speech act is most likely to succeed in a specific context. Thus, form determines the "legitimate" or "official" language use in a way that extends beyond the contexts of explicit rituals or conventions, making all language a "political unit."[18] The competence to produce comprehensible sentences "may be quite inadequate to produce sentences that are likely to be *listened to*, likely to be recognized as acceptable in all situations in which there is occasion to speak."[19]

The lack of such legitimacy or authorization excludes dominated groups of speakers from whole domains of discourse and condemns others to silence. By ignoring this social fact, theories of linguistic competence confuse comprehensibility with social acceptability. This error continues on the pragmatic level in theories of "communicative competence," which falsely confer on the speech act itself the power to produce a social bond or to have a binding force.[20] Even if we reject Bourdieu's claim as reductionistic, we still should accept that there is a difference between comprehensibility and acceptability, offer and uptake. Many intelligible and appropriate utterances will not be taken up in interaction. But this sort of distinction is precisely what illocutionary force is supposed to explain. Indeed, Austin, much like Bourdieu, explains the lack of uptake of a performative precisely in terms of its failure to fit with prevailing social conventions, as in Austin's example of a passerby who christens a ship "Mr. Stalin." So what is the issue here? It is that Bourdieu thinks that illocutionary force has no social referent in actual speech and thus cannot be an explanatory term in a theory of symbolic interaction and power.

Bourdieu does not give anything like a philosophical argument against the theories of linguistic and pragmatic competence that he rejects. Surely, he must do something more than appeal to linguistic "facts," since the very distinction of competence and performance is meant to explain why some comprehensible and competent utterances fail. Competent performance may be successful or unsuccessful, and a theory of speech should be able to explain the difference. The issue then is not that there is a "magical force" in language, but how various theories of communicative competence provide an account of the conditions for failures, infelicities, and distortions of communicative interaction.

Similarly, the conception of illocutionary force does not require a conditionless efficacy of "pure language," as Bourdieu often suggests.[21] The problem is not that illocutionary force suspends all external and non-linguistic social conditions of speech; rather, it means that there can be a force not to the utterance, but to the *reasons* that support the utterance, which in turn are effective in interaction not merely when understood by the hearer, but when understood *and* accepted. While speech act theorists often assume these go hand in hand, there are cases in which speakers demand the reason behind the speech act, if they are to accept it as binding for future interaction. Only rarely is it the case that for a speaker to say in response to a demand for justification that "it is I who say so!" However, for Bourdieu, such commands are precisely the paradigm case for success in speech: an utterance is successful only when a speaker is authorized to perform certain sorts of speech, and this has to do with *who* the speaker is and *who* is listening.

The connection between authorized language and the effectiveness of a speech act is the power of institutions. The judge can say, "I find you guilty!" not because it is backed up by any reasons, but because he is acting on behalf of a group of other agents and with the resources of institutions. "The inquiry into the specifically linguistic principle behind the 'illocutionary force' of discourse thus gives way to the distinctly sociological inquiry into the conditions in which an individual agent can find himself invested with such power."[22] But for all his authority to do so, the judge still must give reasons which conform to practices of justification or have his decision overturned in review. Similarly, Bourdieu claims that the slogans of a party official succeed in his speeches not for any content or reasons, but because he is delegated by the group to speak for them. His words and speech cannot produce this force; that is, no speaker can generate legitimate power but can only find it and employ it.[23] Generating new forms of power would require that other agents recognize the political slogans as normatively correct and legitimate and not merely authorized.

The thrust of these empirical claims about authority is surprisingly like one of the very philosophers Bourdieu rejects; standard criticisms of Austin's analysis of performatives as conventions fit very well with Bourdieu's sociological analysis of power and delegation.[24] The long history of speech act theory after Austin is a movement away from the conventionalism that also characterizes Bourdieu's position. H.P. Grice reintroduces a complex form of intentionality, specifically "reflexive intentions," as necessary for communication; P.F. Strawson goes beyond the oversimplifying alternatives of conventions or intentions and offers a continuum of speech act types between those which are more purely intentional and those that rely on existing conventions. None of these analyses suggest that words necessarily have any causal efficacy with interaction among agents. Continuing Strawson's line of argument, Searle and Habermas introduce a range of irreducible and complex types of speech act, some of which are "institutionally unbound."[25] Such speech acts do not require the backing of institutions nor the existence of an official convention to succeed.

This category of speech acts requires a different account of agency and of social causality. The issue here is the orientation of actors to reasons in many practical situations. This means that actors, and not merely sociologists, are reflexive in ways that are crucial for their ability to become aware of and change the conditions under which they act and speak.

What sort of speech acts are "institutionally unbound"? It may be thought that self-expression provides a paradigm case, but Bourdieu is correct that class and other social relations figure into the modes and styles of such modes of expression. The appropriate paradigm is not a specific type of speech act, but a *level* of communication. It is in reflective, second-order communication, which Habermas calls "discourse," that this potential for language use is most apparent. Discourse is here not a general term for speech and writings, as Bourdieu uses the term. Rather, it is reflective language use, and as such it concerns the ways in which speakers consider and thematize the reasons or claims that are made explicitly or implicitly in speech. Thus, what is required for discourse is not the ability to articulate well-formed sentences, but to give convincing reasons, to back up claims made in speech when challenged by other speakers, and to create institutions and practices in which such public testing is possible. Even the form and style of such discourse may be challenged for normative reasons, for being exclusionary and re-enforcing inequalities of power.

Such discourses typically involve public argumentation of various sorts. Arguments here are not to be interpreted logically and narrowly as compelling inferences, but pragmatically and broadly as self-reflective, reason-giving activities whose social function is to respond to hearers' demands for justifications for why they should accept the claims made by speakers and in so accepting them change their future courses of action. It is the acceptance of such a claim and its reasons by an agent that gives the speech act what Habermas calls its "inter-subjectively binding force,"[26] in that actors can now appeal to it in coordinating future activity and in making further agreements. Certainly, reflection of this sort can facilitate integration and reproduction, particularly through promoting false consensus and unfair compromises. But it can also challenge the basis for antecedent consensus. Furthermore, reflective practices of testing socially accepted reasons and policies can be institutionalized, such as in jurisprudence, science and democracy. In such institutions, language use does not simply function unproblematically and unreflectively, but often works to repair and reconstitute broken-down social relationships and normative bonds.

Although Bourdieu never explicitly considers reflective discourses and practices, he has two possible responses to such criticisms. First, such criticisms might push him in a structuralist direction. According to Bourdieu, *habitus* presupposes a homology "between the structured systems of sociologically pertinent linguistic differences and the equally structured systems of social differences."[27] For example, such a homology may exist between differences in pronunciation and differences in class and would be repeated at every level of language use, including discourse. But this sort of strong homology does not generalize easily to all features of language use. Since there is no mechanism which would produce it, this sort of homology is an assumption, rather than the empirical result, of explanations that appeal to socialization in a *habitus*. The second line of response does invoke a specific mechanism for how one class imposes its *habitus* on others. The "imposition of form" is a plausible mechanism for explaining the effectiveness of modes of expression. But this mechanism is not strong enough to exclude the possibilities that agents could become reflexively aware of its operation and correct for it.[28] Such an imposed constraint on discourse is simply too weak a basis for the rejection of the explanatory power of illocutionary force, now understood as the binding power of the acceptance of reasons.

In order to establish these sorts of limits on practical reflexivity, Bourdieu makes a further assumption about *habitus*: that of "misrecognition" of actors of their own *habitus*, which they inevitably see as natural or appropriate.[29] But this claim raises as many explanatory problems as it solves: it simply makes the cultural reproduction of domination inevitable. Either agents' reflection on their own conditions is structurally determined, or agents are inevitably duped by their culture into misrecognizing its culturally arbitrary and dominating character. In either case, the possibility of innovation and transformation becomes improbable and dependent on external social conditions, such as the breakdown of social conditions due to forces outside of agents' control. Yet, Bourdieu does not deny that such innovative changes occur historically, and in doing so he introduces further ambiguities into his account of power and enculturation.

In an essay on political censorship, Bourdieu raises the problem of innovation and change indirectly, by considering the claims that a theory is independent of the social contexts out of which it emerges; the "theory effect" is the construction of new contexts. One might expect Bourdieu to deny any such independence for the very sorts of reasons that underlie his criticisms of illocutionary force. Instead, Bourdieu does offer a defence of theory as constructive, intellectual practice, one that is put in strong terms indeed. In the next section, I shall show that this strong independence and transformative power granted to theory is inconsistent with Bourdieu's general account of practical reason and cultural constraint. This inconsistency shows that Bourdieu's theory of reproduction only permits radical trans- formation and wholesale change; in political terms, this means that agents await change in a way more akin to Heideggerian *Gelassen- heit*, rather than the reflexive agency and learning of Critical Theory. This is the pernicious political effect of excluding critical reflection on reasons in Bourdieu's one-sided account of inculcated dispositions: only the new sages and sayers – sociological theorists – somehow possess the reflexivity necessary for radical change and the articula- tion of novelty.

The Claims of Theory: Cultural Constraint and Transformative Agency

Bourdieu's criticism of illocutionary force denies that there are ex- planatory mechanisms "intrinsic" to language itself. As opposed to linguistic mechanisms available to all speakers, speech succeeds when the particular speaker is properly situated in social relations of power. But this explanation leaves entirely open how it is that innovation, new forms of expression, and new public justification are possible, all of which could challenge existing institutions, relations of power, and conjunctures of social forces. Bourdieu offers the model of "heretical" or "heterodox" discourse, which challenges the orthodoxy built into the culturally arbitrary character of a *habitus*; but such discourse does not require practically knowledgeable authors or addressees. Rather, the efficacy of heretical discourse, Bourdieu writes, "does not reside in the magic force immanent to language, such as Austin's 'illocutionary force,' or in the person of its author, such as Weber's charisma . . ."[30] Instead, heretical discourses are utopian, "no-where" in the current cultural space.

Among heretical discourses, Bourdieu includes some theories, in particular those which "presage" and "predict" a new social reality, a new social world, a new form of common sense, in which they will succeed. It is significant that Bourdieu chooses the name "heretical" rather than "critical" discourses, since what he demands is that the discourse produces a radically new "sense" of social reality, in a word, a new form of practical reason. But in the absence of any clear account of conflict and change, all that innovation can mean is complete and total transformation of the cultural background. In a word, heretical discourse permits Heideggerian world disclosure, "naming the unnameable, and saying the unsayable" in order to articulate what speakers are not objectively authorized to say.[31] The only real difference between Bourdieu and Heidegger is linguistic: whereas Heidegger clothes his notion of disclosing a new world and breaking with the old one in the nostalgic longing for the past, Bourdieu uses the future oriented language of political utopianism. Both do not adequately equip practical agents with reflective and critical abilities which would make it possible to describe how they might initiate such transformative processes, or to understand how they might succeed in enlisting the cooperation of other agents in transforming social identities and conditions.

The problem is that, despite his constructivist picture of future "worlds," what Bourdieu grants to theories and to sociologists he denies for practical reasoning and for knowledgeable agents. Given that *habitus* constrains action through the operation of power, any strategic move to a "new world" remains within the very same set of constrained alternatives. How might an alternative not in this set gain acceptance? Bourdieu credits some theorists with actually achieving this task, and Marx's theory of class struggle is the clearest example of a "theory effect" of producing the social reality that it "pre-dicts." This sort of effect gives theories a practical status: they are not so much descriptions of how history works, as the orthodox Marxists have it, but visions of different historical possibilities.

As a constructivist, Bourdieu sees theory as successful if it *makes*, rather than corresponds to, the social reality that it describes via the action of powerful agents: "It is only after Marx, and indeed only after the creation of parties capable of imposing (on a large scale) a vision of the social world organized according to the theory of class struggle that one could refer, strictly speaking, to classes and class struggle."[32] This constructivist capability is, however, not tied to special epistemic authority or capacities of theorists, but to the agency of groups already invested with power and backed by institutions. It is only under the proper external social conditions and relations of power that social reality can be constructed or predicted by a theory. Just as the utterance "the meeting is now open," so the assertion "there are two classes" is also a performative, which fails or succeeds according to the backing of social groups and agents. It is here that the consequences of assimilating all forms of speech to performatives and reducing performatives to commands become clear: it eliminates the very possibility of transformation that it is supposed to describe.

Consider Bourdieu's favored example: Marx's theory of class. The constructivist role of theory is not at all apparent in the process by which social reality was made in light of it. There is no clear relationship between Marx's theoretical statements, even understood as performatives, and the political effectiveness of the Leninists and Stalinists who made his theories a political program. Their choice of Marxian theory is primarily strategic: it has no relation to any special reflexive status of the theory nor any significant appeal to its particular emancipatory content. Nor is it clear why workers should accept having this vision of the future "imposed" upon them. Workers stand behind the party's effort to change the social world only if its slogans speak to them and articulate much of what they have already experienced. Thus, the constructivist process crucially requires that workers be convinced of the vision of the future as critically articulating an absent alternative in political discourse. "Creating" the audience for a theory is an interactive process among competent agents who change the theory as a practical tool for their on-going struggles.

The misrecognition of the arbitrary character of one's *habitus* further constrains this process of making a new social world. Misrecognition also governs such attempts to articulate and elaborate alternatives. This pervasive limit on reflection certainly characterized Heidegger's supposed radical break, which Bourdieu declares to be "false." Theories, too, are misrecognized as description of the actual world, not as performatives with practical effects. However, Bourdieu overestimates what the performative character of theory requires. It can be quite consistent with many forms of social science, since even causal descriptions can have practical effect. Amartya Sen shows us that we are wrong to think of famines as merely decreases in the food supply. Although this analysis does not radically alter the constitutive conditions of agency, it does change our practical relation to the social world, modestly, by changing our technocratic beliefs about the ways in which we should intervene in it. Even as a causal analysis of famines, it does provide an alternative to the market-based biases that distort how we think about fulfilling the imperative of creating the "new" world without hunger.

Bourdieu also has a less dramatic way of talking about the transformation of the social world. By articulating what is silent and oppressed, a theory expresses a coherent and compelling vision of the world. In doing so, it "transforms the representation of the social world as well as the world itself" to the extent that it "renders possible practices that refer to the transformed representation."[33] This modest way of speaking of cultural change does not see the theorist as the central, constructivist role in radical transformation. Rather, the theorist has a role in communicating and articulating alternatives, some of which may bind future action and some of which may not. On this communicative and practically oriented account, new representations are not seen as itself constitutive of social change, but only as enabling agents to construct alternative practices themselves. The more modest and practically reflexive view of social theory recognizes that we can change representations of the social world without changing practices. Such a view not only endorses the very descriptive and constative conception of theory which Bourdieu denies, it also requires practical agency for reasoning participants in social discourse that is much like what Bourdieu grants to the sociological theorist. Such practical and transformative reasoning is hardly utopian presaging of a "new world" or a new common sense. All that it requires is reflective agency, the capacities of socially and culturally situated agents to reflect upon their social conditions, criticize them, and articulate new interpretations of them. These conditions include the cultural constraints of power and dispositions, which can be overcome at least piecemeal by reflective agents in the historical present. Without such abilities, theoretical reflection in the social sciences has a different status: because it is *both* descriptive and prescriptive, it can interpret *and* change the world.

Practical Reason and Reflexive Agency: An Alternative Account

In the previous section, I argued that the performative and constructive aspect of social theories cannot be reconstructed on the meager account of reflexive agency that Bourdieu provides. It is historically misleading to grant either to Marx the theorist or to Marxist political parties the ability to construct the reality of class struggle, even if they altered the way agents related to such forms of power. The new social movements of class struggle established themselves without the existing institutions and authority that Bourdieu describes as conditions of success. Bourdieu's account of power and misrecognition make it difficult to explain how such processes work in the historical present, in which the social reality and identity which practical agents project does not yet exist and is still being contested in its future course. Because his theory provides no basis for practical agency, the relation of theoretical articulation to practice is mysterious. In these cases merely uttering a performative hardly makes it so, when dispositions and practices are up for grabs. Without some reference to intentional levels of explanations of what agents see themselves at any historical moment as trying to accomplish in altering the relations of power, constructivism can only suggest that social change is a contingent event, unrelated to the abilities for reflection that the theorist employs. A better explanation would equip agents with the same broader and more effective practical abilities, while at the same time loosening the larger-scale mechanisms of cultural integration and power.

Harry Frankfurt offers a model of hierarchical motivation to deal with related problems of causal determination and volitional reflexivity. No matter how constrained, according to Frankfurt, a will is autonomous to the degree that it is reflective. Autonomy is manifested precisely in second-order desires, that is, in the desire to have or not to have a desire.[34] Such second-order desires might arguably fall under the constraints of one's *habitus*, since those reflexive desires, too, must be constrained by a set of cultural variants. Certainly, some second-order desires reveal the influence of *habitus*, as in the hyper-correctness of petit-bourgeois speakers in France and the non-cooperation of working-class male adolescents in schools in England.[35] In both cases, these desires produce the type of person the actor wants to be. But two quite distinct mechanisms are at work in these different cases, and *habitus* easily conflates them. Second-order desires may be the result of the irrational and unconscious mechanisms such as "adaptive preference formation." Such desires are neither autonomous nor practically rational. But other second-order desires may be the result of deliberations, character formation and planning; these mechanisms are employed most effectively in second-order and deliberate processes of socialization.

There is no place in Bourdieu's one-dimensional account of pre-reflective *habitus* for such deliberate processes and practices, which are historically quite widespread. Various moral and aesthetic disciplines from the Greeks to the Buddhists to the Jesuits show ways in which such care for the self can open up a cultural space for greater self-interpretation and deliberate choice. Certainly, such practices of self-interpretation can only take place in communities and movements. Nonetheless, certain forms of life may permit more variation and free choice in contrast with the prevailing cultural constraints. There is no reason why institutions, such as those in democratic traditions, could not do the same in creating pluralistic citizenship. Cultural practices socialize people to acquire various dispositions; but there is also a normative question in *how* these preferences and dispositions are formed. Second-order socialization permits autonomous and deliberate second-order desires, desires to be a certain sort of person who has particular sorts of desires and goals. It is here that practical reason can be shown to be at work.

Similar mechanisms can also function in belief formation. Here, too, Bourdieu only identifies the sort of mechanism which inhibits deliberation, criticism, and revision, that of cultural misrecognition. But other reflexive and institutionalized mechanisms may work against such biases, even when they are shared by groups. Here public learning can subject beliefs to public testing from diverse points of view; similarly, public deliberation can be institutionalized in complex practices of belief revision and deliberation, such as legal review, scientific peer review, and democratic debate. Such public processes of deliberation are the institutional equivalent of practices of character planning, in which second-order beliefs and beliefs about the demands for justification lead people to reject certain sorts of widely accepted beliefs, such as those that depend on ignoring legitimate protests of others or that could not withstand free and open debate. It is obvious that misrecognition and biases can be built into such public institutions and their practices, especially if groups do not have free and equal access to epistemic authority or effective modes of public expression. However, there is no reason to believe that practical and public reasoning cannot detect at least *some* of these cultural biases and constraints, and that at least *some* reflective agents may be able to convince others that suppressed forms of expression and alternatives absent from deliberation ought to be seriously considered on their merits.

The mechanisms of misrecognition that Bourdieu describes are not always present or effective, and they can even lose their power to impose their form on a *habitus*. Unlike in France, in the United States there has been an enormous debate about linguistic and cultural diversity in educational institutions. The more pluralistic a society is the less likely it is that its integration can be achieved pre-reflectively in common dispositions, even in sub-groups. Cultural pluralism permits much more room for both a wider range of alternatives and deeper conflicts. Different sorts of integrative mechanisms will have to be developed to solve the problems of coordination and conflict that will emerge.[36] In these sorts of societies, inequalities related to participation in public deliberation will play a greater role in reproducing relations of power and domination. But the issue for practical reason in such a situation is the revision of beliefs and desires in explicit ways in accordance with more public and inclusive conceptions of legitimacy and authority. Reflexive agency in such societies requires not only changing beliefs and desires, but also the social conditions under which agents reflect, deliberate and cooperate with each other to widen their universes of discourse. By doing so, they may also change their existing relations of power.

Conclusion

While containing intuitions that ought not to be jettisoned, Bourdieu's rejection of rule-governed and intentionalist accounts of practical reasoning has a high price. While a *habitus* does not constrain through "mechanical determination," it does become indistinguishable from objectivist constraints through "misrecognition" and other mechanisms that culturally limit reflexive agency. I have argued that these mechanisms are not as pervasive as Bourdieu's theory requires and that Bourdieu overemphasizes their effectiveness in imposing the constraints of power and domination on practical reasoning. In light of a more reflexive account of practical reasoning, we can make better sense of both how speech acts bind speakers in interaction and how theory influences social reality. In considering how agents are constrained on the reflective level, Bourdieu emphasizes the operation of one-sided mechanisms very much like adaptive preference formation, while ignoring the possibilities of second-order practices such as public character formation. He one-sidedly emphasizes the suppression of modes of expression through relations of power, rather than the way public institutions could promote voice through open and fair procedures of public justification. Once agents are more fully equipped with reflective abilities for practical reasoning, we can see how they can become more or less reflective about their cultural constraints and how socializing institutions could enable, rather than limit, the use of these practical abilities.

The problem with Bourdieu's explanations is that they are neither richer nor more complete than the ones that he seeks to replace. Many of the phenomena that Bourdieu discusses are better explained intentionally, as in the case of "sour grapes." I have also identified other phenomena that Bourdieu tries unsuccessfully to explain away, such as illocutionary force, or which he must go to extreme lengths to accommodate, such as the practical effects of theories. Such "effects" of the practical relation of theories to social reality are not best explained as the radical construction of the very phenomena they predict, nor is practically changing conditions of domination always dependent on creating an entirely "new world" or "a new common sense."

Rather than settle on a limited range of core phenomena, there is no reason why the explanatory role of practical reason in the social sciences cannot encompass intentional, regulative and constitutive phenomena all at the same time. In my alternative account, I have argued that good explanations of practical reasoning in public institutions and pluralistic societies require all three of these dimensions. For practical reason to be innovative and critical in the way that such institutions require, new forms of socialization of agents are necessary. If agents can be socialized into subordination and submission to authority, then they can also acquire the uses and capacities of practical reason which permit egalitarian and open relations to the self and the social world. Exactly what this non-coercive form of socialization will look like and how it is to be constructed is still an open question, but I have suggested that there are some clear historical precedents. Reflective agents will need to be socialized into a different kind of political culture than the ones Bourdieu so far has analyzed; this new public culture will encourage and enable such autonomous relations to self and others. Autonomous agents cannot be "forced to be free," as in Rousseau's paradoxical formulation. Given that Bourdieu wants to offer "weapons against symbolic domination," his account of socialization leaves us in the same paradoxical position. If Bourdieu's theory is to be a genuinely critical rather than a defeatist one, as he insists it is, he must begin to articulate such a utopia of an open, democratic and egalitarian culture to replace the hierarchies of both symbolic domination and social distinction. This utopia is, however, only consistent with a more thoroughly reflective and interpretive practical reason than Bourdieu has suggested so far.

Notes

1 Carl Hempel, *Aspects of Scientific Explanation* (New York: Free Press, 1965), p. 481.
2 See Steven Lukes, *Emile Durkheim* (New York: Harper and Row, 1973), p. 11–15, for an excellent analysis of the ambiguities of the concept of social facts.
3 See Harold Garfinkel, *Studies in Ethnomethodology* (Englewood Cliffs: Prentice-Hall, 1967); Hubert Dreyfus points out the similarity between these two approaches and their common critique of rule-following in his *Being-in-the-World* (Cambridge: MIT Press, 1991), p. 19, 204–5. Also see Charles Taylor's discussion of *habitus* as an alternative to intellectualist rule following and as part of the "ontological" interpretation of *phronesis*, see his essay, "To Follow a Rule," reproduced in this volume.
4 Richard Miller argues for this sort of analysis of causal claims in the social sciences in *Fact and Method* (Princeton: Princeton University Press, 1987), p. 76. For an analysis of the explanations of rational choice theory using this notion, see James Bohman, "The Limits of Rational Choice Explanation," in *Rational Choice Theory: Advocacy and Critique*, ed. James Coleman and Thomas Fararo (Los Angeles: Russell Sage, 1991), 207–28.

150   James Bohman

5 Bourdieu, *Outline of a Theory of Practice* (Cambridge: Cambridge University Press, 1977), pp. 5–6.
6 Bourdieu, *Language and Symbolic Power* (Cambridge: Polity Press, 1991), p. 43.
7 Ibid., p. 51.
8 Ibid.
9 For the fullest characterization of *habitus*, see *Outline of a Theory of Practice*, p. 72–77; for a comparison between Bourdieu's notion of *habitus* and Habermas's similar, but importantly different, analysis of the *lifeworld*, see my *New Philosophy of Social Science: Problems of Indeterminacy* (Cambridge: MIT Press/Polity Press, 1991), 158–67. I argue that holistic conceptions of cultural backgrounds such as these need to refer to their micro-realizations in social actions, if explanations which employ them are to not to fall prey to the functionalist fallacy and remain incomplete. Habermas's explanation of the "invasion of the lifeworld" is potentially complete. Bourdieu's core explanations of *habitus* could be made so, but only with the modifications of his notion of practical reason that I am arguing for here.
10 *Outline of a Theory of Practice*, p. 55.
11 Jon Elster, *Sour Grapes* (Cambridge: Cambridge University Press, 1983), p. 126ff.
12 Bourdieu, *Language and Symbolic Power*, p. 51.
13 See Harold Garfinkel's discussion of how social theory turns agents into "judgmental dopes," in *Studies in Ethnomethodology*, p. 22. I am arguing that Bourdieu's conception of *habitus* falls under the same critique as Parsons' over-socialized view of man, except here agents are over-enculturated dupes.
14 For this claim, see Bourdieu, *Questions de sociologie* (Paris: Minuit, 1980), p. 13; he also argues that it provides the "means to dominate domination" (p. 49), as if that were possible. This same point also discussed in Pierre Bourdieu and Loïc J. D. Wacquant, *Invitation to Reflexive Sociology* (Chicago: University of Chicago Press, 1992), p. xiv and pp. 50–1, without clarification. Similarly, Bourdieu claims in *The Logic of Practice* (Cambridge: Polity Press, 1990) that it is "liberating" for sociologists to "reappropriate schemes of perception and appreciation that are often at the root of social deprivation," without saying wherein such liberation lies (p. 285, footnote 15). If it helps us denaturalize the social world and our cultural biases, there are many non-theoretical ways to that end.
15 Amartya Sen, *Poverty and Famines* (Oxford: Oxford University Press, 1981).
16 See, for example, Wacquant's description of "reflexive sociology" in *Invitation to Reflexive Sociology* as the "self-analysis of the sociologist as cultural producer" (pp. 36–7). This epistemic form of reflexivity, or self-reference of one's own theoretical enterprise, is no substitute for the practical reflexivity of critical agents which I am arguing for here. I refer

to it as "Wittgensteinian reflexivity." "Postmodern reflexivity" is textual, referring to the textual character of social scientific writing; hence, its proposals are stylistic. Only "critical reflexivity" refers to the practical capacity of agents to become aware of and transform the conditions of social action. I want to argue that Wittgensteinian reflexivity is not enough for a critically oriented social theory.

17 This is not to say that Critical Theorists cannot make common cause with Bourdieu or gain from his analyses of symbolic domination. In particular, there is a great similarity between Bourdieu's criticisms of ethnography and objectivist theory as "spectacle" and Horkheimer's criticisms of "traditional" theory. See, for example, *The Logic of Practice*, pp. 20–1. But my claim is that Horkheimer and Bourdieu part company on issues of reason and agency. The emphasis on theory that still underlies Bourdieu's reflexive turn can be also be seen in his discussion of "The Scholastic Point of View," *Cultural Anthropology* 5:4 (1990), 380–91.

18 See Bourdieu's essays "The Production and the Reproduction of Legitimate Language" and "Authorized Language," in *Language and Symbolic Power*, pp. 43–65 and 107–116, respectively.

19 *Ibid.*, p. 55.

20 Jürgen Habermas, *Theory of Communicative Action*, vol. I (Boston: Beacon Press), p. 278.

21 As Bourdieu claims repeatedly in the essays collected in *Language and Symbolic Power*, as, for example, on pages 31, 107–16 or 170; often such criticism is directed against Habermas. Also see *Invitation to Reflexive Sociology*, pp. 147–8.

22 *Language and Symbolic Power*, p. 75.

23 As Bourdieu puts it: symbolic power "is defined in and through a *given* relationship between those who exercise power and those who submit to it, i.e., in the very structure of the field in which *belief* is produced" (first emphasis mine, second Bourdieu's). *Ibid.*, p. 170. Yet, in a footnote to this very passage, Bourdieu talks about "heterodox" discourse in such a way that it matters what actors believe and that they can "neutralize" the power of the doxa of a habitus to immobilize. If there is a "symbolic power of mobilization and subversion" (ft. 8, p. 277), then symbolic power is not a *given relation* as Bourdieu asserts above. If Bourdieu admits this, then there is no basis for his sociological arguments against illocutionary force, nor is there anything more than a weak imposition of power through the general "structure of the field in which belief is produced." The slogans of the party leader could generate their own symbolic power, as well as their own audience which believes them. This process still needs to be explained, and below I argue that Bourdieu's attempt to do so fails precisely because of the ontological and strategic character of his notion of practical reason.

24 Bourdieu has recently admitted the affinity of his view to Austin's actual theory, now blaming "his commentators" and not Austin himself for

asserting the efficacy of "intrinsic features" of language. See *An Invitation to Reflexive Sociology*, pp. 147–8. Even if that is the case, Bourdieu owes an answer to those speech act theorists who have criticized Austin's conventionalism, starting with Grice's "reflexive intentionality" and Searle's background knowledge as sources of communicative success.

25 For a description of this category, see Habermas, "What is Universal Pragmatics?" in *Communication and the Evolution of Society* (Boston: Beacon Press, 1979), pp. 38–9. This distinction marks the difference between the uptake of those speech acts warranted by convention and those speech acts warranted by reasons, such as between christening a boat and making a well-warranted assertion. I can say "I hereby pronounce this boat Mr. Stalin!" and under proper circumstance have named a boat for most purposes. But I cannot say "I hereby pronounce belief 'x' true!" and expect any effect at all, even if Bourdieu is right that theoretical statements are performatives. It is only on the basis of such a distinction that we could understand how "heterodox discourse" gets accepted at all.

26 Habermas, *Theory of Communicative Action*, vol. I, p. 287ff.

27 Bourdieu, *Language and Symbolic Power*, p. 54.

28 As the discussion of "heterodox" discourse referred to above shows. Bourdieu argues that censorship is "never quite as perfect or as invisible as when each agent has nothing to say apart from what he is authorized to say." But this absence of conflict and contestation is hardly so common an historical experience of oppression from which to generalize. See *Language and Symbolic Power*, p. 138ff.

29 Ibid., p. 170.

30 Ibid., p. 129.

31 For a detailed criticism of Heideggerian world disclosure and an attempt to put critical discourse in its place, see my "World Disclosure and Radical Criticism," *Thesis Eleven* (1994).

32 *Language and Symbolic Power.*, p. 133.

33 *Ibid.*,

34 See Harry Frankfurt's essays on this interpretation of autonomy in *The Importance of What We Care About* (Cambridge: Cambridge University Press, 1988), esp. pp. 11–25.

35 For Bourdieu's discussion of hyper-correctness of the petit-bourgeois, see *Distinction* (Cambridge, Mass.: Harvard University Press, 1984), as well as *Language and Symbolic Power*, pp. 62–3. For the English working class example, see Paul Willis, *Learning to Labor: How Working Class Kids Get Working Class Jobs* (Westmead: Saxon House, 1977).

36 For an analysis of the uses of practical reason in public deliberation under conditions of cultural pluralism (where there is no strong shared culture or society-wide mechanisms of cultural integration), see my "Cultural Pluralism and Public Reason," *Political Theory* (1994).

9

A (neo) American in Paris: Bourdieu, Mead, and Pragmatism

Mitchell Aboulafia

Pierre Bourdieu and George Herbert Mead, separated by several generations, an ocean, national and local traditions, and fields (in Bourdieu's sense of the term), are without a doubt intellectual soul mates. Of course, even mates are not given to a complete sharing of interests, and there are indeed important differences in this pair's views. But while differences would be expected, the affinities – which have not passed unnoticed by Bourdieu – require explanation. Queried about two recent studies that have suggested connections between his thought and Dewey's – the latter Mead's life-long compatriot – Bourdieu responds:[1]

I came across these studies very recently and they stimulated me to take a closer look at Dewey's philosophy, of which I had only very partial and superficial knowledge. Indeed, the affinities and convergences are quite striking, and I believe I understand what their basis is: my effort to react against the deep-seated intellectualism characteristic of all European philosophies (with the rare exceptions of Wittgenstein, Heidegger, and Merleau-Ponty) determined me, unwittingly, to move very close to philosophical currents that the European tradition of "depth" and obscurity is inclined to treat as foils, negative reference points.[2]

Bourdieu notes that among the commonalties he finds is a drive to overcome dualisms, for instance, those of subject/object and internal/external. This is surely on the mark with regard to Dewey and Mead, but there is a good deal more to report. Mead and Bourdieu share, for example: a social conception of mind and agency; a penchant for non-positivistic approaches to the empirical sciences; a dedication to the interdisciplinary; views that link certain kinds of problem solving

behavior to reflection; a commitment to giving the bodily and dispositional their due; a concern with lived, non- scientized, time;
recurrent appeals to "open" systems, improvization, and the role of
conflict in change; a pluralistic vision; a preference for analyzing
language in terms of use; an emphasis on reasonableness as opposed
to a transcendental notion of reason; a willingness to speak the
language of interest and a healthy suspicion regarding views from
nowhere; an insistence on the importance of recognition in social life;
and even similar uses of sports metaphors and analogies. And the list
could go on.

The goals of this article are twofold. First, given the limited understanding and the even more limited acceptance of pragmatism on the
continent, it is of some importance that one of the continent's current
premier intellectuals is echoing themes and ideas addressed some
seventy-five years ago by American thinkers. This confluence is
clearly worthy of illustration.[3] But there is more at work here than
historical or antiquarian impulses. For all of their similarities, there
are indeed important differences between Mead and Bourdieu, and by
exploring them the various strengths and weaknesses of their
approaches become apparent. The second concern, then, is to examine these thinkers with an eye toward how one might eventually use
their strengths and jettison their weaknesses in order to address present-day issues and disputes. I begin with a brief introductory overview of possible avenues for comparing Mead and Bourdieu; in a
second section I discuss in some detail key similarities and important
differences. A caveat, however, is in order. This essay can only hope to
initiate a discussion of the issues involved, for the material here is so
rich that it calls for at least a book-length study.

I

While there are a number of ways one could approach the theoretical
underpinnings of Bourdieu's work, the tension he sets up in *The Logic
of Practice* between so-called objective and subjective orientations is a
natural place to begin comparing him to Mead, for in many ways the
latter's project can be understood as an attempt to find a path
between just such a Scylla and Charybdis. Bourdieu addresses the
tension as one between the subjectivism or finalism (that is, the
projectism) of a Sartre and the determinism or mechanism of structuralism. Both of these approaches fail to grasp the dynamics of an
agent engaged in a social world, of habitus to field, and they fall into
reductive mechanism or myths of (self) creation.

There is an economy of practices, a reason immanent in practices, whose "origin" lies neither in the "decisions" of reason understood as rational calculation nor in the determinations of mechanisms external to and superior to the agents.[4]

As long as we divide the world into subjects and objects, the one confronting the other in an external relationship, we will not be able to avoid falling into mechanism or subjectivism. The way out of this dualism is to understand *habitus* and field. Bourdieu tells us in his "A Lecture on the Lecture" that

the source of historical action ... is not an active subject confronting society as if that society were an object constituted externally. This source resides neither in consciousness nor in things but in the relation between two states of the social, that is, between the history objectified in things, in the form of institutions, and the history incarnated in bodies, in the form of that system of enduring dispositions which I call *habitus*. The body is in the social world but the social world is also in the body.[5]

All of this is, of course, well known to readers of Bourdieu, but what is intriguing here is the extent to which these sentiments would be seconded by Mead and in response to just the sort of unacceptable dichotomy that Bourdieu is attempting to overcome. Mead's penchant for using the terms "subject" and "object" can be quite misleading in this regard, for it may give the impression that he succumbs to a type of dualism that Bourdieu insists on castigating. But when one actually examines Mead's texts in any detail, it is clear that he is in large measure modifying the traditional uses of these terms, using them as shorthands for his own innovations, and in so doing is quite in line with Bourdieu. In fact, Mead was something of a social ecologist for whom traditional Cartesian dualities made little sense, and who thought that one's bodily dispositions – attitudes in his language – shape and are shaped by their immersion in various environments. More on this below.

In order to elucidate just how closely aligned Bourdieu's and Mead's views of the social world are, one might step back a bit to the underpinnings of Mead's ideas, specifically to the work of William James, who influenced both Dewey and Mead. If there was one question that tormented James it was the question of how to approach the issue of freedom vs. determinism, a variant of Bourdieu's mechanism vs. subjectivism. Unlike Mead or Dewey, James never developed a social theory that might have allowed him to address this issue in a fashion that Bourdieu would find compelling. But many of Mead's insights harken back to James's psychology, specifically to his notion of habit and his model of the stream of consciousness. James writes:

Habit is thus the enormous flywheel of society, its most precious conservative agent. It alone is what keeps us all within the bounds of ordinance, and saves the children of fortune from the envious uprisings of the poor. It alone prevents the hardest and most repulsive walks of life from being deserted by those brought up to tread therein.[6]

Bourdieu sees the *habitus* as basically just such a conservative force, yet one that doesn't leave agents mired in the way things were because dispositions can be transferred and utilized in different contexts. James, too, did not view his notion of habit in strictly deterministic terms. For both we can learn to improve our lives by reflecting on the kinds of habits or dispositions that we possess and by making a concerted effort to reinforce or extinguish specific ones through our practices.

Mead can be viewed as developing James's notion of habit in the direction of a social behaviorism, in which repertoires of socially generated behaviors and dispositions crystallize into what he calls the "me," his shorthand for a constellation of attitudes that we associate with particular agents or selves, and which emerges in relationship to specific social contexts. Mead's "me" is comparable to Bourdieu's *habitus*, a connection that we will examine below. Suffice it to say at this juncture that Mead's view of socialization never led him to a mechanistic determinism and that both Bourdieu and Mead agree that reflection and self-awareness stand some chance of helping us to modify unwanted behaviors. There is, however, an additional point of comparison between James, Bourdieu, and Mead that should be noted at this juncture. Habits can be thought of as allies in achieving the good life precisely because they *do not* require reflective operations for their success. James tells us that

the more details of our daily life we can hand over to the effortless custody of automatism, the more our higher powers of mind will be set free for their own proper work. There is no more miserable human being than one in whom nothing is habitual but indecision, and for whom the lighting of every cigar, the drinking of every cup, the time of rising and going to bed every day, and the beginning of every bit of work, are subjects of express volitional deliberation.[7]

Bourdieu shares with many a pragmatist a desire to sing the praises of the non-reflective activities that fill so much of our waking lives and which so much of the western philosophical tradition has found reason to flee. Note in this regard Mead's language in the following passage (which finds him discussing the relationship between scientific endeavors, which are a type of reflective activity) and what he labels the *biologic individual*. The latter can be thought of as living, as Mead would put it, in *the world that is there*, that is, a world of practices and activities that form the ground and horizons of our reflective endeavors.

This immediate experience which is reality, and which is the final test of the reality of scientific hypotheses as well as the test of the truth of all our ideas and suppositions, is the experience of what I have called the "biologic individual." ... [This] term lays emphasis on the living reality which may be distinguished from reflection. . . . [T]he actual experience did not take place in this form [i.e., reflection – M.A.] but in the form of unsophisticated reality.[8]

The appeal to the social construction of reality takes a turn to the bodily with Mead, as it does with Bourdieu; and both exhibit a marked sensitivity to understanding action in terms of bodily dispositions and interests. Yet, as we shall see, there are a number of important differences between their approaches. For example, while both can be viewed as having an Aristotelian strain in their thought, and while both respect the place of habit in practice – avoiding spectator theories of knowledge as they view knowledge as interest-laden – they differ on the degree to which disinterestedness is possible. In this regard Mead is influenced by the British tradition of Adam Smith, while Bourdieu draws on Nietzsche. Mead can even be viewed as falling between Habermas and Bourdieu here. On the one hand, Habermas's neo-Kantian views on morality are too transcendently inspired for Mead. But, on the other, Bourdieu's Nietzschean sensibilities with regard to interest and power would strike Mead as, dare I say it, too relativistic (and as uncharitable to boot). Mead remained something of a secularized Christian in his expectations regarding the possibilities of overcoming and broadening one's interests, and in his belief in mutuality. In discussing the ideal of democracy, he writes rather late in his career:

The most grandiose of these community ideals is that which lies behind the structure of what was called Christendom, and found its historic expression in the Sermon on the Mount, in the parable of the Good Samaritan, and in the Golden Rule. These affirm that the interests of all men are so identical, that the man who acts in the interest of his neighbors will act in his own interest.[9]

A good deal of the differences between Mead and Bourdieu turn on the Nietzschean aspects of the latter's thought, those that allow him to develop tools to analyze power relations that Mead did not possess, but which may prevent him from seeing possibilities for mutuality and reciprocity that Mead could envision.[10]

II

One place to begin a more specific analysis of Bourdieu and Mead is with the latter's well-known "I" and "me" distinction. As we have noted, Bourdieu seeks to avoid the unacceptable choices of mechanism and subjectivism by appealing to habitus and fields. Mead's approach to the dilemma is to speak of the "I" and the "me" aspects of the individual, which he views in functional terms, the "I" being the "source" of innovations that modify the socially constituted "me." But to understand just what Mead was seeking to accomplish with these distinctions, we must back up a bit and address, however briefly, his model of language acquisition and his account of roles.

Mead followed Wundt in emphasizing the birth of human language in gestures between animals, which Mead had a penchant for explaining by appealing to a dog-fight. In such a struggle a first dog may growl and a second may respond by baring its fangs or growling back. Such behaviors can be viewed as gestures, as parts of a social act, for they are behaviors that suggest behaviors to come. An exchange of gestures, in which there is a response by a second organism and a counter-response by the first, is referred to as a *conversation of gesture* by Mead. Meaning in this circumstance is defined in terms of the responses of the organisms, for example, growl means the baring of fangs. This is not to say that animals are (self-) consciously aware of the meanings of their gestures, that is, of the responses that they or other animals will make of their gestures.[11] They are not able to say to themselves: if I do x, y will follow. A (self-) conscious awareness of meaning awaits the presence of human beings who possess language.

Human beings often engage in non-(self-) conscious conversations of gestures of just the sort described above, which Mead illustrates in terms of boxers who must learn how to read cues, gestures, in order to avoid blows. And, interestingly enough, it is in reference to this example that Bourdieu cites Mead, approving of the latter's account of such an exchange. Here are Mead's words describing this type of exchange, which occur right after he presents an account of a dog-fight:

We find a similar situation in boxing and in fencing, as in the feint and the parry that is initiated on the part of the other. And then the first one of the two in turn changes his attack; there may be considerable play back and forth before actually a stroke results. This is the same situation as in the dog-fight. If the individual is successful a great deal of his attack and defense must not be considered, it must take place immediately. He must adjust "instinctively" to the attitude of the other individual. He may, of course, think it out. He may deliberately feint in order to open up a place of attack. But a great deal has to be without deliberation.[12]

This passage not only reveals Bourdieu's affinities to Mead, it sets the stage for points of contention. What Bourdieu likes about Mead's model is that it avoids the false distance from practice that occurs when one is (theoretically) analyzing someone else's practices, a distancing that leads to faulty conclusions regarding the nature of the agent's relation to her practices. Theory about action is quite different from actual encounters, and too often theoreticians forget just how different they are precisely because they are analyzing someone else's practices. This is a luxury that boxers cannot afford.

As for the anthropologists, they would have been less inclined to use the language of the mechanical model if, when considering exchange, they had thought not only of *potlatch* or *kula*, but also of the games they themselves play in social life, which are expressed in the language of tact, skill, dexterity, delicacy or *savoir-faire*, all names for practical sense.[13]

For Mead, as for Bourdieu, much of our lives takes place on a non-thetic level of awareness, one in which we are not actively positing alternative futures. For both, reflection occurs when problems arise that may require reasoned decisions or strategic planning, which is quite different from the non-(self-)conscious reasonableness that guides our daily unproblematic practices. Bourdieu tells us that

there is an economy of practices, a reason immanent in practices, whose "origin" lies neither in the "decisions" of reason as understood as rational calculation nor in the determinations of mechanisms external to and superior to the agents.... In other words, if one fails to recognize any form of action other than rational action or mechanical reaction, it is impossible to understand the logic of all the actions that are reasonable without being the product of a reasoned design, still less of rational calculation; informed by a kind of objective finality without being consciously organized in relation to an explicitly constituted end; intelligible and coherent without springing from an intention of coherence and a deliberate decision; adjusted to the future without being the product of a project or a plan.[14]

Mead also presumes that there is, or can be, a reasonableness to activities that are not undergoing critical evaluation; there is, after all, a *world that is there*. However, differences between Mead and Bourdieu begin to surface when we consider the place of significant symbols – that is, gestures which entail (self-)conscious cognition – in Mead's model.

For Mead, gestures become significant symbols when those using them are capable of becoming aware of their meanings. The key here is the vocal gesture. One can be aware of a vocal gesture in a manner similar to the person that it is directed at. If I say, "Look-out!" as you are about to slip on an icy street, I hear the gesture as you do, and I can respond to my own gesture as you do, for example, by slowing my pace. "Gestures become significant symbols when they implicitly arouse in an individual making them the same responses which they explicitly arouse, or are supposed to arouse, in other individuals, the individuals to whom they are addressed"[15] Vocal gestures allow human beings to (self-)consciously respond as others do to a symbol, which means that they can anticipate what another's reaction to a significant symbol might be.[16] They can even talk to themselves in the absence of the other by taking the linguistic role of the other. The bottom line here for Mead is that this capacity allows one to turn experience back on itself, that is, to reflexively respond to stimuli. This reflexivity is at the heart of what he calls *mind*.

It is by means of reflexiveness – the turning back of the experience of the individual upon himself – that the whole social process is thus brought into the experience of the individuals involved in it; it is by such means, which enable the individual to take the attitude of the other toward himself, that the individual is able consciously to adjust himself to that process, and to modify the resultant of that process in any given social act in terms of his adjustment to it. Reflexiveness, then, is the essential condition, within the social process, for the development of mind.[17]

It is the vocal gesture that allows "mind" to develop, and with "mind" human beings have the capacity to become reflexively aware of increasingly complex social interactions and to develop skills that produce solutions to problems. Although Mead clearly distinguishes the reflective from the non-reflective, he insists that we typically move rather naturally between them in our daily rounds. Of course, the notion of reflexivity is fundamental to Bourdieu's position, for the social scientist depends on it to become aware of his or her own biases. In this regard, reflexion is a methodological tool for producing better social science. But Bourdieu also raises the question of the place of reflexivity in daily life, and here, while bowing to the possibility of requiring it in times of trouble, his rhetorical task is to downplay its importance. So, for example, we find Bourdieu remarking:

And there is every reason to think that as soon as he reflects on his practice, adopting a quasi-theoretical posture, the agent loses any chance of expressing the truth of his practice, and especially the truth of the practical relation to the practice.... In contrast to logic, a mode of thought that works by making explicit the work of thought, practice excludes all formal concerns. Reflexive attention to action itself, when it occurs (almost invariably only when the automatisms have broken down), remains subordinate to the pursuit of the result and to the search (not necessarily perceived in this way) for the maximum effectiveness of the effort expended.[18]

Passages such as this one tend to suggest that Bourdieu is not beyond bifurcating experience into reflective and non-reflective domains in his quest to invoke the pragmatic. This bifurcation is especially troubling because so much of his work centers on overcoming just such dualisms, an overcoming that would do away with the need to valorize one side over another. This is not to say that such a division cannot provide a useful shorthand for a range of experiences. But this is quite different from setting the terms at odds for the purpose of valorizing one of them, and it appears that under the guise of helping to counterbalance misplaced theoretical appetites, Bourdieu has succumbed to just such a temptation. The non-reflective actions of the boxer in the ring or the athlete on the field are seen as having a grace – no, a power – that reflective activities do not have, at least those that are not performed by sociologists setting their biases in order. Here it appears that Nietzsche is at work, or to blame, in leading Bourdieu in the direction of a hyper-aestheticized notion of excellence grounded in some sort of animal naturalness. As the following remark suggests, Bourdieu appears rather comfortable residing in Nietzsche's shadow, echoing as he does the latter's suspicions regarding the "thinker's" contributions to the demise of virtue.[19]

Excellence (that is, practical mastery in its accomplished form) has ceased to exist once people start asking whether it can be taught, as soon as they seek to base "correct" practice on rules extracted, for the purposes of transmission, as in all academicisms, from the practices of earlier periods or their products.[20]

While Bourdieu has claimed that he "never really got into the existentialist mood," it doesn't appear that he has remained immune from the spell of at least one version of the jargon of authenticity.[21]

On one hand, it could be argued that Mead has an advantage over Bourdieu with regard to this dichotomy, for while both tend to bifurcate the reflective and non-reflective, Mead doesn't view reflective activities as somehow opposed to – and less authentic than – non-reflective ones, but as interwined with them in our daily affairs. Reflection is a fundamental type of problem solving behavior for Mead, and problems, in his broad definition of the term, continuously confront us. On the other hand, Bourdieu has been through the fires of Husserl, Heidegger, and especially Merleau-Ponty, and hence insists that the *habitus* entails a non-reflective capacity for anticipatory experience and intelligent behavior, which Mead appears to reserve for the reflective sphere (although there are passages in Mead that can be read as moving in Bourdieu's direction).[22] To further highlight the differences between them with regard to this dichotomy we can invoke the ghost of James once again, in particular his model of the stream of consciousness.

James's chapter on "The Stream of Thought" is found in his *Psychology* immediately following the one mentioned above on habit. James attempts to show that the transitive parts of the stream – the and's, if's and but's of experience and language – are as basic as the substantive, nominalistic, parts. He also seeks to show that there is a fundamental temporal dimension to experience, for each moment – the one that is being focused on – is surrounded by a fringe, where the stream, so to speak, is going and where it has come from. This model would not be unfamiliar to Bourdieu, for it shares a number of similarities with one that he would have encountered as a student of Husserl's work, but without the latter's essentialism. As a matter of fact, Bourdieu draws on Husserl to help support his own account of temporalized *non-reflective* activity, which has an anticipatory dimension.[23] Mead, on the other hand, suggests that the anticipatory is most clearly exhibited in those reflective hiatuses in the stream that arise when we must address problems. Mead's leanings in this direction are already suggested in one of his most important early papers, "The Definition of the Psychical." There he does not view the characteristics of the stream in terms of pre-reflective experience, but places them in the sphere of the problematic that gives rise to reflection.

Are there any characteristics of the stream which are not unmistakably present *when we face any problem* and really *construct any hypothesis?* The kaleidoscopic flash of suggestion . . . the transitive *feelings of effort and anticipation* when we feel that we are on the right track and substantive points of rest, as the idea becomes definite, the welcoming and rejecting, especially the identification of the meaning of the whole idea with the different steps in its coming to consciousness – there are none of these that are not almost oppressively present on the surface of consciousness during just the periods which Dewey describes as those of disintegration and reconstitution of the stimulus – the object.[24] (emphasis added)

For Mead, "feelings of effort and anticipation" are most keen when we must reflect due to problems that we encounter. Bourdieu is trying to avoid just this sort of appeal to reflection in his account of the *habitus.* These matters go to the heart of some of the basic differences between Bourdieu and Mead and deserve to be fleshed out, which we can begin to do by turning to Mead's notion of roles, in order to set the stage for a discussion of the "I" and the "me."

Roles can be understood as constellations of behaviors that are accessible to a reflexive apprehension, and they become so available by utilizing mechanisms similar to those found in the vocal gesture. If I am to play at being a doctor I must (to some degree) be able to view my actions from the perspective of the patient. I must have built into my repertoire of behaviors both sides of an exchange in order to play my side, as I do when I anticipate a response to my vocal gesture. Given how commonplace the notion of role-taking has become, this should all appear straightforward enough, but there is actually a rather large pitfall lurking. Mead uses the expression "taking the role of the other" to describe a number of different kinds of exchanges and many of them are not self-conscious ones, nor do they necessarily entail behaviors as complex as those in the roles that we see acted out on stage. For instance, in caressing a doll a very young child may take the role of certain behaviors of a parent without actually playing at being a parent. As counterintuitive as it at first may seem, Mead's role theory does not lead to all the world being a stage. Gary Cook provides some rather helpful advice here.

We can avoid some of the misleading connotations of the phrase "taking the role of the other" by using in its stead the alternative phrase Mead himself often employs, namely, "taking the attitude of the other." An attitude, he says, consists of a behavioral disposition, a tendency to respond in a certain manner to certain sorts of stimuli, or the beginnings of an action that seek an occasion for full release or expression.[25]

This is actually a rather significant clarification, for Bourdieu is quite critical of traditions in social science that he thinks would proceed as Dilthey might, that is, by putting oneself "empathetically" in the place or role of the other.[26] And given that he lumps phenomenologists and interactionists in the same class, and that Mead is often viewed as the grandfather of interactionism, Bourdieu or his followers might very well be misled by Mead's language. No doubt there is some of this sort of thinking in Mead, but by no means does every use of the phrase "taking the role of the other" suggest an empathy born of ideational understanding or an exchange of feelings entailed in roles of the theatrical sort. To put this in other terms, this clarification is important because it will allow us to more easily see just how similar Mead's "me" is to Bourdieu's habitus in its appeal to the attitudinal. It is worth noting one additional point at this juncture: Mead's model builds in a notion of reciprocity at a very basic level. One must be able to take the attitude of the other in order to speak and fully play one's part. To what degree this activity should be viewed in strategic or manipulative terms is debatable, and represents a potential bone of contention between Mead and Bourdieu. But what is clear is that if one emphasizes this aspect of the model – as opposed to novelty, the dispositional, and systemic entanglements – then the step to Habermas's ideal of a communication community is not a long one.[27]

There are varying degrees of complexity possible in the process of taking the attitude of the other, so that the child learning to take specific attitudes – for example, the relatively isolated behavior of caressing a doll – should be viewed differently from the child playing at being a doctor, which might more properly be called role-playing. The latter requires an internalization of two sets or constellations of "exchangeable" attitudes, that is, doctor and patient. However, even though role-playing of this type entails considerably more complex sets of behaviors than caressing a doll, Mead is careful (at times) to distinguish it from the presentation of a self, or a "me."[28] The terms self and "me" are reserved for yet more complicated sets of behaviors that Mead tries to explain in terms of his neologism, the *generalized other*. If we think of roles as being played in relationship to *specific others*, then selves can be said to arise in relationship to complex networks of interactions with the assistance of a *generalized other*, and these networks or systems bear comparison with Bourdieu's fields.

The organized community or social group which gives to the individual his unity of self may be called "the generalized other." The attitude of the generalized other is the attitude of the whole community. Thus, for example, in the case of such a social group as a ball team, the team is the generalized other in so far as it enters – *as an organized process or social activity* – into the experience of any one of the individual members of it.[29] (emphasis added)

What is important here is not so much the example of a ball team but the phrase, "organized process." We can think of various "systems," such as families or even corporations, as giving rise to generalized others, which in turn produce "me's." While not identical to Bourdieu's fields, such "systems" are clearly homologous to them. The following groups can be said to have generalized others:

Some of them are concrete social classes or subgroups, such as political parties, clubs, corporations, which are all actually functional social units, in terms of which their individual members are directly related to one another. The others are abstract social classes or subgroups, such as the class of debtors and the class of creditors, in terms of which their individual members are related to one another only more or less indirectly.[30]

Such groups give rise to generalized others, and the consciously apprehended "me" arises as one turns back – reflects, so to speak – on one's own behaviors and views them from the perspective of a generalized other. The group, then, is both the source of behaviors and the "place" from which we can "view" our behaviors, in a manner analogous to the way in which we become aware of the meaning of a gesture by viewing it in terms of the other person's response. Various communities give rise to different "me's," and some communities may be thought of as more inclusive than others – for example, political parties or religious orders – because their attitudes permeate other "me's;" hence, they can be thought of as giving rise to meta-selves. Further, even the same communities do not generate identical "me's" because of the (slightly) different positions that each individual has in a group. We are, so to speak, Leibnizian monads of particular social worlds. And this parallels Bourdieu's view that "each individual system of dispositions is a structural variant of the others, expressing the singularity of its position within the class and its trajectory."[31] However, Mead and Bourdieu part company over the importance of self-consciousness for the realization of the "singularity" of an agent. Mead insists that the "me" or the self and self-consciousness go hand in hand. The self is an "object" of cognition, framed by the generalized other, and only by having this object before one's eyes can one properly speaking be said to have a self, as opposed to a bundle of unknown behaviors. Here Mead once again parts with Bourdieu in emphasizing the importance of reflection. While both wish to overcome the Cartesian subject, and while both have a sophisticated view of the individual as a social agent, Mead remains committed to the category of self-consciousness as a key factor in agency and "singularity."

For Mead, to be aware of a "me" requires what he calls the "I." We can think of the "I" and "me" as phases of experience that are the *functional* equivalents of a transcendental ego and an empirical self. One cannot be aware of the "me" unless there is a subject, an "I," present to provide the "consciousness of" the empirical object, that is, the "me." Not only does the "I" allow us to be aware of the "me," it also serves as the "source" of responses. "The 'I' is the response of the organism to the attitudes of the others; the 'me' is the organized set of attitudes of others which one himself assumes."[32] The "I's" responses are (in varying degrees) novel and by definition they cannot be self-consciously appropriated as they take place. Appealing to the example of a game once again, we can say that a play initiated by an "I" is never identical with a past play. Every response is somewhat unique, so one cannot self-consciously appropriate an act until it has taken place. "If you ask, then, where directly in your own experience the "I" comes in, the answer is that it comes in as a historical figure. It is what you were a second ago that is the "I" of the "me."[33] As an historical figure the "I" has become a "me," a response that is now "included" in some systemic "me."

If we think of the "me" as homologous to Bourdieu's habitus, and social groups or communities as comparable to fields, then one is left wondering if there is a category that parallels the "I" in Bourdieu's approach. At first glance it may appear that the "I" is too spontaneous for inclusion in Bourdieu's model, but although the "I" is the source of novel responses, we cannot presume that the "I" exists unmarked by previous experience, for its responses typically draw on learned behaviors. It is also worth noting in this regard that in Mead's model of systemic transformation, a new ("me") system could not arise if events – the "I's" responses, for instance – were so novel that they could not couple with a prior system in order to transform it. (This would be true, for example, in the case of a biological mutation that is so novel that it fails to survive long enough to transform its environment.) So one should not confuse Mead's approach with the extreme self-creationism of Sartre's account of consciousness as nothing in *Being and Nothingness*.[34] Finally, since much of the way we respond to the world is non-reflexive, the "I" – which responds before the individual is self-consciously aware of what she has done – can be said to be the home of our non-reflexive engagement with the world, which Bourdieu places in the realm of the *habitus*. All of this suggests that a good deal of what Mead describes as the "I" is covered in Bourdieu's notion of the *habitus*, and Bourdieu it seems is even willing to speak of *habitus* in terms of spontaneity.

The *habitus* is a spontaneity without consciousness or will, opposed as much to the mechanical necessity of things without history in mechanistic theories as it is to the reflexive freedom of subjects "without inertia" in rationalistic theories.[35]

Because the "I" is not reflexively aware of its actions as it produces them, and because it does so in a rather spontaneous fashion, it can be compared to features of the *habitus*. Yet there are differences. Bourdieu would be quite uncomfortable with the "I's" penchant for novelty and the way in which Mead appears to presume that the "I" and "me" can work together to set up a situation in which novelty and reflexivity are available to an agent, suggesting just the kind of subjectivism that Bourdieu wants to avoid.[36] And it is worth noting that the novelty that Mead locates in the responses of the "I" is not merely an artifact of human activity, for novel events are imbedded in the fabric of nature, the warp in nature's woof. They are the ultimate source of change for Mead and are responsible for the flow of time itself; without them we would be living in a Parmenidian universe.[37] If Mead, for example, were asked to explain the dynamism and ongoing modifications of Bourdieu's fields, he would not focus on exchanges of capital that produce and are produced by fluctuations in power relations, but on the presence of novel events. While Bourdieu and Mead view the agent in terms of constellations of dispositions, for Mead agents are conceived of as sources of novel behaviors that quite often modify these constellations. Bourdieu, on the other hand, tends to emphasize how the *habitus* of an agent manages to place a damper on insurgent novelty.

Early experiences have particular weight because the *habitus* tends to ensure its own constancy and its defence against change through the selection it makes within new information by rejecting information capable of calling into question its accumulated information, if exposed to it accidentally or by force, and especially by avoiding exposure to such information. . . . Through the systematic "choices" it makes among the places, events and people that might be frequented, the *habitus* tends to protect itself from crises and critical challenges by providing itself with a milieu to which it is as pre-adapted as possible.[38]

While a *habitus* that is inclined to welcome novelty with (at least) somewhat open arms would be a rather strange beast for Bourdieu, this doesn't mean that he takes himself to be a determinist, and he has on a number of occasions sought to address the issue. When asked about innovation and agency in the face of the seeming durability of the *habitus* in a relatively recent interview, Bourdieu turns first to flagellating those who are as enraptured with the notion of themselves as creators as they are obsessively preoccupied with their singularity.[39] He then goes on to tell us that

habitus is not the fate that some people read into it. Being the product of history, it is an *open system of dispositions* that is constantly subjected to experiences, and therefore constantly affected by them in a way that either reinforces or modifies its structures. It is durable but not eternal![40]

Bourdieu also assures us that a habitus can undergo modification in the face of different fields or even due to an "awakening of consciousness and social analysis."[41]

Yet, in spite of Bourdieu's protestations (perhaps he doth protest a bit too much here), there is something rather Spinozan about his work, not so much the hard determinism of Spinoza but the latter's appeal to *conatus*, to each "thing's" striving to preserve its own existence, with the understanding that every "thing" is intimately conjoined in a series of relationships (causes) that permit it to be what it is. While Bourdieu may not directly appeal to Spinoza's concept, a comparable notion of the inertial looms rather large in his pluri-verse, a world in which a habitus can be thought of as preserving itself because it follows a given trajectory. It may very well be that those who charge Bourdieu with determinism are in fact detecting recurring invocations of determinism's kissing cousin, the inertial.

When Bourdieu talks about transformations of the social world he tends to emphasize how given dispositions and schemes can be transposed to different contexts. Novelty seemingly has little or nothing to do with the process.

Because the *habitus* is an infinite capacity for generating products – thoughts, perceptions, expressions and actions – whose limits are set by the historically and socially situated conditions of its production, the conditioned and conditional freedom it provides is as remote from creation of unpredictable novelty as it is from simple mechanical reproduction of the original conditioning.[42]

Mead, on the other hand, emphasizes the role that the upsurge of genuinely novel events play in the transformation of the social world. Here he is more influenced by biological models of evolutionary development than is Bourdieu, ones in which mutations or new forms of life manage to introduce themselves into a given ecosystem or organism and create a realignment of prior relationships. As a matter of fact, Mead develops a whole analysis of the process of the transformation of systems based on the introduction of a novel event (or organism) into an existing system. Yet as different as they may seem, there is clearly a sense in which they share a similar understanding of transformation. For if novelty is defined as the displacement and mapping of one set of dispositions or schemas onto another, then both agree that "novelty" can be a major source of change.

So for both Bourdieu and Mead novelty may arise due to the transpositions of schemas and habits into different contexts, but for Mead it also emerges due to the unpredictably idiosyncratic, which has its locus in the individual. Individuals can introduce change into social systems for Mead. But this is not all. Individual human beings actually have something of an obligation to do so, and this calls for self-assertion.

The "I" is the response of the individual to the attitude of the community as this appears in his own experience. His response to that organized attitude in turn changes it. . . . But if the response to it is a response which is of the nature of the conversation of gestures, if it creates a situation which is in some sense novel, if one puts up his side of the case, asserts himself over against others and insists that they take a different attitude toward himself, *then there is*

something important occurring that is not previously present in experience.[43]
(emphasis added)

Note that one asserts oneself not only for one's own interest, but because by so doing something important occurs "that is not previously present in experience." Mead reveals his attachment here to a tradition that places a strong positive valence on creativity; and individuals, as originators of novel responses, are viewed in a favorable light when they promote novelty in conversations with others. While Mead would not have spoken in Buber's language regarding the spark of the divine in the other, there is a sense in which individuals are a source of continuing wonder to him because of their capacity to say and do novel things, because they can exceed our anticipations. And, of course, this sensibility, shared to a degree by Buber and Mead, is quite in line with Judaic and Christian teachings that link creation and irreducible individuality. So, in spite of the apparent lack of Christian humbleness in Mead's insistence on self assertion, it would be misleading to read Nietzsche into his comments. Notwithstanding Mead's secular turn, a good deal of his early contact with a liberal, Mid-western, progressive Christian tradition remained ingrained.[44]

There are additional connections to this tradition in Mead's thought that are worth highlighting at this juncture. Conversations of gestures – whether reflective or non-reflective (as in the case of the boxer that Bourdieu so liked) – not only promote novel responses, they also nurture mutuality. For Mead, a conspicuous feature of our everyday social and linguistic exchanges is that we continually take the perspective of others, and by doing so we develop our capacity for tolerance, the descriptive and the prescriptive being closely affiliated. Bourdieu would want to place some distance between himself and models that emphasize this sensibility, not only because they do not seem sufficiently sensitive to objective conditions, but because they appear insufficiently attuned to the nature of interests or *illusio*. For Bourdieu, we can never escape our interests, and must even ask what interests universalism serves. To be a social actor is to have a stake in a certain game.

To understand the notion of interest, it is necessary to see that it is opposed not only to that of disinterestedness or gratuitousness but also to that of *indifference*. To be indifferent is to be unmoved by the game: like Buridan's donkey, this game makes no difference to me. Indifference is an axiological state, an ethical state of nonpreference as well as a state of knowledge in which I am not capable of differentiating the stakes proposed. Such was the goal of the Stoics: to reach a state of ataraxy (*ataraxia* means the fact of not being troubled). *Illusio* is the very opposite of ataraxy: it is to be invested, taken in and by the game. . . . Each field calls forth and gives life to a specific form of interest, a specific *illusio*, as tacit recognition of the value of the stakes of the game as practical mastery of its rules.[45]

Since it is hard to imagine how one could exist for Bourdieu without at each moment being immersed in some field, it is also hard to imagine how one could ever escape from "interestedness." Mead, following James's lead, is also quite convinced that a transhistorical rationality that would allow us to escape our interests is simply not in the cards for mere social and historical beings such as ourselves. That we are perspectivally bound creatures should alone give us pause when we hear claims to disinterested observations from the mount. Nevertheless, there is considerable difference between Mead and Bourdieu here, as the following statement by Mead makes patently clear.

We are definitely identified with our own interests. One is constituted out of his own interests; and when those interests are frustrated, what is called for then is in some sense a sacrifice of this narrow self. This should lead to the development of a larger self which can be identified with the interests of others. I think all of us feel that one must be ready to recognize the interests of others even when they run counter to our own, but that the person who does that does not really sacrifice himself, but becomes a larger self.[46]

No doubt the skills involved in the sharing of attitudes and interests can be used in manipulative or strategic ways, and not just for the "enlargement" of the self. And Bourdieu is quite versed in attuning us to the ways in which we are continually shuffling capital and mischievously employing such skills in the service of our interests. Mead, however, was something of a babe in the woods in this regard. He believed that the modern world might very well see the rise of so-called "abstract groups" that would be increasingly open to participation by those removed in time and place.[47] He believed in his own pragmatized version of Kant's enlarged mentality, one that did not seek to deny interests but expand them through shared (or potentially shareable) experiences. He continued to believe in the merits of a secularized version of the Christian commonwealth of his youthful dreams, where all human beings would be brothers and sisters who would be able to see their interests as the interests of their neighbors. And, in a rather Jamesian fashion, he continued to believe that our belief in this ideal was part and parcel of the practice that could help to make it happen. Bourdieu, of course, would find all of this as unconvincing as it is quaintly American and provincial. Ideas and practices cannot avoid being tainted by (unspecified) interests, and he would be moved to unmask any pretensions to the contrary.

Notes

1　Victor Kestenbaum, *The Phenomenological Sense of John Dewey: Habit and Meaning* (Atlantic Highlands, N.J.: Humanities Press, 1977) and James M. Ostrow, *Social Sensitivity: A Study of Habit and Experience* (Albany: SUNY, 1990).

2　Pierre Bourdieu and Loïc J. D. Wacquant, *An Invitation to Reflexive Sociology* (Chicago: University of Chicago Press, 1992), 122. Bourdieu goes on to say:

> At bottom and in short – I cannot consider here all the relevant common-alities and differences – I would say that the theory of practical sense presents many similarities with theories, such as Dewey's, that grant a central role to the notion of habit, understood as an active and creative relation to the world, and reject all the conceptual dualisms upon which nearly all post-Cartesian philosophies are based: subject and object, internal and external, material and spiritual, individual and social, and so on.

(In contrast to the Platonic vision of like nurturing like, perhaps we should refer to Bourdieu's speculations here as his prototheory of the reactive habitus: opposition to the same breeds the similar.)

3　Given Bourdieu's repeated disparagements of theory for theory's sake, or the mere comparison of theories for the sake of contrasting them, I find myself in a bit of a quandary. Bourdieu would no doubt prefer that my time be spent utilizing his approach to investigate the genesis of fields that could produce such similarities. Since this is neither the place nor the time to analyze or dispute Bourdieu's complex relationship to the theoretical, I suggest that those who share his aversion to the merely theoretical view this piece as supplying information for a possible future study. See, for example, *Invitation*, 159–60.

4　Pierre Bourdieu, *The Logic of Practice*, tr. Richard Nice (Stanford: Stanford University Press, 1990), 50. Hereafter referred to as *LP*.

5　Pierre Bourdieu, "A Lecture on the Lecture," in *In Other Words: Essays Towards a Reflexive Sociology*, tr. Matthew Adamson (Stanford: Stanford University Press, 1990), 190.

6　William James, *Psychology: The Briefer Course*, ed. Gordon Allport (New York: Harper and Row, 1961), 10.

7　James, *Psychology*, 11–12.

8　G. H. Mead, *Mind, Self, and Society: From the Standpoint of a Social Behaviorist*, ed. Charles W. Morris (Chicago: University of Chicago Press, 1934), pp. 352–3. Hereafter referred to as *MSS*.

9　G. H. Mead, "Scientific Method and the Moral Sciences," in *Selected Writings: George Herbert Mead*, ed. Andrew J. Reck (Chicago: University of Chicago Press, 1964), 258. See also, "Philanthropy from the Point of View of Ethics," *Selected Writings*, 397.

10   Bourdieu would in all likelihood respond to Mead on ethics and politics as he has to Dewey on art and education.

Dewey, however laudable his stances in matters of art and education, did not escape this kind of moralism [that is, by rejecting the dichotomy between popular and high culture one could make it disappear – M.A.] fostered by both his epoch and his national philosophical and political traditions. (*Invitation*, 84).

11   The parentheses around "self" are meant to draw attention to the distinction between a fully developed consciousness of self, in which one is directly reflecting on who one is – that is, one's identity – and the awareness one has of one's actions or the meaning of one's words. In the latter case the parentheses will be used. This distinction is suggested by Mead's approach; whether and to what degree it can be maintained is beyond the scope of this paper.

12   *MSS*, 43.

13   *LP*, 80.

14   *LP*, 50–1.

15   *MSS*, 47.

16   Mead is well aware of the fact that hand sign languages allow one to respond to their own gestures as the other does because one can see and feel a hand sign as the other sees it. Mead, however, views the vocal gesture as ultimately more suited to this task.

17   *MSS*, 134.

18   *LP*, 91.

19   Socrates, as Nietzsche glibly and humorously teaches, was a dialectician and educator, and as such a degenerate, one who fell from true excellence, which needs none of his rhetorical strategies. Nietzsche, *Twilight of the Idols*, in *The Portable Nietzsche*, tr. Walter Kaufmann (New York: Viking Press, 1968), 473–9.

20   *LP*, 103.

21   Bourdieu, *In Other Words*, 5.

22   Rosenthal and Bourgeois read Mead as very close to Merleau-Ponty in their book, *Mead and Merleau-Ponty*, hence they tend to see a pre-reflective sphere in Mead's thought that has many of the attributes of Merleau-Ponty's lived body. My own view is that Mead bifurcated the reflective and non-reflective to an unnecessary degree, but I agree with Rosenthal and Bourgeois that there is a sensitivity to experience in Mead that could easily be developed in the direction of Merleau-Ponty's work. Our disagreement is over the degree to which he actually accomplished this end. I discuss the pre-reflective and reflective in my book, *The Mediating Self: Mead, Sartre, and Self-Determination* (New Haven: Yale University Press, 1986). See, Sandra B. Rosenthal and Patrick L. Bourgeois, *Mead and Merleau-Ponty: Toward a Common Vision*, (Albany: SUNY, 1991).

23   See, for example, *Invitation*, 137n. 91 (editor's note). Bourdieu, in discussing the difference between reasonable and rational actions, states:

One should recall here the Husserlian distinction between protension, the positing of a future immediately inscribed in the present, as an objective potentiality and endowed with the doxic modality of the present, and project, the positing of a future grasped as such, that is, as contingent, liable to come to pass or not. (*In Other Words*, 109). Bourdieu by no means denies the possibility of operating with a project in view, he simply believes that the Sartreans have seriously over-estimated the importance of (self) conscious goal oriented activity.

24   Mead, "The Definition of the Psychical," *Selected Writings*, 42–3.
25   Cook, *Mead*, 79.
26   *LP*, 19.
27   Jürgen Habermas, "Individuation through Socialization: On George Herbert Mead's Theory of Subjectivity," in *Postmetaphysical Thinking: Philosophical Essays*, tr. William Mark Hohengarten (Cambridge: MIT Press, 1992).
28   There are times that Mead is rather loose with these terms and is willing to call both the "I" and "me" a self, while at other times the "me" does not appear to require quite the level of sophistication that is suggested here. Part of the problem lies in the fact that so much of what we have from Mead is drawn from students' or Mead's lecture notes. Mead never published a book on his social psychology or philosophy. In addition, it appears that he wanted to retain some flexibility in his functional distinctions.
29   *MSS*, 154.
30   *MSS*, 157.
31   *LP*, 60. Bourdieu goes on to tell us that " 'personal' style, the particular stamp marking all the products of the same *habitus*, whether practices or works, is never more than a deviation in relation to the style of a period or class."
32   *MSS*, 175.
33   *MSS*, 174.
34   Bourdieu appears to associate project oriented or "controlled" sponta-neity with Sartre, but the absence of a posited self on the pre-reflective level for Sartre complicates this reading.
35   *LP*, 56.
36   Whether Mead can succeed here is beyond the scope of this paper. See, *The Mediating Self*.
37   G. H. Mead, *The Philosophy of the Present*, ed. Arthur E. Murphy (Chicago: University of Chicago Press, 1980; Open Court, 1932), 1, 33. No doubt the metaphysical questions surrounding the status of novelty – just how novel is novelty? – are rather breathtaking and worthy of attention, but are clearly beyond the scope of this paper.
38   *LP*, 60–61.
39   *Invitation*, 132–3.
40   *Invitation*, 133. He goes on to say:

Having said this, I must immediately add that there is a probability, inscribed in the social destiny associated with definite social conditions, that experiences will confirm habitus, because most people are statistically bound to encounter circumstances that tend to agree with those that originally fashioned their habitus.... From [the categories already constructed by prior experiences – Bourdieu]...follows an inevitable priority of originary experiences and a *relative* closure of the system of dispositions that constitute habitus."

This is not Bourdieu's complete answer. He goes on to talk about the relation of *habitus* to certain social structures.

41 Bourdieu, "A Reply to Some Objections," in *In Other Words*, 116.
42 *LP*, 55.
43 *MSS*, 196.
44 This, of course, would not surprise Bourdieu, who has few compunctions about categorizing Dewey's moralism in terms of American cultural traditions. See note # 10 above.
45 *Invitation*, 116–17. This reference to the stoics brings to mind Adam Smith, who was influenced by them. Bourdieu seems to take a special delight in criticizing what he takes to be the notion of the *impartial spectator*, which suggests to him objectivity from the mountain top, the aloofness of the theoretician (*LP*, 31). Mead, on the other hand, would feel comfortable with this phrase if it were understood in the spirit of certain aspects of Adam Smith's work, that is, not as objectivity from on high but as a constant claim on us to attempt to move into the perspective of others, and thereby gain some distance from our own interests. Smith may have increasingly moved toward a notion of the Judge on high as he revised successive editions of his *Theory of the Moral Sentiments*, but from the first there was a strong social bent and practical impulse behind the phrase.
46 *MSS*, 386.
47 Membership in these groups allows for:

definite social relations (however indirect) with an almost infinite number of other individuals...cutting across functional lines of demarcation which divide different human social communities from one another, and including individual members from several (in some cases from all) such communities. (*MSS*, 157)

Mead took this process to be part and parcel of the growing interdependence of the modern world. He did not view such groups as necessarily destroying more localized ones, but as existing at different levels of abstraction.

10

Bourdieu Nouveau

William Earle

...la condamnation de l'éclectisme a souvent servi d'alibi à l'inculture....

Pierre Bourdieu[1]

This is no time for people who say: this, this, and only this. We say: this, and *this*, and *that* too.

James Fenton[2]

Une autre [impolitesse], de Haig un peu plus tard, qui se plaint de la chaleur régnant dans l'Orangerie: *Ces Français, au lieu de parler de haute technologie, ils feraient mieux d'apprendre a installer la climatisation!* Climatiser l'Orangerie? Sommet de la civilisation....

Jacques Attali[3]

What I really wanted was to break through the veil of mythologies drawn over our image of society, so that people could act more reasonably and better.

Norbert Elias[4]

I

The arrival, in the United States, of Beaujolais nouveau is always something of an event, enhanced no doubt by the stagemanagerial expertise of American vintners, but an event nonetheless. In the same way, and with appropriately academized (and so genteel) advance publicity, we can picture Pierre Bourdieu arriving in one of the many places he is these days invited to appear, to give a lecture (whatever the ostensible subject matter at least as much now about himself and his own work) and to chat with the natives. We had one such event at my own university (CUNY) a few years ago with a standingroom-only crowd drawn from many academic disciplines as well as some freelance New York intellectuals, but pretty much excluding local philosophers. (The philosophers, even if not now so purely analytic as they were a while ago, are still attempting a kind of purity which certainly involves isolation, in the full medical sense, from trendy[5] foreign intellectuals.)

I went to Bourdieu's lecture because I had come to believe, and still believe, that his "theory of practice" is what Wittgenstein would have had had Wittgenstein not, aristocratically and arbitrarily, disdained all theory in philosophy and imposed upon himself, in a kind of reverse delusion of grandeur, the exclusive examination of the fine-grained logical grammar of our form-of-life-embedded ordinary language.

I start anecdotally, but only because the anecdote can (and should) be viewed, to use the phrase of Bachelard so often cited by Bourdieu, as a "cas particulier du possible."[6] My philosophical colleagues did not stay away from Bourdieu because they are particularly narrow or generally intolerant of the different. Indeed, away from philosophy, they are apt to be great readers of European literature, people of wide culture and broad sympathies. The explanation is, rather, that which Bourdieu has worked out in detail in the case of Heidegger[7] and which can be applied to Wittgenstein as well as to American analytic philosophers. These constitute three cases, for all their differences, of the same "possible" – the same general form or structure.

In all three cases, a philosopher or group of philosophers is caught up in the objective necessity[8] of maintaining the integrity, the impermeability, the autonomy, of the philosophical field or *champ*[9] against external competitors as well as maintaining, or improving, his (or their) position within the field. (*Champ* designates two of Bourdieu's central concepts and will be discussed in the next section.) Perhaps the main external competitor in the modern era has been science – one would, were this less summary, have to say something about the various (and various kinds of) impingements of the various sciences, natural and human, at particular points in philosophical space – which is why Heidegger ventured to say, what is of course laughable, that "Science does not think" and concocted a dubious, dubiously useful, metaphysics of Being or why Wittgenstein imagined forms of lives of fictive tribes and the language games they may be conceived to have played while eschewing help from real ethnography which actually carries forward the descriptive project – the "natural history" of diversely situated humans – to which Wittgenstein was himself committed.[10]

In the remarks that follow, I shall be looking, mainly, though not exclusively, and certainly not with a Bourdieu-naive eye, at one of Bourdieu's most recent works *Raisons Pratiques: Sur la théorie de l'action* – hence my titular "nouveau" – which collects (i) talks given between 1986 and 1994 at Tokyo, East Berlin, Madison (Wisconsin), Princeton, Amsterdam, Lyon; (ii) contributions to international conferences, one at the Freie Universität Berlin focussed on Bourdieu's work, one at Locarno (Switzerland) devoted to the history of science; (iii) an interview published in Japan; (iv) an essay that appeared in a Robert K. Merton *Festschrift*. This list, itself, suggests something of where his *trajectoire* has brought Bourdieu, the *vieillissement social*[11] he has undergone. Both the thinker and the thought have become rather more world-historical than they used to be.

II

Champ, or field, is associated by Bourdieu with two distinct concepts. *Champ*$_1$ is "global social space"[12] within which each person has a series of better or worse addresses which constitute his/her social trajectory. The most explicit acknowledgement of social space, at least in the United States, is in the idea (and talk) of upward or downward mobility, though "mobility" makes social space sound too external to the lives and identities of those who move through it. Address in social space is determined by "position in the statistical distributions according to the *two principles of differentiation* which, in the more advanced societies like the United States, Japan, and France, are doubtless the most efficient: economic capital and cultural capital."[13] People are made both objectively and subjectively alike, *simpatico*, electively affine, of "our crowd," and even potential lovers and marital partners, by having the same combination of capital assets. This is why, despite considerable congressional liberty (The Studio 54 Syndrome), few friendships flourish, and even fewer marriages are contracted, between parties from different social "neighborhoods."

"Neighborhood" must, of course, be understood as a set of adjacent points in social space, occupied by people who enjoy – relatively – easy access to each other even if, in ordinary space, they may (as in the rather extreme case of the "jet set") reside dispersively in a dozen world-class cities.[14] This point can, and should, be made in a more formal and general way: Social space, with its abstract addresses and neighborhoods, is a construction of social theory with as many dimensions as there are socially significant – that is, explanatorily significant – variables.

It is not an empirical discovery that people inhabit social space; but the concept of social space, as it comes to be defined by Bourdieu, provides the framework for research. More precisely, global social space (*champ*$_1$) along with its circular definers, the various kinds of capital, PLUS the relatively autonomous (and in so-called advanced societies, at least) highly differentiated social worlds (*champs*$_2$) within global social space PLUS *habitus*, an individual's "second nature" which is entirely a consequence of locations within *champ*$_1$ and some, typically only one, *champ*$_2$ TOGETHER constitute the conceptual framework within which Bourdieu has worked. ("People inhabit social space" might be viewed as, in Wittgenstein's sense, a grammatical remark.[15])

This set of framework concepts must be handled with considerable theoretical caution. *First*, although the concepts in question are of philosophical interest,[16] we (interested philosophers) should resist the temptation to "philosophize" the concepts themselves, ablating the research program they animate, and providing for them, instead, concise, not to say schematic, verbal definitions which have the effect of rendering them absolutely *a priori*. Essentialized, it is easy enough either to make deflationary comparisons (Isn't *habitus* merely habit, disposition, *hexis*? Isn't *champ*$_1$ merely socio-economic class all over again? Etc. Etc.) or to demonstrate their trivial, or tautological, character – as Raymond Boudon attempts in the case of *habitus*.[17] What Bourdieu attempts consistently to avoid (which can make him sound antiphilosophical which he is not) is what Bachelard described as "une philosophie claire, rapide, facile, mais qui reste une philosophie de philosophe."[18] Bourdieu's own definitions are slow and cumulative and are no more meant to be free-standing, or self-sufficient, than sentences in scientific papers which refer to experiments, technical apparatus, laboratories, accomplished research.[19] Bourdieu's verbal formulations of the framework concepts are, in other words, implicitly indexical.[20]

It would be a crude mistake – this is the *second* place we need to be cautious – to suppose that, if the framework concepts do not record empirical findings, they are arbitrary or adventitious or indeed unimportant. Concepts compete against other concepts that might be, or might have been, developed and deployed in their place. The process of conceptual elaboration, as undertaken by Bourdieu, embodies a set of *defensible* theoretical choices. This is a long story, but here are some excerpts.

(i) *Champ*$_1$, global social space, is designed as an alternative to class in the Marxist sense. The concept of class, at least in the political vulgate of the left, is ambivalent between something that is *input to* and something that is *output from* political processes. For Bourdieu, a class, that is, a group with a certain distribution of class consciousness and the acknowledgement, also distributed among its members, of authorized spokespersons, is always the result of processes of class formation.[21] In contrast, locations in social space, which are always conceived comparatively (or *par leur extériorité mutuelle*[22]) with other possible – worse or better – locations, are markers for individual portfolios of capital, of socially effective (and, in the case of symbolic capital, socially recognized) advantages. In understanding *champ*$_1$, we can appreciate the two complementary aspects of Bourdieu's approach. *First*, Bourdieu condemns, and actually avoids, *apriorism*, the philosophical fantasy that knowledge of an object, O, is possible without the examination of O. As he tells a Japanese audience: "I will talk about a country I know well, France, not because I was born there or speak French, but because I have studied it extensively."[23] But, *second*, an individual object of study, contemporary France for example, as a "particular case of the possible," should allow us "to seize the invariant, the structure, in the observed variant." Ethnography should be made to yield "l'histoire comparée," "l'anthropologie comparative."[24] The interplay of the ethnographic and the anthropological, the variable and the universally valid, is nicely brought out in the following passage which is worth quoting at length:

Nothing permits us to suppose that the principle of differentiation is the same at all times and in all places, in Ming China and contemporary China or, again, in the Germany, Russia, or Algeria, of today. But with the exception of the least differentiated societies (which nevertheless reveal differences, less easy to measure, in symbolic capital), all societies reveal themselves as social spaces, that is, structures of differences which cannot really be comprehended without contructing the generative principle on which such differences are objectively based. The principle is nothing other than the structure of the forms of power and types of capital which are efficacious in the social universe considered – and which vary according to places and moments.[25]

As a particular instance, in addressing an audience in East Berlin (as it happens, about two weeks before the opening of the Berlin Wall), Bourdieu points out that in understanding the societies of the Soviet Union and eastern Europe, as they existed until recently, it is necessary to introduce "an index of specifically political capital" retained by members of the political Nomenklatura: "Where other forms of accumulation are more or less completely controlled, political capital becomes the primordial principle of differentiation. . . ."[26] A form of capital which in western societies would be dominant within the "political world," one world (or *champ₂*) among many and limited by other autonomous worlds external to it, each with a set of competitive implicit judgements about what counts, what makes a difference, incarnate in a variety of *champ₂*-specific *habitus*,[27] in a globally, and overly, politicized Soviet-style society, will run rampant, like an animal without natural enemies, destroying, or at least compromising, the integrity, the separateness, of every social sphere.

(ii) Even in societies where money is everything, it isn't the only thing. In highly differentiated societies – France, Germany, the United States, Japan, Bourdieu's most common examples – each *champ₂* assigns to economic capital, cultural capital, and a form, or a few forms, of *champ₂*-specific symbolic capital [for a fuller discussion of symbolic capital, *see* next section], not only their degree of relative importance, but their acceptable, or nondisqualifying, role in intra-*champ₂* competition. James Merrill, the distinguished American poet, whose father happened to be the Merrill in Merrill Lynch (a major international brokerage and financial services corporation), could be bought a superior education, and could buy himself freedom from teaching, but he could not have bought a press to publish his books of poems nor – equally unthinkably! – have run an advertisement in *The New York Times*, paid for out of his own pocket, to publicize one of them. In any case, in Merrill's chosen world, commercial success counts for nothing or negatively; the poetry world is a very pure one – Bourdieu speaks of "l'artiste 'pur', sans autres 'clients' que ses propres concurrents"[28] – in which the only thing that counts is the judgements of other poets, the judgements of one's peers.

But even in Hollywood, there are rules about what money can and cannot do: one can't finance a movie out of one's own pocket. I have been told by an entry-level poet and a Hollywood insider, respectively, that neither of these points is unqualifiedly true. This may be. Autonomy, that is to say, the relative autonomy, of a particular field, is always, as Bourdieu always emphasizes, an historical accomplishment. A chapter in *The Rules of Art: Genesis and Structure of the Literary Field* is entitled "The Conquest of Autonomy."[29] And what has been conquered can, of course, be lost. There are – current – complaints from within various fields – the fine arts and the sciences being the two most conspicuous examples – of permeation by extraneous factors including those that are crudely economic. But the fact that the complaints arise and that the extraneous factors are judged inappropriate and generate resentment testifies to the continuing struggle, waged by insiders, to maintain purity. I should add that insiders' perceptions of purity, though they may give rise to narcissistic delusions, also reflect the real, though limited, functional separateness of their $champ_2$.[30]

The Hollywood example is a little different, since the movie business (or "the industry" as it is invariably referred to by players) is after all continuous with the economic world at large, but even so you cannot buy credibility even in a town where everything seems to be for sale, though the more you have of it, the more rules you can flaunt.

There is also the possibility, at least for extremely powerful or successful players, of turning boundary violations and $champ_2$ trespass to good account. The perfect French example is Sartre, described brilliantly by Bourdieu:

Transgressing the invisible, but almost intransversible frontier which separates professors, philosophers or critics, and writers, petit-bourgeois scholarship students and heirs of the bourgeoisie, academic prudence and artistic daring, erudition and inspiration, the gravity of the concept and the elegance of writing [écriture], but also reflexivity and naivete, Sartre really invented and incarnated the figure of the *total intellectual*, thinker-writer, novelist-metaphysician, artist-philosopher, who deployed in the political battles of the moment all these forms of authority and competence united in his own person.[31]

Andy Warhol provides an interesting American example. Warhol managed, within the fine arts microcosm of *ars gratia artis*, to present himself as naively, if not simple-mindedly (but perhaps ironically – no one could be quite certain) commercial, calling his atelier "The Factory," answering the question "What is art?" "A boy's name," and, not only not hiding, but openly revealing an attitude epitomized by this observation from his postumously published *Diaries*: "Some blacks recognized me a few times this weekend, and I'm trying to figure out what they recognized so I can somehow sell it to them, whatever it is."[32]

In fact, what they (and everybody else) recognized, in Warhol, was his recognizability, or the *celebrity* of "being famous for being famous," which constructs its own demi-monde or pseudo-$champ_2$, a world in which the purest, or most perfectly contentless, form of symbolic capital rules and in which there is a promiscuous commingling of people who are "well-known" for something, something like actual accomplishment, in a real $champ_2$, and a variety of *dolce far niente* types (for example, displaced aristocrats and deposed royalty) who exist only to be recognized by the doorpersons of fashionable night clubs and discotheques.

The pseudo-*champ₂* of celebrity (against which worlds of "genuine" accomplishment, at least in the United States, feel themselves on the perpetual defensive) can help, by contrast, to illuminate the nature of a real *champ₂*. Celebrity, which is not even the same thing as real social standing (that is, social standing in the *Social Register* sense which defines a world of birth privilege and discretion and which obeys a version of the Epicurean "Live hidden!" maxim counselling a "lady," for example, to appear but thrice in the newspapers on the occasions of birth, marriage, and death), is generated by extracting a small payment (a moment or maybe fifteen minutes of attention) from everybody in complete indifference to social, or professional, standing. In contrast, all real *champs₂* function as closed corporations whose already, or some of whose already, consecrated members retain the exclusive right to consecrate new members. Ph.D.'s in philosophy – more precisely, those "twice selected" members of graduate faculties – make new Ph.D.'s in philosophy. In less juridically institutionalized, or explicitly regular, worlds, like the *champ₂* of poets or the *champ₂* of painters, there is an analogous process of consecration.

Suppose one goes "directly philosophical" here, and asks, what might be referred to as a Euthyphro question, "Is X a poet because X is recognized by (already recognized) poets or is X recognized by (already recognized) poets because X is a poet?" Euthyphro questions are likely to strike philosophers as getting at the heart of the matter: answers enforce absolute conceptual dependence or independence, as in the original case (*Euthyphro* 10d) where piety [*hosion*] either is or isn't totally distinct from the appreciative proclivities of the gods. On earth, however, things are messier and more circular, and Bennett M. Berger's remark about Bourdieu is apt: "he knows that the determining property of an independent variable and the determined property of a dependent variable are often mysterious or ambiguous..."[33] where "mysterious" (I take it) means, not definitively indescribable or indefeasibly unanalyzable, but just not obvious to untutored common sense – which is why sociology is, as Bourdieu always says, esoteric for all seeming exotericism.[34] These matters will be pursued in the next section in connection with "symbolic capital."

III

Bourdieu is not interested in a taxonomy of capital; and "symbolic capital" should not be thought of as a kind of capital, but as way of emphasizing certain relational features of capital in general. Let me start with what definitely *isn't* symbolic capital. Money, although it too is a social creation and is indeed subject to massive devaluation by mere belief, if general, in its worthlessness, has nevertheless a kind of autonomous causal efficacy. $50,0000, whoever possesses it and however acquired, just has the *purchasing power* of $50,000. According to Bourdieu, in one brief formulation, "Symbolic capital is capital with a cognitive foundation, which rests upon knowledge and recognition."[35] "Knowledge and recognition" ["la connaissance et la reconnaissance"] has, I think, to be construed as kind of *hendiadys* working more like "nice and warm" than like "scotch and soda," though the distinctive cognitive modality Bourdieu has in mind is difficult to characterize abstractly. The clerk at Macy's who recognizes a proferred twenty-dollar bill as a twenty-dollar bill is *not* exercising the kind of discernment in question. Why not? Two reasons. *First*, the clerk, in recognizing the bill, doesn't distinguish himself from anybody else in the United States of America. *Second*, the owner of the bill, in owing it, doesn't distinguish herself from anybody else either. Possession of a twenty-dollar bill is not like possession of a Platinum American Express Card. Here is a longer explanation and an example:

> ...honor in Mediterranean societies is a typical form of symbolic capital, which exists only through reputation, that is, the representation which others make of it, to the extent that they share just the set of beliefs which makes them perceive and appreciate certain properties and forms of conduct as honorable or dishonorable.[36]

Definitionally, symbolic capital provides the basis for making invidious comparisons and unflattering distinctions through "categories of perception which are the product of the incorporation of oppositions and divisions inscribed in the structured distribution of the species of capital in question...."[37] The courtesans around Louis XIV, who pursue "la vie de cour" are, in virtue of their incorporated *habitus*, hypersensitive to "all the little differences, the marks of subtle distinction in etiquette and rank," and are (as Bourdieu sums them up) "prêts à mourir pour une affaire de bonnets."[38]

The millinery – and, more generally, sartorial – matters that agitated courtiers will strike us as paradigm cases of the trivial, but this is not because we have a better grasp of what is really important, but because we are not courtiers. It is easy enough to achieve Stoic *ataraxia* (which signifies, in Bourdieu's words, "the fact of not being troubled"[39]) relative to any world which is not one's own. Even "what is reported [I am quoting Bourdieu] in the society columns of *Figaro*, *Vogue*, or *Jours de France* ceases to be, as we ordinarily think, exemplary manifestations of the idle life of the 'leisure class' or 'conspicuous consumptions' of the well-off, and appears as a particular form of social labor which requires an expense of time and money and a specific [that is, a *champ*$_2$-specific: WJE] competence, which tends to assure the reproduction, or enlargement, of social capital."[40] This same point is made by Norbert Elias, the magisterial historical sociologist of "*die höfische Gesellschaft*": "Court etiquette which, by the values of bourgeois-industrial societies, may well seem something quite unimportant, something merely 'external' and perhaps even ridiculous, proves, if one respects the autonomy of the structure of court society, an extremely reliable instrument for measuring the prestige value of an individual within the social network."[41] Prestige, in court society is no more arbitrary, in the sense of creatable *ad libitum* or *ex nihilo*, than authority or credibility within a particular scientific field. For this reason it is not true to say of some X that X is prestigious because X is accorded prestige. No one can quite think he is recognizing something that is entirely the product of that very recognition. The courtiers will have had a *realist* conception of prestige just because they will have felt – altogether sensibly – their judgments controlled by something external to themselves and also liable to be mistaken and, accordingly, corrigible.

Of course, what controls and corrects the courtiers' judgments is not a form of – what Andrew Pickering calls – "natural agency," something that could causally interact with, and so be detected by, a piece of equipment as particles were by Glaser's quenched xenon bubble chamber or charges on quarks by Morpurgo's magnetic levitation electrometer.[42] But – this is the other side of the same story – the value, *qua* scientific demonstration, of Glaser's or Morpurgo's scientific papers is not something that is machine-detectable or algorithmically decidable, though it is nonarbitrarily ascertainable by members of the relevant physics community. In this respect, it resembles other things cared about in social worlds such as credentials, names, titles, carriage, bearing, voice, linguistic competence, erudition, grace, and *savoir faire*.[43] These are all matters of recognition in just the sense in which Bourdieu can write of "the great success of *Nausea*, which we immediately recognized as a 'magisterial' synthesis of literature and philosophy."[44] But *was* it? Was it *really?*, the philosopher armed with "Euthyphro questions" will ask. And the most accurate – short – answer will strike such a philosopher as alarmingly circular: it had to be because it was recognized to be, but could not have been recognized to be unless it was.

I should, in this final section, say a few words about *habitus*. Put in terms of its French intellectual context, the concept of *habitus* (understood nonschematically in the total research program for which it is a framework concept), allows Bourdieu to pursue a middle way, "une voie médiane"[45] between the structuralist cancellation of agency and the – fantasized – omnipotent agents of the pure philosophical tradition from Descartes to Sartre. "I wanted [Bourdieu said in a 1985 interview] to reintroduce agents that Lévi-Strauss and the structuralists, among others Althusser, tended to abolish, making them into simple epiphenomena of structure."[46] Again, this must be done without recidivism to "the imaginary anthropology of subjectivism"[47] associated with Sartre.[48]

In *Raisons pratiques*, *habitus* is described – I deliberately avoid the word "defined" – as "this sort of practical sense of what is to be done in a given situation – what in a sport one calls the feel for the game [le sens du jeu], an art of *anticipating* the future of the game which is inscribed, virtually, in the present state of the game."[49] I should now – if I am a competent player of *this* game, *my* game – be writing this sentence very spontaneously and, in a certain sense, shocking as this may sound in philosophy, thoughtlessly. This is the profit of long immersion in a specific *champ*$_2$. Novices (beginning students, for example) nervously, and generally awkwardly, think up their thoughts, betraying the effort one can also see on the faces, in the body language, and in the more-or-less inappropriate results, of *parvenus* to any social world. The *parvenu*, lacking the *habitus* orchestrated by, and to, the social world he seeks to enter, must rely on rules, if rules can be found. But social games – including those constitutive of being a philosopher, sociologist, or physicist[50] – are not, and could not be, played by agents who are following explicit rules. Complex practices are codified, if at all and certainly always incompletely, only when it is too late for the codification to do much good on the cutting edge of play.

There are also deeper, or more intrinsic, reasons why rule-following, by itself, cannot explain behavioral regularities, patterned human action. These reasons are hinted at, with characteristic ellipsis and indirection, in the famous passages (Articles 197 through 214) of Wittgenstein's *Philosophical Investigations* devoted to rule-following. These passages have given rise to a whole – far from uncontentious – literature[51] and are presently seeping into discussion, both English and French, of Bourdieu.[52] I shall here limit myself to a few brief remarks. First, one has to take account of Wittgenstein's conception of philosophy: "Philosophy simply puts everything before us, and neither explains nor deduces anything. – Since everything lies open to view there is nothing to explain. For what is hidden, for example, is of no interest to us."[53] Whether or not one accepts this as an interestingly ascetic vision of philosophy, it could hardly be a worse, or more wrong-headed, characterization of intellectual activity in general, whether in ordinary life or scientific inquiry.

Wittgenstein is right that "there is a way of grasping a rule which is *not* an *interpretation*" (para. 201) and that "'obeying a rule' is a practice" (para. 202), but there is no explanation of what makes the practice possible, of why we are not in practice bogged down in hermeneutic uncertainty. The missing explanatory concept is precisely that of *habitus*, an individual's acquired, relatively durable system of dispositions which "generate and organize practices and representations that can be objectively adapted to their outcomes without presupposing a conscious aiming at ends or an express mastery of the operations necessary to attain them."[54] Wittgenstein says, "Following a rule is analogous to obeying an order. We are trained to do so; we react to an order in a particular way." But the reaction is mediated by *habitus* acquired in the common circumstances, local and historically specific, of our social world. That is why there is something misplaced about Wittgenstein's next question: "But what if one person reacts in one way and another in another to the order and the training?" (206). *Habitus* is Bourdieu's way of cancelling the abstract possibilities that haunt subjectivist accounts of action that picture agents acting *ex nihilo* and with unbounded freedom. We may regret, narcissistically, that our *Handlungsspielraum* or "marge de manoevre" (to use Norbert Elias's term[55]) is stubbornly finite, but we must nevertheless avoid the illusion of Kant's dove: "The light dove, cleaving the air in its free flight, and feeling its resistance, might imagine that its flight would be still easier in empty space."[56]

Notes

1   Pierre Bourdieu, *Questions de Sociologie* (Paris: Minuit, 1984), p. 24: "...the condemnation of eclecticism has often served as the alibi for a lack of culture...."
2   James Fenton, *Out of Danger* (New York: Farrar Straus Giroux, 1994), p. 96.
3   Jacques Attali, *Verbatim I: 1981–1986* (Paris: Fayard, 1993), pp. 242–3.
4   Norbert Elias, *Reflections on a Life*, trans. Edmund Jephcott (Cambridge: Polity Press, 1994), pp. 36–7.
5   "Trendy" is a pejorative term for a style of cultural appropriation in which interest in a figure or topic is generated by interest, at least interest

expressed by the "right" people in the "right" places – as "right" is defined by the appropriating community. Interest (one hopes) can also be generated, independently of trendiness, by cognitive utility relative to intellectual projects, scientific research programs, philosophical perplexities.

6   Pierre Bourdieu, *Raisons Pratiques: Sur la théorie de l'action* (Paris: Seuil, 1994), p. 16: "The whole of my scientific project has, in effect, been inspired by the conviction that one cannot grasp the logic of the social world, at the deepest level, without emerging oneself in the particularity of a historically situated and dated empirical reality but in order to construe it as a 'particular case of the possible', in Gaston Bachelard's phrase. . . ."

7   Pierre Bourdieu, *L'ontologie politique de Martin Heidegger* (Paris: Minuit, 1988); *The Politcal Ontology of Martin Heidegger*, trans. Peter Collier (Stanford, CA: Stanford University Press, 1991).

8   The *necessity* is conditional and not absolute, conditional, precisely on the kind of investment in a given field which is the *sine qua non* of being, and being regarded as, a serious player in that field; the necessity is *objective* in that it operates independently of, and often more effectively without, conscious motivation or design.

9   This is in fact what, in the next section, will be distinguished as $champ_2$.

10 Richard Shusterman makes this critique of Wittgenstein but also of Austin in arguing that Bourdieu's empirical turn advances their idea of understanding language is through study of its actual use in real social contexts. See Richard Shusterman, "Bourdieu et la philosophie anglo-américane," *Critique* 579–80 (August–September, 1995), a special issue of *Critique* devoted to Bourdieu's work, edited by Christiane Chauviré and including also the papers of Charles Taylor and Jacques Bouveresse, which appear in this book.

11 Bourdieu, *Raisons Pratiques*, pp. 88–9.

12 Bourdieu, *Raisons Pratiques*, p. 55: "l'espace social global."

13 Bourdieu, *Raisons Pratiques*, p. 20.

14 Of course addresses, in the ordinary sense, reveal (because they are, within certain natality constraints, largely determined by) positions in social space. A writer like Angus Wilson, hypersensitive to social nuance, will use address to convey social standing. A character in the story, "Saturnalia" is described as "too intent upon the cultivation of a Knightsbridge exterior with a Kensington purse" and a few sentences later "'It's too shamemaking', she said in her deep contralto, she had managed to get that new book *Vile Bodies* from the library and was making full use of the Mayfair slang before it was too widely known in S. W. 7." In Angus Wilson, *The Wrong Set* (New York: William Morrow, 1950), p. 70. This is – one assumes, disingenuously – denied by The Human Resources Administration of the City of New York which advertises its Food Stamp Program with the adcopy "Hunger knows no neighborhood."

15 This probably has to be qualified since, for Bourdieu, the process of concept formation is much less "willkürlich" than Wittgenstein can make it sound. See, for example, *Philosophische Grammatik* (Oxford: Blackwell, 1969), p. 184: "Die Grammatik ist keiner Wirklichkeit Rechenschaft schuldig. Die grammatischen Regeln bestimmen erst die Bedeutung (konstituieren sie) und sind darum keiner Bedeutung verantwortlich und insofern willkürlich." *Philosophical Grammar*, trans. Anthony Kenny (Oxford: Blackwell, 1974), p. 184: "Grammar is not accountable to any reality. It is grammatical rules that determine meaning (constitute it) and so they themselves are not answerable to any meaning and to that extent are arbitrary." Wittgenstein's own "insofern" ("to that extent") should, of course, be given its full weight.

16 What this means, I hope, is that consideration of these concepts, with all their surrounding lore, is helpful (cognitively rather than merely decoratively) relative to the research projects of people in the discipline of philosophy.

17 Raymond Boudon, *La place du désordre* (Paris: Presses Universitaires de France, 1984), pp. 69–70.

18 Gaston Bachelard, *La philosophie du non* (Paris: Quadridge/PUF, 1988; originally, 1940), p. 8; *The Philosophy of No*, trans. G. C. Waterson (New York: Orion Press, 1968), p. 8.

19 This style of defining can be misconstrued as it is, for example, by Jeffrey C. Alexander, *Fin de Siècle Social Theory* (London: Verso, 1995), p. 136: "Like Bourdieu's other key concepts, habitus turns out not merely to be loosely defined – the criticism so beloved by scientism – but to be ambiguous in what can only be called a systematic way." This is itself an ambiguous comment (Is Alexander actually making the criticism beloved by scientism?). What is, in fact, systematic in Bourdieu is the attempt to overcome a set of standard social science antinomies.

20 This is all said very well by Bourdieu himself who seems, in reflective remarks, to understand himself quite well. For example, in Bourdieu and Loïc J. D. Wacquant, *An Invitation to Reflexive Sociology* (Chicago: University of Chicago Press, 1992), pp. 95–6: "I do not like professorial definitions much.... [M]any of the gaps or shortcomings for which I am sometimes reproached are in fact conscious refusals and deliberate choices. For instance the use of *open concepts* is a way of rejecting positivism – but this is a ready-made phrase. It is, to be more precise, a permanent reminder that concepts have no definition other than systematic ones, and are designed to be *put to work empirically in systematic fashion*. Such notions as habitus, field, and capital can be defined, but only within the theoretical system they constitute, not in isolation." For the French version, see Bourdieu and Wacquant, *Réponses* (Paris: Seuil, 1992), p. 71.

21 Bourdieu, *Raisons pratiques*, p. 28: "Ce qui existe, c'est un espace social, un espace de différences, dans lequel les classes existent en quelque sorte à l'état virtuel, en pointillé, non comme un donné, mais

comme *quelque chose qu'il s'agit de faire.*" ["What really exists is social space, a space of differences, within which classes exist in a sort of virtual state, or sketchily, not as a given, but as something that is to be constructed."]

22 See Bourdieu, *Raisons pratiques*, p. 20.
23 Bourdieu, *Raisons pratiques*, p. 15.
24 Bourdieu, *Raisons pratiques*, pp. 16–17.
25 Bourdieu, *Raisons pratiques*, p. 54.
26 Bourdieu, *Raisons pratiques*, p. 34.
27 *Habitus* is used as the plural of *habitus*.
28 Bourdieu, *Raisons pratiques*, p. 75.
29 Pierre Bourdieu, *The Rules of Art: Genesis and Structure of the Literary Field* (Cambridge: Polity Press, 1996).
30 Bourdieu speaks (*Raisons pratiques*, p. 77) of "les interprétations qui, par un 'court-circuit', s'autorisent à passer directement de ce qui se passe sans le monde à ce qui se passe dans le champ [interpretations which, by a 'short-circuit', allow us to move directly from what happens in the world to what happens in the $champ_2$]." A good illustration is the rather casual and indeed careless and highly assumptive left-academic critique of British social anthropology. I cite Jack Goody's comment in rebuttal. In *The Expansive Moment: Anthropology in Britain and Africa. 1918–1970* (Cambridge: Cambridge University Press, 1995), p. 39: "Much has been made in recent years of the role of British anthropologists working under colonial regimes, supported by a conservative social theory known as structural-functionalism. [. . .] But the attempt to show structural-functionalism as the necessary ideology of the colonial regimes and anthropologists as their instruments comes up against a number of difficulties when we look at the actual history of the participants, for in many cases their attitudes and roles were very different from what these holistic assumptions would predict. That is because such pronouncements ignore the internal contradictions of colonial rule as well as the relative autonomy (however limited) of fields of knowledge."
31 Bourdieu, *Les règles de l'art*, p. 293.
32 Andy Warhol, *The Andy Warhol Diaries*, ed. Pat Hackett (New York: Warner Books, 1989), p. 58.
33 Bennett M. Berger, *An Essay on Culture: Symbolic Structure and Social Structure* (Berkeley, CA: University of California Press, 1995), p. 92.
34 For a good discussion (very much in the spirit of Gaston Bachelard) of the necessity of breaking with common sense and fighting against "l'illusion du savoir immédiat," see Pierre Bourdieu, Jean-Claude Chamboredon, Jean-Claude Passeron, *Le métier de sociologue*, 4th edn (Paris: Mouton, [1968] 1983), esp. the section entitled "La rupture," pp. 27–34.
35 Bourdieu, *Raisons pratiques*, p. 161.
36 Bourdieu, *Raisons pratiques*, pp. 116–17.
37 Bourdieu, *Raisons pratiques*, p. 117.

38 Bourdieu, *Raisons pratiques*, p. 161.
39 Bourdieu and Wacquant, *An Invitation to Reflexive Sociology*, p. 116; *Reponses*, p. 92.
40 Pierre Bourdieu, *Questions de Sociologie* (Paris: Minuit, 1984), p. 56.
41 Norbert Elias, *The Court Society*, trans. Edmund Jephcott (New York: Pantheon Books, 1983), p. 8; *La Société de Cour*, trans. Pierre Kamnitzer and Jeanne Etoré (Paris: Flammarion, 1985), p. xxxix; *Die höfische Gesellschaft* (Frankfurt am Main: Suhrkamp Verlag, 1983 [originally, 1969]), p. 19.
42 Andrew Pickering, *The Mangle of Practice: Time, Agency, & Science* (Chicago: University of Chicago Press, 1995). "Natural agency" is used throughout the book; on the bubble chamber, see chapter 2; on the electrometer, see chapter 3.
43 This list is from Bennnett M. Berger, *An Essay on Culture*, p. 93: "The currency deployable in status markets is 'cultural capital'. By this term Bourdieu means to distinguish between the power exercised by money (economic capital) and the power exercised by resources inherited or acquired chiefly from family and educational systems: credentials, names, titles, carriage, bearing, voice; linguistic competence, erudition, grace, savoir faire – in short all the skills and facilities that function as assets (and liabilities in some contexts) in the cultural performances of everyday life."
44 Bourdieu, *The Rules of Art*, p. 211.
45 "Une voie médiane: l'habitus" is a chapter title in Francois Dosse, *Histoire du structuralisme*, tome 2: *Le chant du cygne. 1967 à nos jours* (Paris: Éditions la Découverte, 1992), p. 378.
46 Pierre Bourdieu, *In Other Words: Essays Towards a Reflexive Sociology*, trans. Matthew Adamson (Stanford, CA: Stanford University Press, 1990), p. 9; *Choses dites* (Paris: Minuit, 1987), p. 19.
47 This phrase is the title of chapter 2 of Pierre Bourdieu, *Le sens pratique* (Paris: Minuit, 1980); *The Logic of Practice*, trans. Richard Nice (Stanford, CA: Stanford University Press, 1990). This chapter is mainly about Sartre though also considers "rational action theory" à la Jon Elster.
48 Bourdieu resorts to the notion of *habitus* in order to try to find a middle way between the objectivism with which he reproaches structuralists like Lèvi-Strass and the spontaneity that "Philosophies of the subject" try to oppose to structuralism. See Jacques Bouveresse "Rules, Dispositions, and the *Habitus*," in this volume, p. 50.
49 Bourdieu, *Raisons pratiques*, p. 45.
50 For an example of work in history/ethnography of science making use of Bourdieu, see Yves Gingras, "Following Scientists Through Society? Yes, But at Arm's Length!" in *Scientific Practice: Theories and Stories of Doing Physics*, ed. Jed Z. Buchwald (Chicago, IL: University of Chicago Press, 1995), p. 140: "In order to understand why and in which circumstances scientists or engineers can move from the laboratory to the minister's office, one must start from the observation that scientists are

subjected to a disciplinary training that gives them a set of tools that define an intellectual horizon. Social actors socialized to live in a particular field can rarely transfer their knowledge and skills directly to another field. To use Pierre Bourdieu's concept, their habitus is the product of a trajectory in a particular field and is best 'adjusted' to function inside it. Each of these fields and the relations between them are the product of a past history of social relations and are, in this sense, a social construction. Thus, far from being homogeneous, the social space must be seen as composed of many relatively autonomous fields having their own logic: the plurality of fields is a plurality of worlds."

51 For an example of a pair of books by well-known philosophers, with radically divergent interpretations of Wittgenstein, see Saul A. Kripke, *Wittgenstein: On Rules and Private Language* (Cambridge, MA: Harvard University Press, 1983); and Colin McGinn, *Wittgenstein on Meaning* (Oxford: Basil Blackwell, 1984).

52 For example, Charles Taylor, "To Follow a Rule," reprinted in this volume.

53 Ludwig Wittgenstein, *Philosophical Investigations*, second edition, trans. G. E. M. Anscombe (New York: Macmillan, 1958), p. 50e.

54 Bourdieu, *The Logic of Practice*, p. 53; *Le sens pratique*, p. 88.

55 In English, "Scope for action." See *The Court Society*, p. 15; *Die höfische Gesselschaft*, p. 30; *La société de cour*, p. xlix.

56 Immanuel Kant, *Critique of Pure Reason*, though I am quoting this from Arthur L. Stinchombe, *Creating Efficient Industrial Administrations* (New York: Academic Press, 1974), to which it serves as epigraph. There is also Wittgenstein's version of the same thought, *Philosophical Investigations*, p. 46e: "We have got on to slippery ice where there is no friction so in a certain sense the conditions are ideal, but also, just because of that, we are unable to walk."

11

Bourdieuean Dynamics: The American Middle-Class Self-Constructs

Chuck Dyke

The best way to praise and appraise Bourdieu's work is also the most straightforward: use it. So the substantive body of this paper is the examination of an important moment in the cultural self- construction of the American middle class. But, in addition, it's important to take advantage of this opportunity to show how Bourdieu's methods settle comfortably among a whole family of related methods developed over the last few years in the natural sciences. The study of nonlinear dynamical systems arose out of dissatisfaction with the reductive simplifications of traditional methods as a set of tools with which organized diachronic complexity could be confronted seriously. It is quite apparent that Bourdieu's theorizing was similarly motivated. Not surprisingly, the resulting new methods are compatible and complementary. This has to be emphasized in order to take advantage of the mutual support and legitimation they offer to each other.

The Tradition

In the old days, when our sense of explanation was based largely on the paradigm of the various totalizing rationalisms, the link between explanatory generality on the one hand, and determinate "real world" phenomena on the other was thought to be the "link" between laws and their instances. This sense of explanation produced a clear demarcation between successful and unsuccessful sciences: those that could discover laws and demonstrate the range of phenomena for which the laws "held", and those sciences that could not do so.

The social sciences were, in general, humiliated under this scheme. Their successes were trivial, and their failures legion. In retrospect, it's not hard to see why. The law/instance scheme works only for repetitive phenomena, phenomena whose next recognizable occurrence is identical to the last. Social phenomena are seldom repetitive in the required – clockwork – sense.

Similarly, the star attraction of the explanatory scheme of law and instance is the controlled experiment in which one group of scientists proves that it can make the same thing happen over and over again, and invites other groups to satisfy themselves that they can do so as well. This is rarely possible in the social sciences, and when it is possible we find that the grounds of the possibility are the truncation and constraint of normally complex social circumstances so as to convert them to laboratory simplifications whose relevance for normal human activity is entirely problematic.

In Bourdieu's case, there were two residues of the old patterns of explanation to be confronted: *a priori* structuralism, and a collection of law/instance rationalisms built around the concept of rules. In the case of nonlinear dynamics, the habits that had to be overcome were the search for the single narrowly deterministic trajectory, and the assumption that point equilibria are the normal eventual states of systems.[1] In both cases these old schemes are replaced with theories of the historical generation of durable pattern.

Histories are the playing out of organized, that is, nonrandom, possibilities. Thus social systems are only what they can be. To say this is to make reference to assemblages of organized possibility as primary explanatory circumstances. It is also, of course, to flirt with tautology. However, this isn't by itself a deterrent to hopes of explaining. *Every* general statement of an overall explanatory strategy involves the same sort of flirtation. Vacuity is avoided just insofar as it's possible to exhibit a system of transformations from *determinate* circumstances to *determinately* patterned outcomes. This is true of the explanation of a ballistics trajectory in terms of a determinate initial position and momentum. It's true of the explanation of the adaptive transformation of the distribution of phenotypes within a population in terms of a determinate set of genetic and epigenetic possibilities in interaction with a determinate environment. It's true of the explanation of the behavior of a particular institution in terms of its historically determinate response potentials *vis-à-vis* a determinate challenge. In fact, with respect to this general observation, there is a continuity between explanations of the simple and explanations of the complex. Discontinuities between the simple and the complex are to be found *within* this generality as we find how many different ways determinate explanatory circumstances can be related to what they explain. Simple repetition turns out to be exceptional.

When setting up a dynamical model, one of the first questions you have to ask is "What are the dimensions of significant change?" What differences make a difference? Bourdieu's general answer to this question is that various forms of capital – social, cultural, and economic – make a difference as individuals pursue trajectories and assume positions within a generalized social space. The choice of "capital" as the fundamental designater of social dimension is, of course, a nod to the Marxian tradition from which Bourdieu emerges at several generations remove. But it is no mere gesture. It is a well-considered decision with respect to a grouping of the causes of social movement. We can pause for a moment to compare the Bourdieuean decision to the comparable decisions in the dynamics of physical systems.

The most typical state spaces of dynamics are characterized in terms of positions and momenta. These "state variables" characterize systems *completely* from a particular dynamical point of view (that we may call "Newtonian"). Two centuries or so of thinking about "mechanical" systems lies behind the choice of position and momentum as the canonical dynamical variables, and the scientific success of a wide range of subfields underwrites the choice. A good part of the reason for success lies in the fact that characterizing a system in terms of the positions and momenta of its constituent parts fits rather neatly with the parallel choice of *energy* as the basic causal dynamical term. Things move because of differentials and gradients in energies, and these differentials and gradients tend to become transparent in the canonical position/momentum representations.[2] Furthermore, position/momentum representations are general with respect to the particular *kinds* of differentials and gradients present in any given system. Gravitational gradients, temperature gradients, and all sorts of other gradients will result in systems whose state at any given time can be characterized in terms of positions and momenta.

The trick, then, in spatially representing social spaces, is to find a characterization of social states (watch the puns here) linked closely enough to the causes of movement to offer the possibility of explanation without being so tightly linked to a particular (usually reductive) theory of social causation to prejudice the answers to some very difficult questions. We want, in other words, to watch trajectories through social space, and be able to say why we see *these* trajectories rather than others, without reducing this last question to the identification of an "independent variable."

We can see the sense in Bourdieu's generalized conception of capital if we remember how capital is normally defined in the orthodox economics textbooks: as the capacity to command labor. This definition is then built into a highly structured system in which the players of various roles in a highly stylized game are identified. There are established traditions in terms of which "labor", "capital", etc. are identified. So it is never a matter of very much dispute as to who (or what) can command labor (identified and distinguished from other activity).

But this narrow definition of explicitly economic capital begins to lose its usefulness in two sorts of very common circumstance. The first is where the highly stylized game of market capitalism is not present, and the second is where it is present, but so interactively intertwined with other dimensions of life that demarcation of independent dimensions is inconsistent with an adequate account of observed trajectories. This latter circumstance is, of course, absolutely characteristic of nonlinear systems.

Outside its normal home, the concept of capital has to lose two of its surface features in order to take on its explanatory role. First, we have to consider that all sorts of action, not just labor, are "commanded." Second, "command" is an awkward word to use for the interactional alterations of movement through social space that constitute social dynamics. But, then, I would say, it's awkward in its primary use as well.[3] We'll pursue these issues later as we use Bourdieu's generalized conception of capital to help us organize the cultural space of the nineteenth century United States.

Edges

We can further the comparison between Bourdieu's theory of practice and nonlinear dynamics by noting that social systems are always poised between stability and change. For this reason, static structural models have had limited success in accounting for social phenomena, since they eventually founder against the manifest capacities of societies for change, even structural change. Similarly, models built to conform to the assumptions of voluntarist individualism founder on the manifest structural constraints forming the matrix within which individuals as social agents are constructed. Bourdieu's analysis, with the concepts of *habitus* and structured structuring structures as its cornerstones, is designed precisely to deal with the intricacies of this situation, and is, in fact, the only analysis to have emerged from the social sciences with any promise in this regard.

On the other side we have the advances of the last two decades in nonlinear dynamics and nonequilibrium thermodynamics. They have been developed precisely to deal with natural systems poised between stability and change. The typical nonlinear system is deterministic in the sense that it can be characterized by a system of differential equations, yet is unpredictable, in the sense that knowledge of initial conditions is never sufficient to determine uniquely future states of the system very far into the future. Initial knowledge of the system's precise trajectory decays exponentially. This means that we are potentially in possession of rigorous models from the heart of the "hard" sciences to apply to human systems that exhibit not repetition, but pattern, creativity, and improvization. Bourdieu's "orchestra without a conductor" (Bourdieu 1977, p. 72) is, in a firm sense, typical of a far broader range of phenomena than we might have imagined.

The typical system stabilized far from equilibrium, moreover, explores a determinate space of organization and reorganization over a lifetime sustained by a matter and energy flux. Bourdieu's structured structuring structures are not confined to the social realm. The general conception of these processes is most easily illuminated by an examination of *edges* of various sorts. The most interesting edges to have been identified by the dynamicists are called fractal basin boundaries.

Imagine the following, not implausible, situation. Two people start a stroll down a street, one on one side; the other on the other. Each is whistling a tune – over and over again. The street is crowded, as are the open windows looking out upon it. We can further imagine that after the passage of the two, the tunes linger. There may be added whistlers; there may be humming; or there may just be one tune or the other going around in various heads. When a tune lingers in *any* of these ways, we will say that an entrainment has taken place. There are obviously two possible entrainments – for there are two tunes. Some people will be entrained to one, and some to the other. We'll leave out of account those people who become entrained to neither.

If two particular people are differently entrained, we will say that they are on opposite sides of a boundary, or, equivalently, that one is in one "basin" and the other in another "basin." We then rise majestically to a vantage point from which we can identify the occupants of the two basins, all down the street, and trace out the boundaries between them. The trace is likely to be *very* convoluted. In fact, it *could* happen that no matter where we found a person in one basin of entrainment, we could also find, as close by as we pleased, another person entrained in the *other* basin. In such a case we would say that the basin boundary is *fractal*.

We could then begin to look for patterns in the entrainments, even as convoluted as the boundaries between them might seem to be. For the spatial distribution of entrainments that we see from our aerial vantage point is only one among potentially many distributions. The situation is intrinsically multidimensional. In fact, even the spatial distribution is multidimensional. For instance, we might find that there are significant differences distributed, on average, on the two sides of the street. This could indicate nothing more than the superior likelihood of hearing the tune being whistled on your side of the street, and failing to hear the other. While the boundary is fractal, the core could concentrate on a single tune. Nonetheless, as long as the boundary is really fractal, this single simple account can't satisfy us fully. There must be other conditions for determining the pattern of entrainment. Furthermore, even if the boundary wandered fairly reliably down the middle of the street, mere differences in the probability of hearing one tune or the other need not provide the significant story. Are there differences, for example, between the people typically on one side of the street from those typically on the other? If we were witnessing a *passegiata* in a Mediterranean country, there would undoubtedly be such differences. In some cases, women might typically be on one side of the street, and men on the other. Or, it might be that the upper crust could be found, by and large, on one side of the street, and *hoi polloi* on the other. This could have a lot to do with the tune entrained, typically, here or there.

In another case, say a street in the Bronx in the 'thirties, one might have found nearly everyone on one side of the street to be Irish, and nearly everyone on the other side Jewish. Nu? Well, begorrah, they may be whistling different tunes. But of course we can imagine indefinitely many particular situations, each of which might well offer a broad range of potentially significant determinants of the pattern of entrainment.

Further, of course, there are many features of the tunes themselves that could affect the pattern of entrainment. If one of the whistlers were whistling the viola part from Bartok's fourth string quartet, and the other were whistling "Pop Goes the Weasel", the fractal character of the boundary would probably, in fact, disappear. On the other hand, if one were whistling "La ci Darem la Mano" and the other "I Wanna Hold Your Hand" the fractal pattern might be quite interesting, with many dimensions of significance to be discovered. Some tunes are just catchier than others, after all, and attract for that simple reason, independent of the cultural space the tunes normally occupy.

Without beating this poor dead horse any more, I think we can see that even simple entrainments can be very multidimensionally produced. It might take a whole lot of careful research to account fully for the pattern of entrainments we found. The conditions for entrainment can be looked at as the ground against which the potentially entraining signals are played – or whistled. We could distinguish between *kinds* of ground conditions. Among the kinds we would surely find an array of durable dispositions inscribed in the various people along the street, durable dispositions mulched down so deeply that they seldom if ever became a matter of conscious thought. In one way of speaking we could call these dispositions the pretuning of potentially entrainable oscillators, in another way of speaking we could call them habitus. I think that if we're smart we'll take advantage of both the traditions of thought giving rise to the two formulations.

As a next step, we can imagine a diachronic expansion of our simple scenario. For "tunes running around in our heads" are obviously standing in, here, for all sorts of cultural and social signals to which we become entrained. And some tunes have an abiding impact on us. They can even retune us. An obvious case is when we become infatuated with a tune because it's pretty, and catchy, and then find that it comes from a genre of music with which we have little acquaintance. Lured to deeper acquaintance, we explore the genre with lasting effects. For example, many people are led to opera in this way, or to rap. But to be led to a new musical genre is often to be led to a new region of cultural space in many other senses as well, as we all know. Fairly extensive cultural retunings can occur along these lines.[4]

In short, the expansion to the diachronic account leads us directly on the one hand to Bourdieu's conception of structured structuring structures, and on the other hand to the nonlinear dynamics of structural self-organization and reorganization whose study has advanced so much in the last few years.[5] It needs to be emphasized that in both these cases structure is to be understood as historically contingent necessity, not transcendental order. It's often hard for people brought up as strict rationalists to make sense of contingent necessity. This is one of the main reasons why it's worth emphasizing the relationship of Bourdieu's theory to parallel developments in other areas. For if we look at what current physics, chemistry and biology have to say about the structural features of the world they take as objects of investigation, we find that a strong sense of contingent necessity has developed there too. Atoms, for example, are stable structures only under particular boundary conditions. If it's too hot, they don't exist. But once a universe gets set off on a trajectory of expansion and cooling, it's inevitable that atoms are going to emerge as conspicuous structural elements of it, but not all universes need be on such trajectories, and may, for example, never evolve to the point where atoms form. The same sort of thing is true in spades of galaxies, whose presence in a universe is contingent upon an extremely precise range of boundary conditions holding. And we could continue this same story all the way to the existence of life on earth, contingently emerged structures in the presence, again, of a very precise set of ambient conditions. So when Bourdieu provides us with a theory of the emergence and evolution of social structures, this simply falls right into line with what's true at virtually every level of complexity. Emergent social structures are no longer to be thought of as scientific anomalies, but are, on the contrary, perfectly ordinary.

Now, aside from anecdotal piquancy, are there any good reasons to translate familiar lore about social structure into the language of attractors and basin boundaries? Yes. And the reasons are almost without exception Bourdieuean ones. Traditional methods associate social structure with static typology. Bourdieu, in contrast, conceptualizes them as the patterned results of the interplay between many differential potentials, enabled and constrained by "underlying" durable dispositions. Attempted explanation of the patterns by the traditional search for independent variables "causally" associated with predictable outcomes with "lawlike" regularity traditionally fails. Put another way, no identification of a Millean difference explaining why a given outcome occurs in one case and not another can be found. Or, rather, only in rare cases can such a Millean difference be found, and, when it is, it can be shown how a normally complex situation has been radically simplified.

It's worth putting this point rather formulaicly, for the sake of clarity: To say that some process is a linear causal process is to explain why nothing interesting is happening. And, in general, the enforcement of linear causality, as a social strategy, is a preventative measure calculated to ensure that nothing interesting will happen. For example, we design measures to ensure that nothing interesting will happen to our bullet on the way to the target, or our money on the way to the bank. The design of ballistics devices is *precisely* the design of linearizing devices.

The "interesting" phenomena referred to are the "spontaneous" emergence of structure (*autokatakinesis*) and the transformation of existing structure into new structure. That is the kind of phenomena Bourdieu is interested in. But Bourdieu is also out in front with respect to the way in which "structure" is to be understood, and especially the way that structural edges are to be understood. The edges of structure are the homes for the marginal: the unstably entrained, the socially mobile for whom the eventual occupation of a region of social space is problematic – extremely sensitive to ambient contigencies.

Under normal conditions, obviously, social experimentation is extremely problematical. It turns out that there are two relatively general sorts of case. The first is where a social regime has been stabilized through the imposition of enough linearizing constraints to allow prediction on the basis of a careful specification of initial position and "impressed force." For example, we might well be able to be rather specific about what it would take for a child of the black ghetto to end up a success in one of the professions. *Certain* rigidities are attainable for societies, and in their presence we might be able to introduce a "Millean" condition differentially, thus approaching experimental conditions. The second sort of case is where such stability has not been achieved, and the differential trajectories are not predictable even though possibly (nonlinearly) deterministic.

A hypothesis whose examination could exhibit the differences between the two cases would be, say, that children born with a silver spoon in their mouths are extremely unlikely to fail, despite a myriad of possible differences in whatever "variables" we looked at; children from the ghetto are extremely likely to succeed, despite the same sort of myriad of variables, but that prediction for those "in the middle" was a chancy business at best. That is, the dynamics at the boundary between rich and poor is active and fractal, while that lying deep in the attractors of wealth and poverty is constrained and predictable. In fact, for modern industrial "democracies" this is probably the typical structural state of affairs.

The traditional rationalist dogma says that the proof of distinction is at the boundaries: definitions decide doubtful cases. This is a consequence of the fundamentally static universe demanded by this tradition, and its corollary, that identity criteria, applicable diagnostically again and again, are the standard device for ascertaining boundaries. Against this, it has been pointed out that the *last* thing definitions can do is decide borderline cases. But more concretely, the sorts of structures we are interested in have dynamical edges, not static ones.

Of course any careful reader of Bourdieu will react against the grossness of the distinction between rich and poor in the last paragraph. We have learned to think in terms of class fractions – regions in a highly differentiated social space. A primary distinction between a dominant class and a dominated class is further articulated by the identification of a dominant and a dominated fraction of each class.

Historically, this complex structure emerged out of an earlier one, apparently more susceptible of conceptualization in terms of the simple distinction between rich and poor, but in fact more complex than that simple distinction would imply. In dynamical terms, the transition to the more complex system of class fractions was (is) a dynamical process. The most important dynamics in the emergent transformation are those at the edges. As those in the unstable regions between rich and poor seek to distinguish themselves, they must do so by using the species of capital at their command, and, under the right circumstances, can manage to do so. Usually capitalizing on a generalized recognition of the value of the assets they possess, they can concentrate these assets and gain control over the future distribution of them. The best examples, of course, are the learned professions, but in the modern world athletes and entertainers have also succeeded in exploiting their assets to move from the margin into identifiable and exclusive regions of social space.

In order to understand these transformations we have to contrast the conceptualization of class fractions as static structures with their conceptualization as attractors, and the conceptualization of their boundaries as hard edges between exclusive sets with their conceptualization as dynamically active regions. Two analogies from biology can help us.

First, a well-known cautionary tale is told about generations of failure to understand biological membranes, obvious boundaries. For generations they were thought of as hard edges. This was due partly because of the drive for nomenclatural neatness endemic to standard typological thinking, and partly because of a tradition of investigation that led biologists to study dead organisms, "fixed specimens." Living function was typically inferred from dead structure. As techniques for investigating living organisms (or living tissue) were developed, it became clear that membranes were dynamically active elements of open systems rather than the hard edges of closed ones. The parallel to a dominant style of social theorizing is obvious. "Classes" and other social structures were conceptualized typologically, and investigated by techniques that rendered them fixed specimens. Function was then inferred from dead structure, with baleful results a good deal of the time. The Bourdieuean proposal in the context of a theory of practice is that the edges of social structures are dynamically active.

Second, developmental biologists produce what they call fate maps. These are trajectory diagrams tracing the lifetimes of an initial population of cells and their progeny as growth and differentiation take place.[6] The cells are initially identical, but in the developmental process some become dedicated skin cells, nerve cells, sex cells, etc. Given a decently detailed fate map, the dynamics of differentiation and dedication can then be addressed. Humans too have fate maps, and like the cells of a zygote, initially identical humans, in circumstances as identical as you please, can end up on different trajectories. *However*, some fates are relatively predictable, and others unpredictable, reflecting the different potential dynamics of various regions in social space.

The fact that the "boundaries" between, say, class fractions are dynamically active means that no definition will provide necessary and sufficient conditions for class fraction inclusion, nor will it provide a universally reliable predictive base. The "system" of class fractions is at least nonlinear enough to make the edges between class fractions fractal. Or, to put it another way, the world is more fine grained than any definition we might provide. As conceptually near to any given person fated for one trajectory is another person fated for a different trajectory and destination in social space. Near the center of each social attractor are people whose habitus is so deeply ingrained as to be stable. For them we will be able to predict the structural future with fair certainty. But those at the edge of any dimension of this habitus will have futures unpredictable on the basis of any characteristic we might pick out. During centuries of gender asymmetry, a truly beautiful woman had the opportunity to embark on an unusual trajectory, given her initial position in social space. But still there was no predicting which of two beauties would make her fortune. Call it luck, if you like, but much of our talk of luck is folk recognition of the instability of fractal edges.[7]

Now, given the fractal unpredictability at the interpenetrating edges of social attractors how do we investigate social systems with any reliability? How do we make sense of the differential trajectories, or differential entrainments that we notice as pervasive features of the social systems we look at? Experiment and the detection of reliable regularity are possible only under conditions constrained so tightly that they don't allow such differences in the first place.

One method is to "send in a probe," that is send a signal through the system and record the pattern of responses it elicits. While this won't get us to the point of prediction, it can often tell us a lot about the pattern of structures in place at a given time. It is, of course, not always easy to find an appropriate signal – the right tune to whistle. What we need is some Bourdieuean fine print. Readers of Bourdieu are familiar with his insertion of material on, say, the Kabyle into an otherwise theoretical discussion. In just this vein I will draw on some work I've been doing on the formation of the

American middle class in the nineteenth century to help us see some patterns of cultural entrainment.

The Fine Print

The appearance of the work of John Ruskin in the United States over a period of about four decades beginning in the late 1840s will serve as the introduced signal. Its differential reception will constitute the data. Ruskin's project – in his terms – was the aesthetic edification of an expanding cultured public. The project in our terms was that of drawing the emerging middle classes into a high cultural attractor where they could distinguish themselves in terms of superior taste and sensibility. In the American context, the Ruskinean signal had relevance for the edges between the following: high culture, popular culture; European culture, the culture of others; the civilized, the savage; middle class, working class; the educated, the ignorant; the godly, the ungodly.

The pervasive Ruskinean rhetoric is that of the evangelist preacher.[8] In its European context, the evangelical voice was directed toward the formation of a cultural ethos to replace that of the declining European aristocracy. For the rising middle class there was no *intrinsic* reason to support the arts. Success was defined in other terms, and the life of work in God's vineyard can well be exemplified and recognized without opulent display. In such circumstances, some authoritative discourse in support of high culture had to be found, and Ruskin was ready with the voice of theological and moral exhortation. Moral exhortation may indeed have been the only available motivational resource. The evangelical voice has to be contrasted with the historically simultaneous voice of revolution, the voice exhorting the working class to cast off the chains of wage labor; and the voice of democratic melioration. Unlike Morris a generation later, Ruskin wanted no part of these voices of change. But with the voices of revolution and reform unavailable, only the evangelical voice remained.

Of course when this voice began to be heard in America, the neopromised land, it found a certain number of nearly perfectly tuned ears. The voice of the evangelical preacher had long since been established as the dominant American style. The liberation rhetoric of the Revolution established it as the language of politics, a place it retains to the present (though Job has replaced God). It is constantly reinforced by the explicitly evangelistic religious practices that persist as a pervasive part of American culture.

First, the evangelist preaches sacrifice. The architecture of a Godly culture must exhibit on its face the sacrifice of those who dedicate precious resources to it. As this theme played itself out in the New Calvinist Republic this meant, for the rising coalescing middle class, patronage of exemplary architecture to the extent of straining their material resources, for "God never forgets any work or labor of love...Therefore, though it may not be necessarily the interest of religion to admit the service of the arts, the arts will never flourish until they have been primarily devoted to that service – devoted, both by architect and employer; by the one in scrupulous, earnest, affectionate design; by the other in expenditure at least more frank, at least less calculating, than that which he would admit in the indulgence of his own private feelings" (Ruskin, n.d., pp. 26–7)

There is a promise here of salvation for the patron. For the working classes, in contrast, the requirement was that they sacrifice themselves to the culture abuilding. This leads us to an important edge. During the nineteenth century the United States became a nation of ex-peasants. *"Gli scalzi"* crossed the seas to be shod. The old-world peasant aspiration to cross the threshold of respectability by achieving a stable place in the middle class, thwarted in the land of origin, retained all its power in the neopromised land. The life of the ex-peasant in the new land was in all respects a life of self-sacrifice in pursuit of the achievement of middle class status. But what good is status in a dump? Not only must the life of self-sacrifice ratchet the individual up the social ladder, but the social ladder itself must be made worth the effort. A new nation had to be built. It didn't require a Ruskin to link this nation building to the work ethic, but his insistence on the edification of the new nation through great architecture fit seamlessly into a much broader set of imperatives.

Sacrifice is a particularly interesting source of dynamical constraints. We could never talk of sacrifice unless we could talk of alternative allocations of the various sorts of social capital. We also need a clear way to distinguish between more or less direct benefit to the sacrificing individual and benefit to others or to some extrapersonal goal. Thus one of the most common patterns of sacrifice is that of present benefit for future benefit, and, especially, the benefit of "future generations." Thus, a non-trivial conception of sacrifice requires seriously qualitative differences in the conduct of life. Ruskin was trading on a traditional qualitative difference established within the Christian tradition. There is a whiff of honorable martyrdom in his injunction, especially in the American context, where the activity of individuals is enjoined to subordination to the godly task of building a new Christian nation. But we must remember that this injunction is issued while the indigenous population is being sacrificed to the dreams and projects of the European colonizers of the Americas. The cultural capital of Christian godliness is affirmed in its value so as to legitimize a system of sacrifices of genocidal proportions.

The next moral injunction is to truth. One of Ruskin's axioms was that architecture must not deceive. There are three broad classes of architectural deceit:

1st. The suggestion of a mode of structure or support, other than the true one; as in pendants of late Gothic roofs.
2d. The painting of surfaces to represent some other material than that of which they actually consist (as in the marbling of wood), or the deceptive representation of sculptured ornament upon them.
3d. The use of cast or machine made ornaments of any kind. (p. 39)

We do have to notice that it's another Puritan narrative, and deeply imbedded in the prohibition against graven images. Thus it is part of the Old Testament revival characteristic of the Puritan ethos from the time of the *First* Calvinist Republic.[9] But, of course, for Ruskin the strictures against ornamentation do not at all lead to the spare, eremitic starkness of the Dutch church of the seventeenth century, but is, instead, one of the threads meant to lead us back to the Gothic (though not, of course, to the degenerate late Gothic of pendanted roofs). After all, Ruskin's diatribe against ornamentation is directed against *deceiving* ornamentation. Carven leaves and integrated statuary executed and placed properly are ornaments to be prized, and are beautiful.

The Ruskinian injunction to truth had an active role to play in defining the boundary between the cultural fractions represented in nineteenth-century America. We can sketch this role very simply. It became demonstrably bad taste to be Italian. The stiff-backed Protestant asceticism, so intellectually refined in its circulation through high culture became xenophobic as it issued exactly the same judgments on exactly the same principles on the streets of the immigrant-gathering cities. The spare and unadorned became a mark of distinction in the classic Bourdieuean sense, a mark of superiority. Ruskin's diatribes against deceiving ornamentation and the Renaissance fell on receptive ears.

Here we can pause to appreciate some subtle differentiations of social space. Ruskin's message may be thought to have resonated in reinforcement with Anti-Catholicism *per se*, but that's not true. German and Irish Catholicism on the one side have to be contrasted with Latin Catholicism on the other. German and Irish Catholicism (not to mention Dutch Catholicism) are pretty thoroughly Calvinized in conscience and culture. The trajectory of their assimilation into American society is quite different from that of the Italians, and, of course, other Latins. Irish or German Catholic churches can be as stark as any Congregational church, crucifices to the contrary notwithstanding. Equally important, canons of personal adornment along with light skin allowed Irish and German Catholics to entrain in the North American attractor without having to seal themselves off as Italians did. (The one exception to this was the city of Boston, where the entrenched Calvinist ethos was powerful enough to require the Irish to ghettoize themselves.) The alterity of the Italian immigrants, then, was reinforceable by the Ruskinean message as racial differences were parsed as differences of taste and style. The North American attractor was made even more inhospitable to Latin culture by high cultural sanction.

Included among Ruskin's seven lamps of architecture is the lamp of power, a megawatt illuminator of the disciplinary role architecture can play. Presented by Ruskin as an element in an aesthetic, power is the quality of architecture to engender a feeling of awe in us. In Ruskin's view, the genuinely fine instances of power are those that focus the awe toward the power and glory of God and the human mind. Truly monumental architecture, in a setting where it can be seen as a whole, is the architecture of power. Again, we have a message that circulated among sympathetically tuned nodes, reinforcing their natural frequencies and entraining them.

Every culture has recognized the power of monumental architecture to discipline. Architectural monuments are the clearest possible show of strength a dominant society or class has at its command. Further, as we know, they are the demonstration of the command of a surplus that can be diverted from the quotidian to the eternal. In short, in Bourdieuean terms, monumental architecture is the outward and visible sign of social capital, clearly distinguishing the centers of power.

However, as congenial as Ruskin's general evocation of architecture as power may have been, his choice of an architecture of power failed to entrain. There were two firmly established architectures of power in the US at the time of Ruskin's first message: the neoclassical of Jefferson, the buildings of state, the plantation, and banks, and the stark Gothic of the spired New England church. The Ruskin message resonated with the second, of course. But Ruskin's animadversions against neoclassicism just couldn't budge it from its established place as the entrenched style of the architecture of public and economic power. Statehouses continued to be temples as state after state entered the union, and so did banks.

Notice that the *failure* of the Ruskinean signal to resonate with the existing architectural language of power is very nearly diagnostic with respect to the structure of the dynamical system we're considering. For, as we think of the attempted transmission of the Ruskinean signal through the circuit of the public architecture of power in an experimental intervention, we find a subsystem that proved intractable to his message. The message failed to retune the circuitry, failed to produce entrainment. At the level of architectural design, the historical messages of Rome and Athens were virtually hardwired into the semiotics of power. Ruskin could succeed – or, more accurately, Pugin and Ruskin could succeed – with the Houses of Parliament in the superconfident British constitutional monarchy, but, in the still young American republic, implied continuity with the ancients remained imperative.[10] So, with few exceptions, domed neoclassical edifices persisted as the visible mark of the march of European culture across the land.

Ferro-concrete and steel eventually constituted the material conditions for a Ruskinean triumph in the twentieth-century architecture of economic power. There is no need here to spell out this observation. It's become a commonplace. But we can add the further observation that if Ruskin's chapter on the lamp of power is the textbook on the architecture of power, then his teaching reaches fullest consummation in the preferred architecture of Mussolini and the Rockefellers. In *that* architecture the entrainment of his signal succeeded.[11]

Another diagnostic component of the Ruskinean message was the Romantic conception of nature at the core of his aesthetic. Its differential resonances are somewhat paradoxical. Famously, he had argued that the beauty of nature required a human presence for its fulfillment. But the circuitry of American aesthetics of nature was tuned to the *wilderness*, the awesome, mysterious unknown as the potential site for adventure. True, this was (and is) typically tied to religious awe and the Romantic aesthetic of the sublime. Nature is read as the evidence of the power and glory of God.

But here, of course, we find ourselves at one of the most familiar edges, in fact an intersection of edges. The Romantic aesthetic of nature became the nearly exclusive property of high culture, for example in the painting of the Luminists and the Hudson River School and in *Moby-Dick*. In popular culture the aesthetic of the wilderness was the picturesque. Further, the conceptualization of nature that most successfully entrained the dominant culture was not asesthetic at all. A European way of life was being installed from coast to coast. American nature had to be turned to that task.

Nature had to appear in the light of agricultural and extractive enterprise. God's gift was not a gift to the higher contemplative faculties of the new Americans, but a gift to enterprise and well-being. Locke had said, about a century and a half before, in the famous account of the acquisition of property, "Thus in the beginning all the World was *America*...,"[12] and by God it was, in the early nineteenth century, from sea to shining sea.

In other words, nature became capital in the basic economic sense of the term, and, as we know, became economic capital so deeply that any claims of, say, aesthetic worth were definitively subordinated. The transformation of American nature into economic capital – real estate – had begun at least as early as the purchase of Manhattan Island, and it continues. In the face of this fundamental orientation, the high cultural subtleties of the sublime became a limp wristed irrelevancy in the dynamics of cultural formation.

Thus "nature" balanced on the edge between high culture on the one hand, and both popular culture and the anti-culture of economism on the other. Yet the edge must remain. The resources of high culture are too important to cast aside. Bourdieu has shown us their importance in the attainment of distinction, especially for the dominated fraction of the dominant class. But, in addition, the immigrant Americans were close enough to the savage wilderness to require well grounded affirmations of their intrinsic civilization. The European tradition of high culture was useful in this, but the preservation and transmission of this cultural tradition needed to be managed.

Traditions are obviously the locus of the most important structured structuring structures. They define the thinkable and unthinkable, what is done and what is not done. An ethos is transmitted through tradition. Normally the conduits of tradition are virtually invisible – subdoxic in the way of the habitus. In the US the situation is quite different. We are a disparate collection of immigrants and imports, and traditions either came over with us from the old country or evolved here in a quite visible way. For *us*, the high culture of Europe had to be *installed*. The instrumentalities for doing so in cultural centers such as Boston, Philadelphia, Richmond, Charleston, and later St. Louis and San Francisco are obvious and straightforward. But focusing on these cultural centers would lead us to omit the most important conduits of the European high culture, the griots of American culture, the small town school teachers. Strung out across the US was a thin network of heroic defenders of music, literature, and the arts.[13] They were the true managers of the boundary between high culture and everyday life.

The context in which they worked (and *still* work, for all that) was never propitious. There were always more pressing tasks than the acquisition of cultural fluency. Tocqueville had already remarked on the neglect of cultural education that itself had become a sort of tradition in the US. Life was full even for the emerging middle classes, and the acquisition of high culture is always an activity of leisure. Furthermore, the provincial schoolmaster was competing for whatever leisure time there was with what we would now call popular culture. For example, the folk music brought over from the old country was the basis for the dancing, socializing, and courtship constituting the core of small town culture. Bourdieu offers the sage advice that we ought to engage in anthropologies of our own culture and sociologies of alien cultures instead of the other way around. From that perspective we have to recognize that cultural production detached from courtship practices is very tenuously linked to the society in which it struggles to thrive. The sharing of subcultural fluency is one of the ways in which mating patterns are constrained. But except for the dominated fraction of the dominant class, high culture has never figured as a constraint on mate selection in the US. The schoolmasters and schoolmarms could reproduce *themselves* in modest numbers by the installation of high cultural tastes, but except in urban cultural centers these tastes were irrelevant to everyone else. Then as now, the cultural forms linked to courtship were forms of popular culture. Of course, the sheer lack of availability of the means of "classical" music was a problem in small towns and rural areas, but it was not the decisive factor in the failure of that music to penetrate to a wide public.

The cultivation of tastes for literature was similarly difficult. For one thing, few pursued an education long enough to reach the stage of enjoyable reading of the canon – generally Shakespeare – that was offered them. Even later as secondary and post secondary education became available, the typical pattern of aspiration was for a professional education at, say, one of the land grant universities, and the acquisition of high culture remained of distinctly secondary importance. Thus was the *Dorfschulmeister* beset. But he was nonetheless the conduit for the European high cultural message whenever it needed to be remembered. If the Ruskinean message was to resonate in, say, the choice of an architecture for the local courthouse, it was through the agency of the schoolmaster or schoolmistress that the message got through.

Before we dismiss the schoolmaster/mistress with a lament, we have to note that he/she lives on in our school systems and, especially, in the humanities divisions of our universities, and in the pages of the

New York Review of Books as the intellectual leader of the dominated fraction of the dominant class. The recent flurry of concern for humanistic education ought to remind us that while the middle class really feels no need to be cultured themselves, they insist on living in a society that perpetuates the high culture of the past.[14] The present-day schoolmasters/mistresses, like those of the past, are meant, for example, to hold the fort against the totalizing incursion of popular culture by, for example, witholding the blessing of serious aesthetic criticism from the popular arts.[15] They are the designated cultural conservatives, and abandon this stance at great risk of the provisional legitimacy the dominant culture grants them. They must manage the basin boundary, try to achieve entrainments at the edge of high culture.

To Conclude

We return to large print only long enough to underline briefly what the fine print has shown. At the level of particular analysis, we have been able to interdigitate the characteristic Bourdieuean patterns of explanation with those typical of the analysis of nonlinear dynamical systems. The edges of social and cultural formations are best consid-ered as dynamical fractal basin boundaries between complex attrac-tors with relatively hard cores. The processes resulting in the occupation of these attractors in social and cultural space are not linear causal ones, but, rather, to be considered as processes of entrainment.

Since we were looking at a period of nation *building*, including culture building, we are not surprised to find that the durable disposi-tions of *habitus* were less stably entrenched than they would typically be in other contexts. In contrast, we find transitions from diffuse scattered distributions of response to organized patterns of response. These are processes of *self*organization within a loosely coupled open system in the process of becoming more tightly coupled, more co-hesive, through a dynamics of its own. Areas of local entrainment could be found as the emerging culture differentiated into groups (sometimes classes, sometimes regional cultures, sometimes centers of preserved ethnic identity) attempting to find ways of distinguishing themselves and marking off dimensions of alterity. Edges emerged, boundaries that needed to be defended, and still need to be defended. The concept of what it is to be an American was in the process of formation, so part of the dynamics consisted in the search for ways to buffer interaction at the edges that emerged. The rhetoric of the melting pot, however unsuccessful it may have been, was an attempt at such buffering. But more deeply, the rhetoric of respectability, upstandingness, and success as the dominant selfconceptualization of wave after wave of entrants to the middle classes itself required the smoothing of edges. The rhetoric of opportunity was strictly speaking inconsistent with the persistence of difference, however much differences were exploited in the actual climb to success. So local entrainment was always constrained by the requirement of uniformity.

But where *habitus* is weak, other systems of discipline must be provided. In nineteenth-century America, as always, the process of self-construction involved the contraction of the available social space. To recall Ruskin, we can note that from a dynamical point of view, the exhortation to sacrifice has the effect of contracting any potential state space of social action. Any system of discipline has this effect. In fact, in dynamical terms, discipline could be defined as a system of constraints confining a system to subregions of its state space. In general, we could say that if societies and cultures are considered to be exploring the state space of possible ways of life, then the extent of this exploration is always highly constrained, and there are many sources of constraints that we would be foolish to conflate in the search for a canonical general theory of how "societies work." As Bourdieu has argued, the search for social understanding is not a search for the instantiation of "social laws."

This last point allows us to summarize the major insight of Bourdieu's theory of practice in a new way. Social structure is not typological, but dynamical. This, ultimately, is the powerful message in the phrase "structured structuring structures." It is an easy transition from this fundamental insight to the language of "attractors," "basin boundaries," the fractal interpenetration of differential trajectories", and so on, that is, the standard language of nonlinear dynamics. On this basis, the unity of the natural and social sciences is not the reductive unity forced by positivism. In fact, positivists think of themselves as the modern champions of empiricism, the stalwart defenders of the respect for data. Nothing could be farther from the truth. Positivism has constantly to distort dynamical data to force it into static typological frameworks. Positivism is Platonism in drag.

The natural and social sciences are united not by a reductive ontology, but by a tradition of investigative techniques. The tradition itself is a system of structured structuring structures, expanding and elaborating in its own dynamics. The unity is that of living learning science, not dead omniscient science. Science is a practice, not a canon. Learning is not a passive absorption of eternal truths but a trajectory of transformations of self and world in constant interaction. Once we realize that we are free to learn, we can join Bourdieu in the dynamical praxis of understanding ourselves and our societies.

Notes

1   This is to suppress, for the purposes of simplicity, the way in which both Bourdieu's theory and the study of nonlinear dynamics are both explicit rejections of dogmatic individualisms of one sort or another – atomisms.
2   The transparency that can be gained by choosing a felicitous representation is wonderfully demonstrated in Martin C. Gutzwiller, *Chaos in Classical and Quantum Mechanics* (New York: Springer, 1990), ch. 5.
3   The replacement of "command" in a definition of capital is exactly parallel, if not equivalent to the Foucauldian replacement of traditional concepts of power with that of the microphysics of power; *and* with the replacement of the linear independent variable, the Newtonian "impressed force," with the nonlinear interactions of modern dynamics.
4   For example, the scenario of the street in the Bronx in the thirties is the *Abie's Irish Rose* scenario. On its basis we might be able to account for any number of apparent anomalies, for example the presence of John Roche in the Brandeis Politics department in the fifties – tossing off the Yiddish almost as effortlessly as Irving Howe, teaching in the room next door.
5   Stuant Kauffman, *Theories of Order: Self-Organization and Selection in Evolution* (New York, Oxford University Press, 1993).
6   For surrendipitous reasons, the nematode *Caenorhabditus elegans* is nearly perfect for tracing the fates of the initial cell population, and to all intents and purposes the *entire* fate map of *C. elegans* is known. Knowledge is far sketchier for all other (multicelled) organisms.
7   It remains to note that a recognition of the ubiquity of contingent necessities and fractal boundaries makes the old familiar rationalist strategies of reduction obsolete. Whether there are new, more sophisticated, strategies of reduction available remains to be seen. There are lots of reasons, that I won't go into here, for thinking that no such strategies are going to show up, at least if they attempt to do the old reductionist jobs. To say this, of course, is not to say that anything *transcends*, say, the second law of thermodynamics. On the contrary: some of the most powerful anti-reductionist arguments come precisely from a careful consideration of the way that law works in an evolving world. See, for example, Rod Swenson, "Emergent Attractors and the Law of Maximum Entropy Production: Foundations to a Theory of General Evolution", *Systems Research*, vol. 6, no. 3, pp. 187–97, 1989.
8   John Ruskin, *The Seven Lamps of Architecture: Lectures on Architecture and Painting* (New York: A. L. Burt Publisher), n.d. Of course this point

was amply noted at the time. See Roger B. Stein, *John Ruskin and Aesthetic Thought in America, 1840–1900* (Cambridge, MA: Harvard University Press, 1967). Joseph Rykwert, *The First Moderns: The Architects of the Eighteenth Century* (Cambridge, MA and London: The MIT Press, 1983); Nikolaus Pevsner, *An Outline of European Architecture* (Harmondsworth: Penguin, 1943); and *Studies in Art, Architecture and Design Victorian and After* (Princeton: Princeton University Press, 1968). For the American scene, see Leland M. Roth, *A Concise History of American Architecture* (New York: Harper and Row, 1979); and the contributors to Roth, ed., *America Builds: Source Documents in American Architecture and Planning* (New York: Harper and Row Publishers, 1983).

9   See, for example, Simon Schama, *The Embarrassment of Riches: An Interpretation of Dutch Culture in the Golden Age* (New York: Knopf, 1987).

10 The same had been true of the Florentine Republic and the resurgent Rome of the Renaissance, contributing to the synergisms of Humanism and Classical revival that define the period. Machiavelli and Guicciardini are especially important people to read in this light.

11 Amongst feminist critics of modern culture the blatant phallic character of Fascist and Rockefeller architecture will inevitably lead to a reassessment of the Ruskinean message in those terms. Such a reassessment is likely to be extremely fruitful. In the context of this paper, this would mean assessing the degree to which the structural dynamics of the cultural constitution of the American middle class have an important sex/gender dimension. I think that they do, and the fact that I don't go into it here is a mark of the limitations to be recognized in any single attempt to provide a "full" analysis, something I have neither the room nor the wit to do.

12 John Locke, *Two Treatises of Government*, ed. Peter Laslett (Cambridge: Cambridge University Press, 1964), p. 319.

13 See Linda Smeins, "National Rhetoric, Public Discourse, and Spatialization: Middle Class America and the Pattern Book House", *Nineteenth-Century Contexts*, vol. 16, no. 2, 1992, pp. 135–64, and the references therein.

14 See Allan Bloom, *The Closing of the American Mind* (New York: Simon & Schuster, 1987), and C. Dyke, "The Praxis of Art and the Liberal Dream", in John Fisher, ed., *Essays on Aesthetics: Perspectives on the Work of Monroe C. Beardsley* (Philadelphia, Temple University Press, 1983).

15 But see Richard Shusterman, *Pragmatist Aesthetics: Living Beauty, Rethinking Art* (Oxford: Blackwell, 1992).

12

Bourdieu on Art: Field and Individual

Arthur C. Danto

In *Question de methode*, an essay in which he endeavors to assess the relationship of Existentialism to Marxism – and which serves as preamble to his sprawling and only sporadically brilliant *Critique de la raison dialectique* – Jean-Paul Sartre writes as follows: "Valéry is a petit bourgeois intellectual, no doubt about it. But not every petit bourgeois intellectual is Valery." In these two sentences, he adds, "the heuristic inadequacy of contemporary Marxism is contained."[1] How then to explain the gifted individual who seems to transcend the class which otherwise accounts for so many of his beliefs and values? We must resort, Sartre held, to "existential psychoanalysis," which seeks to identify what he terms the "original choice" each of us makes, and which defines, in a total way, how we are to respond to the world for the entirety of our lives. Sartre's study of Flaubert – again sprawling and only sporadically brilliant – set out to explain *Madame Bovary* against the background of the great novelist's original choice, and to account for how he lived and what he wrote, and why his life and work were different in every relevant detail from the lives of other writers whose class location paralleled his. "It becomes impossible to connect *Madame Bovary* directly to the political-social structure and to the evolution of the petite bourgeoisie," Sartre wrote. "The book will have to be referred back to contemporary reality insofar as it was lived by Flaubert through his childhood" (SM, p. 64).

It is one of Pierre Bourdieu's polemical aims to challenge Sartre's scheme of free original choice – what he contemptuously describes as "this sort of conceptual monster...a free and conscious act of auto-creation" (p. 188).[2] Bourdieu does this by identifying, in massive detail, precisely the social and historical structures within which choices are made and what he terms "cultural products" are created.

"God is dead, but the uncreated creator has taken his place" (p. 189). And a kind of *illusio* (p. 167) "directs the gaze toward the apparent producer – painter, composer, writer – and prevents us asking who created this 'creator' and the magic power of transubstantiation with which the 'creator' is endowed." But "it is enough to pose the forbidden question to perceive that the artist who makes the work is himself made, at the core of the field of production, by the whole ensemble of those who help to 'discover' him and consecrate him as an artist." The *piece de resistance* of Bourdieu's recent text, *The Rules of Art: Genesis and Structure of the Literary Field* is clearly a challenge to Sartre, and a brilliant reading of Flaubert's *L'Education sentimentale* against the complex of literary and artistic practices and attitudes which made Flaubert Flaubert.

Le bon Dieu est dans les details was one of Flaubert's bright sayings, adopted as a working motto by the Warburg Institute and certainly put into practice in Bourdieu's study. He describes corresponding structures in the literary and the art worlds of France in the nineteenth century, and readers familiar with high modernism will take particular interest in the provenance of the concept of artistic purity, and especially of "pure painting" which was to play so considerable a role in its aesthetics and its rhetoric, and, correlative with this, "the model of the pure artist" whose painting "was set up in opposition to the academic tradition and freed from the obligation to serve some purpose or simply to mean something" (p. 135). In the course of the century "there develops at the heart of each genre a more autonomous sector – or, if you will, an avant-garde. Each of the genres tends to cleave into a research sector and a commercial sector" – between avant-garde and Kitsch, we might, since Greenberg, say – "two markets...defined in and by their antagonistic relationship" (p. 120).

Indeed, part of the beauty of Bourdieu's marvelous analysis lies in the way in which we can see the formalist critical practice, not to mention the ethics of artistic production so influentially affirmed by Greenberg and internalized as aesthetic truth by those who followed him, emerge institutionally through the world which created Flaubert and Manet. "The history I have tried to reconstruct in its most decisive phases by using a series of synchronic slices leads to the establishment of this world apart – the artistic field or the literary field we know today" (p. 141). Since these worlds are ours, Bourdieu's work could hardly be more illuminating.

Analytical philosophers have tended to resist the "death of the artist" by insisting on the role of artistic intention in identifying and explaining works of art, without realizing that a further step must be taken in order to explain the intentions themselves. We cannot, that is, form just any intention whatever. Bourdieu introduces the idea of a *field* – "a network of objective relations ... between positions – for example the position corresponding to a genre like the novel ... or from another point of view, the position locating a review, a salon, or a circle." But "each position is objectively defined by its objective relationship with other positions" (p. 231). To be an artist is to occupy a position in the field known as the art world, which means that one is objectively related to the positions of critics, dealers, collectors, curators, and the like. It is the field which "creates the creators" who internalize what is possible in reference to the other positions.

Fields, of course, are always in the process of historical change, so the intentions which can be formed at one stage in their evolution cannot be formed at earlier or later stages. The "field" is an immeasurably more nuanced structure than whatever it is that philosophers, who subscribe to what is called "The Institutional Theory of Art," have so far sought to make explicit. One of the chief architects of the Institutional Theory, the philosopher George Dickie, has recently given particular prominence to the role of the artist in determining what can and what cannot be a work of art. But he failed to appreciate that there is a prior question of who is an artist, and for this one must refer to the field for an answer. Since fields are objective structures, the question of what is art and who are artists are themselves objective matters, and Bourdieu has sought to put in place the kind of science required for understanding both: it is an historical science of cultural fields.

It is not clear that Sartre's question of what makes Flaubert Flaubert has been answered, inasmuch as the field will account for everyone, great or good or competent, who exists in it at any given time. There is an implied criticism that this sort of social scientific analysis might "somehow have the effect of 'levelling' artistic values by 'rehabilitating' second-rate authors" (p. 70). The Musée D'Orsay opened to cries of indignation for seeming to give the same degree of prominence to the lesser contemporaries of great artists as to those artists themselves. To this Bourdieu offers a compelling response: "Everything inclines us to think that, on the contrary, one loses the essence of what makes for individuality and even of the greatness of the survivors when one ignores the universe of contemporaries with whom and against whom they construct themselves" (p. 70). Yes and no. It is certainly true that we get a definite perspective on Courbet's masterpiece, *The Studio*, when we see it in the context the Musée D'Orsay provides. But I incline to the view that its greatness is somehow independent of that understanding, and that the work's power is present in it however much or little we may happen to know about the field which made Courbet and which Courbet in turn transformed. There are autonomous experiences with art, which does not entail that art itself is autonomous. There are statements in Bourdieu's text which make me certain he would indignantly resist this claim, but however the issue is to be settled, I find his aesthetic theory, and particularly the idea of a field, consistently interesting and sometimes enthrallingly interesting.

I have often found convincing the thought that every philosophical position is sooner or later going to be occupied by some thinker. The concept of a field helps explain why. Consider classical Chinese philosophy. Its central question was the moral identity of human beings, and it was disclosed as a field when Confucius advanced a thesis that human beings are essentially good. Even a thief, the ancient example held, will spontaneously and with no concern for reward, reach out to pull back a child teetering on the edge of a well. Confucius's claim generated four possible positions: human beings are good, are evil, are both good and evil, are neither good nor evil. The ancient debates revolved around these positions, with followers of Lao Tzu, Han Fei Tsu, and Hsun Tzu attacking one anothers' arguments and proposing counter-examples. The field had a remarkable stability – it lasted in that form for perhaps eighteen centuries, until a challenge came from a direction no one had anticipated, namely Buddhism, which entered China in about the twelfth century, radically destabilizing the four-fold structure of Chinese thought. That challenge was in part met by the Neo-Confucian thinker, Chu Hsi, who transformed the field, opening a set of positions internal to Confucianism itself, leaving the classical alternatives to it to wither into mere treatises. Perhaps this was because of the way Confucianism had penetrated Chinese institutions, making it a matter of social urgency that some way be found for assimilating the appeal to Buddhism to it, whereas nothing quite like this was true of the other positions. Or it may have been that no one who occupied either of the remaining three positions was deep enough a thinker to undertake such a task (Taoism was of course fairly close already to what was found almost irresistibly appealing in Buddhism). If that were the case, the field cannot explain the originality of Chu Hsi, who in effect created a new field by melding Confucianism with what seemed its irreconcilable other. Before him, Buddhism challenged the field from without. After him a field had been created in which it had somehow been assimilated to one of the classical positions. Thereafter, if there was a field, it was within Neo-Confucian philosophy itself: with Wang Yang-ming and Yen Yuan taking up positions in relationship to that of Chu Hsi.

We can identify a comparable historical structure in Western philosophy if we think of the relationship between reason and experience, which pivoted on what role to assign the senses in the enterprises of knowledge. Rationalism and Empiricism were locked in a deep struggle – think of Locke and Leibniz on innate ideas! – until Kant demonstrated that we need reason *as well* as experience, and the pragmatists, who believed they stood to the field in something like the relationship in which Buddhism stood to Chinese philosophy in its entirety, turned out merely to have occupied the fourth available position, i.e. "none of the above." And there the field has remained, mainly perhaps because there is no unoccupied position in it, and nothing to challenge it from outside, though Marxism perhaps thought it had.

In New York painting in the 1950s, there was a polar opposition between Abstraction and Figuration, with an open space for a kind of abstract figuration, and for something which was neither. The challenge, as it turned out, came from Pop, and it is a matter of interpretation whether it occupied the fourth position or simply challenged the whole field, making the arguments used by occupants of the two main positions decreasingly relevant to the subsequent forms of artistic creation. Today Abstraction and Figuration are simply modalities of painting, much marginalized in a field whose complexity, at present writing, is difficult to grasp. How many positions in it are there? In a way, we can hardly say until they get occupied, and we recognize that a possibility has been actualized. Can this be explained relative to the field? I mean: can the field explain the individual who sees what we subsequently acknowledge as an opening? My sense is that the moment one sees that one's work merely fills an empty place, one loses interest. But the power of the field as a coefficient of artistic creativity may be underscored by the fact that outsiders have no perceivable artistic merit until the field admits their work somewhere into the structure because enfranchised artists find ways of using folk art, children's art, the art of outsiders, and the like.

These desultory observations bear on fields internally considered, from the perspective of their logic. When one brings in the social constraints of markets and audiences, things get at once messier and less logical. But I do think that the concept is of the very greatest value in thinking about transformations as well as the internal dialectic of positions, and it gives us a structure it is possible to understand as real. It explains how we think and how we act as cultural beings, and how these modes of thought and conduct change. Whether it can explain the transformations when they occur is quite another matter. Whether Flaubert's greatness is in any sense indexed to the position others less great occupied with him is moot – though we can, I suppose, imagine Flaubert being born into a world in which no positions enabled his remarkable gifts to prosper. But that gets us into the perplexities of counter-identity, which we are best off to leave untouched. The alternative of course may yield a proposition that *Le champ c'est moi*, said by each of us.

Notes

1   J. P. Sartre, *Search for a Method*, trans. H. Barnes (New York: Vintage, 1968), 56; Henceforth abbreviated as SM.
2   Pierre Bourdieu, *The Rules of Art: Genesis and Structure of the Literary Field* (Cambridge: Polity Press, 1996), 188. Future page references to this book appear parathetically in my text.

13

The Social Conditions of the International Circulation of Ideas

Pierre Bourdieu

What can one do today, if one has a genuine desire to further the internationalization of intellectual life? People often have a tendency to think that intellectual life is spontaneously international. Nothing could be further from the truth. Intellectual life, like all other social spaces, is a home to nationalism and imperialism, and intellectuals, like everyone else, constantly peddle prejudices, stereotypes, received ideas, and hastily simplistic representations which are fuelled by the chance happenings of everyday life, like misunderstandings, general incomprehension, and wounded pride (such as might be felt at being unknown in a foreign country). All of which makes me think that a truly scientific internationalism, which to my mind is the only possible ground on which internationalism of any sort is going to be built, is not going to happen of its own accord.

Regarding culture, my beliefs are the same as those I hold for everything else: I don't believe in laissez-faire. What I hope to show here is that all too often, in international exchanges, the logic of laissez-faire favours the circulation of the very worst ideas at the expense of the best. And here, as so often, I find myself inspired by that most out-moded of ideas in this post-modern world – a deeply held belief in scientism. And this scientism leads me to believe that if one understands social mechanisms, one is not necessarily master of them, but one does increase one's chances of mastering them, by however small an amount, particularly when the social mechanisms in question rest largely on misunderstanding. I say largely, as the "intrinsic force of true ideas" is perpetually met by resistance from all quarters, in the shape of interests, prejudices and passions.

International exchanges are subject to a certain number of structural factors which generate misunderstandings. The first factor is that texts circulate without their context. This is a proposition that Marx noted in passing in the *Communist Manifesto*, an unusual place to look for a reception theory... Marx notes that German thinkers have read French thinkers very badly, seeing texts that were the result of a particular political juncture as *pure* texts, and transforming the political agitators at the heart of such texts into a sort of transcendental subject. In the same manner, many misunderstandings in international communication are a result of the fact that texts do not bring their context with them. For example, at the risk of surprising and shocking you, it seems to me that only the logic of this structural misunderstanding can explain the staggering fact that a President of a French Socialist Republic awarded a decoration to Ernst Jünger. Another example might be the consecration of Heidegger by certain French Marxists in the 1950s. I could equally use contemporary examples. But because I would often be implicated in these examples myself, I shall refrain from doing so, as it might be thought that I was taking advantage of the symbolic power invested in me here today to avenge myself on absent adversaries.

The fact that texts circulate without their context, that – to use my terms – they don't bring with them the field of production of which they are a product, and the fact that the recipients, who are themselves in a different field of production, re-interpret the texts in accordance with the structure of the field of reception, are facts that generate some formidable misunderstandings and that can have good or bad consequences. From this account, which I believe to be objective, one could draw either optimistic or pessimistic conclusions. For example, if someone who is an authority in his own country does not bring that authority with him abroad, then foreign readers and commentators sometimes have a liberty not to be found in the country where the text originates, where a reading might be subject to a variety of symbolic or real constraints. All this lends some credibility to the idea that foreign judgments are a little like the judgments of posterity. If, in general, posterity is a better judge, it is doubtless because contemporaries are competitors and often have a hidden interest in not understanding, or even in preventing understanding from taking place in others. Foreign readers, like posterity, have in some cases a distance and autonomy regarding the social conditions of the field. In fact this effect is often slightly illusory, and it does happen that institutionalised authorities, Pascal's "grandeurs d'établissement" cross frontiers very well, as there is an all-too-real international old-boy network that functions with great efficiency.

So the sense and function of a foreign work is determined not simply by the field of origin, but in at least equal proportion by the field of reception. First, because the sense and function of the original field are often completely unknown, but also because the process of transfer from a domestic field to a foreign one is made up of a series of social operations. There is a process of selection (what is to be translated, what is to be published, who it will be translated by, who will publish it), a process of labelling and classification (often the placing of a label on a product that previously has no label at all) by the publishers, the question of the series in which it is to be inserted, the choice of the translator and the writer of the preface (who in presenting the work will take some sort of possession of it, and slant it with his own point of view, and explain how it fits into the field of reception, only rarely going so far as to explain where and how it fits into its field of origin, as the difficulties presented by such an enterprise are too large); and finally the reading process itself, as foreign readers are bound to perceive the text in different ways, since the issues which are of interest to them in the text are inevitably the result of a different field of production.

I shall look at each of these points in a little more detail. The conditions and manner in which texts enter a field of reception is an urgent and important area that needs further research, for both scientific and practical reasons, particularly as our aim is to facilitate and improve communication between different countries. I hope sometime to organise a conference to look at these selection processes, and find out who these people doing the selecting (who were recently termed "gate-keepers" by an American sociologist of science) actually are. Who are the discoverers, and what interest do they have in discovering these things? I am aware that the word "interest" might shock here. But I do believe that anyone, no matter how well intentioned, who appropriates an author for him or herself and becomes the person who introduces that author to another country inevitably has some ulterior motive. It may be sublime, or it may be sublimated, but it should be revealed, as it is clearly a determining factor in what is being done. (I think a little materialism isn't at all out of place here, and won't take away the enchantment). What I am calling "interest" may simply be a sort of affinity through the occupation of a similar or identical place in the different fields. To take one example, it surely isn't by accident that the great Spanish novelist Benet is published in France by Les Éditions de Minuit. To publish what one loves is to strengthen one's position in a certain field, whether one likes it or not, whether one is aware of it or not, even if that effect was not part of the original intention. There is nothing wrong with this, but it should be more widely recognised. Choices which seem pure of other interests, and are mutually agreeable, are often made on the basis of similar positions in different fields and in fact correspond to homologous interests and styles where the intellectual background or project is concerned. These exchanges can be understood as alliances, and function in the same way as relations involving force, hence they might be used to reinforce a dominated or threatened position.

Besides these elective affinities between "creators" (for which, as you have probably worked out, I feel a certain indulgence), there are also the mutual admiration societies which seem somewhat less legitimate as they exercise a temporal power in a cultural or spiritual sphere, and thus correspond to Pascal's definition of tyranny. One thinks for example of the establishment mafia, and of the series of exchanges that go on between people who hold important academic positions. A large number of translations can only be understood if they are placed in the complex network of international exchanges between holders of dominant academic posts, the exchanges of invitations, honorary doctorates, etc. The question that must then be asked is how it comes about that a certain writer or editor becomes the importer of a certain thought. Why is writer X published by publisher Y? For it is obvious that there will always be some sort of profit involved. Heretical imports are often the work of marginals in the field, bringing a message, a position of force from a different field, which they use to try and shore up their own position. Foreign writers are often subject to such instrumental use, and forced to serve purposes which they would perhaps refuse or reject in their country of origin. One can often use a foreign thinker to attack domestic thinkers in this way.

Heidegger is a case in point. Doubtless, many people here today wonder how it was that the French became so interested in Heidegger. There are many reasons of course, perhaps too many, but one particular reason leaps out to the eye: the fact that Sartre held the intellectual field in a stranglehold throughout the 1950s (as Anna Boschetti has demonstrated quite convincingly in her book *Sartre et les Temps Modernes*). One of Heidegger's major functions for the French was to diminish Sartre's impact, with teachers saying for example that all of Sartre's major ideas were already there in Heidegger, where they were better elaborated. On the one side there was Beaufret, who must have been a contemporary of Sartre's at the École Normale Supérieure, in a position of rivalry with him, taking the "khâgne" classes at the prestigious Henri IV school, preparing students for the rigorous entry exams to the Grandes Écoles, managing to create a sort of status for himself as philosopher by bringing

Heidegger to France. Elsewhere, in the literary field, there was Blanchot. And there was also a third category, in the review *Arguments*, the minor Marxist heretics. As straight Marxism was too obviously proletarian, they constructed a modish mixture of Marxism and Heidegger.

Very often with foreign authors it is not what they say that matters, so much as what they can be made to say. This is why certain particularly elastic authors transfer so well. All great prophecies are polysemic. That is one of their cardinal virtues, and explains how they have such general applications, and are transmitted so well across cultures and down the generations. Such elastic thinkers are manna from heaven when it comes to serving expansionist strategic uses.

After this process of selection and choice, there comes the attaching of a label which finishes the work. Hence we don't for instance simply get Simmel, we get Simmel with a preface by Mr. X. The time is ripe for a comparative study of the sociology of the preface. They are typical acts of the transfer of symbolic capital, or at least this is what they most commonly are, as for instance when we find Mauriac writing a preface for Sollers. The elder statesman writes the preface, handing on the symbolic capital, demonstrating that he still has both the ability to recognise new talent, and the generosity to protect an admiring younger generation where his influence is to be discerned. A whole series of exchanges is going on (where bad faith is playing an enormous role) which any objective sort of sociology would render much more difficult. But the direction in which the symbolic capital is circulating is not always the same. For instance, relying on the idea that the writer of the preface is identified with the author of the book, Lévi-Strauss wrote a preface to Mauss where he effectively appropriated for himself the symbolic capital of the author of the famous essay on the gift. I leave you to draw your own conclusions here.

At the end of all this, the imported text receives another new label. The cover of the book acts as a sort of brand name. Seasoned academics have a good understanding of the sorts of covers that different publishers use, and even of the sense of the different series published by the publisher in question. One knows what they all mean, and how they fit into the general scheme of scholarly publishing. If, for example, one were to replace a Suhrkamp cover by one from Seuil, the new brand that the product is marked with would change its meaning dramatically. When there is a sort of structural homology, the transfer can happen quite unproblematically. But there are often failures here, and writers who fall awkwardly by the wayside as a result, sometimes simply by chance, sometimes by ignorance, but often too because they are unwittingly objects of a process of appropriation. In such cases even the cover itself is already a symbolic imposition. Chomsky is an excellent example here, published by Seuil in a philosophy series. To my mind, Seuil as publishers are basically left-wing Catholic, and very much personality-based. So Chomsky found himself with a new brand name, as a result of a typical expansionist project. For Seuil to publish Chomsky, in an environment where Ricoeur's influence was extremely powerful, was to combat what was known as "subjectless structuralism" with a creative, generative personality. And by the insertion of Chomsky's book into such a series, by the addition of a preface, by the contents of that preface, and by the position of the author of the preface, a whole series of transformations took place, whose end result was to considerably alter the sense of the original message.

In actual fact all sorts of transformations and deformations linked to the strategic use of texts and authors are constantly going on, independently of any intention to manipulate information. The differences are so great between historical traditions, in the intellectual field per se as well as in the ensemble of the social field, that the application to a foreign cultural product of the categories of perception and appreciation acquired from experience in the domestic field can actually create fictitious oppositions between similar things, and false parallels between things that are fundamentally different. To demonstrate this, one could analyse in detail the links between French and German philosophers since the 1960s and show how similar intentions have resulted, through reference to starkly different intellectual and social contexts, in the adopting of apparently opposing philosophical positions. To put this in a more striking but more fanciful manner, one might ask oneself whether Habermas would not have been much closer to Foucault than he appears to be, if he had been trained and brought up as a philosopher in France of the 1950s to 1960s, and whether Foucault would not have been much less different from Habermas, had he been been trained and brought up as a philosopher in Germany at the same time. This is to say, by way of an aside, that both thinkers, while appearing to have great freedom in their contexts, are in fact both deeply marked by the context in which they found themselves, partly because (through their hegemonic intentions) they came into conflict with the intellectual traditions particular to their own countries, which were of course profoundly different.

Another instructive example. Before becoming self- righteously indignant, like certain German scholars, at the use to which certain French philosophers (notably Deleuze and Foucault) have put

Nietzsche, one must understand the function that Nietzsche – for Foucault the Nietzsche of *The Genealogy of Morals* – fulfilled in a certain field of academic philosophy which was dominated at the time by a sort of subjective, spiritual existentialism. *The Genealogy of Morals* offered a sort of philosophical guarantee and philosophical respectability both to apparently old-fashioned scientific, positivist ideas (incarnated in the fading image of Durkheim) and to the sociology of knowledge and the social history of ideas. Thus, in an effort to combat ahistorical rationalism by founding a historical science of historical reason (complete with the idea of "genealogy" and a notion like that of the *episteme*), Foucault was thought to be contributing to a movement which, when viewed from Germany, where Nietzsche had a totally different meaning, appeared to be a restoration of irrationality, against which Habermas, amongst others (like Otto Apel, for instance), set up his whole philosophical project.

If I were to add my own contribution to this debate, I would say that the opposition is considerably less radical than it first seems, between, on the one hand, the rationalist and historicist approach that I pursue (with the idea of a social history of reason, or of the scientific field as the place of the historical genesis of the social conditions for the production of reason) and, on the other hand, a neo-Kantian rationalism, which attempts to transform itself into a scientific sort of reason by basing itself on linguistic arguments, as in Habermas and Apel. I am sure that a rationalist relativism and a sort of enlightened absolutism can be of great mutual assistance in the defence of the *Aufklärung*. Perhaps the intention is the same, and it is merely the means that are different. Of course, I exaggerate a little here. But I do believe that these differences are not as great as they have long been imagined to be, by people not taking account of the workings of the prism effect when work is transferred from a field in one country to another, and when a different set of categories and thought are actually at work.

The logical Realpolitik of which I am a ceaseless advocate must above all have as its aim an intention to work towards the creation of social conditions permitting rational dialogue. In this context, this means working at raising awareness and knowledge of the ways in which different national fields function, for the greater the ignorance of the original context, the higher the risk that the text will be used in a different sense. This project will only appear banal so long as we fail to enter into the details of its realisation. The aim must be to produce a scientific knowledge of national fields of production and the national categories of thought that originate there, and to diffuse this knowledge as widely as possible, notably by ensuring that it forms a component of studies of foreign languages, civilisations, and philosophies. To give an idea of the difficulty of the enterprise, one could do worse than begin by examining the attitudes to be found among specialists in these fields. All too often, the so-called specialists in international exchanges have developed their own private sociologies to explain differences between national traditions. Germanists and Romance specialists, for example, constantly produce and reproduce attitudes which have their basis in ill-thought-out half-truths: people who "know them pretty well," "who aren't so easily fooled," who "find them awful, but love them all the same." Such convictions are particularly common among specialists of foreign civilisations (like "orientalists" or "japanologists") and betray attitudes which result in a sort of condescending amusement which is ultimately quite close to racism.

Freedom where national categories of thought are concerned – through which we think the differences between the products of such categories – can result only from a sustained effort to think out these categories and render them quite explicit. It can only come from a social history, and a reflexive sociology which would be critical in the Kantian sense, whose goal would be a scientific socio-analysis to illuminate the structure of a national cultural unconscious. Through a rigorous reconstruction of the different national histories, and above all through a history of educational institutions and the fields of cultural production, it would unveil the historical foundations of various categories of thought, and the problematic areas that social actors unwittingly reveal ("it is history which is the true unconscious" as Durkheim said) through acts of cultural reception or production.

If there is no question of denying the existence of profound intellectual nationalisms, based on what are perceived as important intellectual national interests, there is also a less obvious point worth noting. The international struggle for domination in cultural matters and for the imposition of the dominant principle of domination (I mean by this the imposing of a particular definition of the legitimate exercise of intellectual activity, for example, Germany's valorization of ideas of *Kultur*, depth, philosophical content, etc., over what they saw as the French stress on *Civilisation*, clarity, literature, etc.), this struggle inevitably finds its roots in the struggles within each national camp, in struggles where the dominant national definition and foreign definition are themselves involved. They are not simply arms in a struggle, but are also themselves stakes of a struggle.

We can see why such conditions make philosophical confusion and misunderstandings more the rule than the exception in the international scene, as another example could show. A considerable amount of intellectual independence and theoretical lucidity is necessary to understand that Durkheim, revolting against a dominant intellectual order which included men like Bergson, is actually in the same camp as Cassirer (who in *Myths of State* made an explicit link between his "symbolic forms" and Durkheim's "primitive forms of classification"), while Cassirer was a target against whom Heidegger developed a variation of Bergsonian *Lebensphilosophie*.

One could multiply almost indefinitely such chiastic effects, which not only facilitate alliances or hostilities based on mutual misunderstanding, but also serve to problematize or minimize the accumulation of historical data on different traditions or on the internationalization (or de-nationalization) of the categories of thought, which ultimately must be the primary conditions for a true intellectual universalism.

Selective Bibliography of Pierre Bourdieu, 1958–1998

Note: This bibliography, which is limited to French and English publications, is based on the complete bibliography of Bourdieu's works prepared by Yvette Delsaut and Marie-Christine Rivière. Entries are grouped into books, articles, oral presentations, interviews, and miscellaneous writings (reviews, prefaces, postscripts, and tributes).

Books

Sociologie de l'Algérie, Paris, PUF, Coll. 'Que Sais-je', 802, 1958, new rev. and corr. edn, 1961. Published in English as *The Algerians* (tr. A. C. M. Ross), Boston, Beacon Press, 1962.

Travail et travailleurs en Algérie, Paris and The Hague, Mouton, 1963 (with A. Darbel, J. P. Rivet, C. Seibel).

Le déracinement, la crise de l'agriculture traditionnelle en Algérie, Paris, Éd. de Minuit, 1964 (with A. Sayad).

Les héritiers, les étudiants et la culture, Paris, Éd. de Minuit, 1964, new augm. edn, 1966 (with J. C. Passeron). Published in English as *The Inheritors, French Students and their Relation to Culture* (tr. R. Nice), with a new Epilogue 1979. Chicago-London. The University of Chicago Press, 1979.

Les étudiants et leurs études, Paris and The Hague, Mouton, Cahiers du Centre de sociologie européenne, 1, 1964 (with J. C. Passeron).

Un art moyen, essai sur les usages sociaux de la photographie, Paris, Éd. de Minuit, 1965, new rev. edn, 1970 (with L. Boltanski, R. Castel, J. C. Chamboredon). Published in English as *Photography: A Middlebrow Art* (tr. S. Whiteside). Cambridge, Polity Press, 1990.

L'amour de l'art, les musées d'art et leur public, Paris, Éd. de Minuit, 1966, new augm. edn, *L'amour de l'art, les musées d'art européens et leur public*, 1969 (with A. Darbel, D. Schnapper). Published in English as *The Love of Art: European Art Museums and their Public* (tr. C. Beattie, N. Merriman), Cambridge, Polity Press, 1990.

Le métier de sociologue, Paris, Mouton-Bordas, 1968 (with J. C. Chamboredon, J. C. Passeron). Published in English as *The Craft of Sociology* (tr. R. Nice, B. Krais ed.), Berlin, New York, Walter de Gruyter, 1991.

La reproduction. Éléments pour une théorie du système d'enseignement, Paris, Éd. de Minuit, 1970, new augm. edn with preface, 1989 (with J. C. Passeron). Published in English as *Reproduction in Education, Society and Culture* (tr. R. Nice), London-Beverley Hills, *Esquisse d'une théorie de la pratique, précédé de trois études d'ethnologie kabyle*, Genève, Droz, 1972. Pages 162–89 in 'The Three Forms of Theoretical Knowledge', *Social Science Information*, XII, 1, 1973, pp. 53–80; also, *Outline of a Theory of Practice* (tr. R. Nice), Cambridge, Cambridge University Press, 1977; also, pp. 3–9, 72–3, 'Structures, Strategies, and the Habitus', in *French Sociology, Rupture and Renewal since 1968*. C. Lemert ed., New York, Columbia University Press, 1981, pp. 86–96; also, 'Structures, Habitus, Power: Basis for a Theory of Symbolic Power', in N. B. Dirks, G. Eley, S. B. Ortner (eds), *Culture, Power, History. A Reader in Contemporary Social Theory*, Princeton, Princeton University Press, 1994, pp. 155–99.

Algérie 60, structures économiques et structures temporelles, Paris, Éd. de Minuit, 1977. Published in English as *Algeria 1960* (tr. R. Nice), Cambridge-Paris, Cambridge University Press/Éd. de la Maison des sciences de l'homme. 1979, pp. 1–94.

La distinction. Critique sociale du jugement, Paris, Éd. de Minuit, 1979; new augm. edn with an introduction, 1982. Published in English as extracts (tr. R. Nice): pp. 9–61, 'The aristocracy of culture', *Media, Culture and Society*, vol. 2, 3 (July 1980), pp. 225–54; also, in *Media, Culture and Society, A Critical Reader*, London, Sage Publications, 1986, pp. 164–93; pp. 139–44, 'A diagram of social position and life-style', *Media, Culture and Society*, vol. 2, 3 (July 1980), pp. 255–9; complete publication, *Distinction. A Social Critique of the Judgement of Taste* (tr. R. Nice), Cambridge (Massachusetts), Harvard University Press, 1984; paperback edition, London, New York, Routledge & Kegan Paul, 1986.

Le sens pratique, Paris, Éd. de Minuit, 1980. Published in English as *The Logic of Practice* (tr. R. Nice), Cambridge, Polity Press, 1990, 333 pp.: also, (extract). 'Structures, Habitus and Practices', in *The Polity Reader in Social Theory*, Cambridge, Polity Press, 1994, pp. 95–110; also, (extracts: 'L'action du temps', 'Le capital symbolique', 'Les modes de domination'), 'The work of time', 'Symbolic Capital', 'Modes of Domination', in A. D. Schrift, *The Logic of the Gift*, New York-London, 1997, pp. 190–230.

Questions de sociologie, Paris, Éd. de Minuit, 1980; [collected texts: 'L'art de résister aux paroles' [1979]; 'Une science qui dérange' [1980], 'Le sociologue en question' (unpublished); 'Les intellectuels sont-ils hors jeu?' [1978]; 'Comment libérer les intellectuels libres'? [1980]; 'Pour une sociologie des sociologues' [1976]; 'Le paradoxe du sociologue' [1977]; 'Ce que parler veut dire' (also, 'Savoir ce que parler veut dire' [1978]; 'Quelques propriétiés des champs' (unpublished – ENS-Paris, 1976); 'Le marché linguistique' (unpublished – Geneva, 1978); 'La censure' [1977]; 'La "jeunesse" n'est qu'un mot' [1978]; 'L'origine et l'évolution des espèces de mélomanes' [1978]; 'La métamorphose des goûts' (unpublished – Neuchâtel, 1980); 'Comment peut-on être sportif?' [1978]; 'Haute couture et haute culture' [1974]; 'Mais qui a créé les 'créateurs'?' [1980]; 'L'opinion publique n'existe pas' [1971]; 'Culture et politique' (unpublished – Grenoble, 1980); 'La grève et l'action politique' (unpublished – MSH-Paris, 1975); 'Le racisme de l'intelligence' [1978])]. Published in English as *Sociology in Question*, London, Sage Publications, 1993, 184 pp.

Travaux et projets, Paris, Centre de sociologie européenne, 1980.

Leçon sur la leçon, Paris, Éd. de Minuit [1982]; *Leçon inaugurale*, 90, Paris, Collège de France, 1982. Published in English (with *Choses dites*; Y. Delsaut, *Bibliographie des travaux de Pierre Bourdieu. 1958–1988*, Paris, Centre de sociologie européenne, 1989), as *In Other Words. Essays towards a Reflexive Sociology*, Cambridge, Polity Press, 1990. 223 pp.

Ce que parler veut dire. L'économie des échanges linguistiques, Paris, Fayard, 1982. (Extracts: 'La production et la reproduction de la langue légitime'), published in English as 'The Production and Reproduction of Legitimate Language', in *Language and Symbolic Power*, Cambridge, Polity Press [1991], pp. 43–65; (extract: 'La formation des prix et l'anticipation des profits'), 'Price Formation and the Anticipation of Profits', *op. cit.*, pp. 66–89; (extract: 'Le langage autorisé: les conditions sociales de l'efficacité du discours rituel'),

'Authorized Language: The Social Conditions for the Effectiveness of Ritual Discourse', *op cit.*, pp. 107–16; (extract: 'Les rites d'institution'), 'Rites of Institution', *op. cit.*, pp. 117–26; (extract: 'Décrire et prescrire: les conditions de possibilitié et les limites de l'efficacité politique'), 'Description and Prescription: The Conditions of Possibility and the Limits of Political Effectiveness', *op. cit.*, pp. 127–36; (extract: 'Censure et mise en forme'), 'Censorship and the Imposition of Form', *op. cit.*, pp. 137–59; (extract: 'La force de la représentation'), 'Identity and Representation: Elements for a Critical Reflection on the Idea of Region', *op. cit.*, pp. 220–8.

Homo academicus, Paris, Éd. de Minuit [1984]. Published in English as *Homo academicus* (tr. P. Collier), Preface to the English Edition (pp. xi–xxvi), London, Polity Press, 1988

Choses dites, Paris, Éd. de Minuit [1987]; [collected texts: ' "Fieldwork in Philosophy" ' [1986]; 'Repères' [1983]; 'De la règle aux stratégies' [1985]; 'La codification' [1986]; 'Sociologues de la croyance et croyances de sociologues' [1987]; 'Objectiver le sujet objectivant' (unpublished – Strasbourg, 1984); 'La dissolution du religieux' [1985]; 'L'intérêt du sociologue' [1984]; 'Lecture, lecteurs, lettrés, littérature' [1981]; 'Espace social et pouvoir symbolique' (unpublished – San Diego, 1986); 'Le champ intellectuel: un monde à part' (unpublished – radio interview, Hambourg, 1985); 'Les usages du "peuple" ' (unpublished – Lausanne, 1982); La délégation et le fétichisme politique' [1984]; 'Programme pour une sociologie du sport' (unpublished – CEMA-Paris, 1983); 'Le sondage: une "science" sans savant' [1985]]; also, (extract: pp. 203–16), 'Program for a Sociology of Sport' (tr. J. McAloon, A. D. Savage), *Sociology of Sport Journal*, 5, 1988, pp. 153–61; (extract: 'Espace social et pouvoir symbolique'), 'Social Space and Symbolic Power' (San Diego, 1987) (tr. L. Wacquant), *Sociological Theory*, 7(1), spring 1989, pp. 14–25; also, in *The Polity Reader in Social Theory*, Cambridge, Polity Press, 1994, pp. 111–20.

La noblesse d'Etat. Grandes écoles et esprit de corps, Paris, Éd. de Minuit [1989], 568 pp. Published in English as *The State Nobility. Elite Schools in the Field of Power* (tr. L. C. Clough), Stanford, Stanford University Press, 1996, 475 pp.

Language and Symbolic Power (tr. G. Raymond, M. Adamson – J. B. Thompson, ed.), Cambridge, Polity Press [1991]; [collected texts translated in English: 'La production et la reproduction de la langue légitime', 'La formation des prix et l'anticipation des profits', 'Le langage autorisé', 'Les rites d'institution', 'Décrire et prescrire',

'Censure et mise en forme', 'La force de la représentation', in *Ce que parler veut dire* [1982]; 'Vous avez dit populaire' [1983]; 'La représentation politique' [1981]; 'La délégation et le fétichisme politique' [1984]; 'Espace social et genèse des "classes"' [1984]; 'Sur le pouvoir symbolique' [1977]].

Social Theory for a Changing Society, P. Bourdieu and J. S. Coleman (eds), Boulder-San Francisco-Oxford, Westview Press, New York, Russell Sage Foundation, 1991, 387 pp.

Réponses. Pour une anthropologie réflexive, Paris, Éd. du Seuil [1992], 267 pp. (with L. Wacquant). Published in English as *An Invitation to Reflexive Sociology* (tr. L. Wacquant), Chicago, University of Chicago Press, 1992, 332 pp.

Les règles de l'art. Genèse et structure du champ littéraire, Paris, Éd. du Seuil [1992], 480 pp. Published in English as *The Rules of Art* (tr. S. Emanuel), Cambridge, Polity Press, 1996, 410 pp.; also, Stanford, Stanford University Press, 1996, 408 pp. (extract: 'Note brève sur les rapports entre les luttes artistiques et les luttes littéraires', 'The Link between literary and artistic struggles' (tr. D. Dorday), in P. Collier, R. Lethbridge (eds), *Artistic Relations, Literature and the Visual Arts in Nineteenth-Century France,* New Haven-London, Yale University Press, 1994, pp. 30–9).

The Field of Cultural Production. Essays on Art and Literature (ed. R. Johnson), Cambridge, Polity Press, 1993, 322 pp.; [collected texts translated in English: 'The Field of Cultural Production, or: The Economic World Reversed' [1983]; 'La production de la croyance: contribution à une économie des biens symboliques' [1977]; 'Le marché des biens symboliques' [1977]; 'Is the Structure of *Sentimental Education* an Instance of Social Self-analysis?' (unpublished – Christian Gauss Seminars in Criticism, Princeton, 1986); 'Field of Power, Literary Field and Habitus' (unpublished – Christian Gauss Seminars in Criticism, Princeton, 1986); 'Principles for a Sociology of Cultural Works' [1992]; 'Flaubert's Point of View' [1988]; 'Eléments d'une théorie sociologique de la perception artistique' [1968]; 'L'institutionnalisation de l'anomie' [1987]; 'The Historical Genesis of a Pure Aesthetic' [1987]].

La misère du monde, Paris, Éd. du Seuil, 1993, 948 pp. (et al.); [collected texts: 'L'espace des points de vue', pp. 9–11; 'La rue des jonquilles', pp. 13–32; 'L'ordre des choses', pp. 81–99; 'Effets de lieu', pp. 159–67; 'La démission de l'Etat', pp. 219–28; 'Une mission impossible', pp. 229–44; La mauvaise foi de l'institution', pp. 245–7; 'Porte-à-faux et double contrainte, pp. 249–56 (with G. Balazs);

'La fin d'un monde', pp. 407–11; 'Vu d'en bas', pp. 433–45; 'Un équilibre si fragile', pp. 477–86 (with G. Balazs); 'Suspendue à un fil', pp. 487–98; 'Une vie perdue', pp. 519–31; 'Les exclus de l'intérieur', pp. 597–603 (with P. Champagne); 'Oh! Les beaux jours', pp. 605–20; 'Les contradictions de l'héritage', pp. 711–18; 'Le rêve des familles', pp. 795–807; 'Comprendre', pp. 903–39; 'Post-scriptum', pp. 941–9]. (Extract: 'Comprendre'), published in English as 'Understanding' (tr. B. Fowler). *Theory, Culture and Society*, 13(2) mai 1996, p. 17–37.

Libre-échange, Paris, Éd. du Seuil, 1994, 147 pp. (with H. Haacke). Published in English as *Free Exchange*, Cambridge–Oxford, Polity Press–Blackwell Publishers, 1995, 144 pp.

Raisons pratiques. Sur la théorie de l'action, Paris, Éd. du Seuil, 1994, 252 pp.; Paris, Éd. du Seuil [1996], 248 pp.; [collected texts: 'Espace social et espace symbolique' (unpublished – Todaï, 1989); 'Le nouveau capital' (unpublished – Todaï, 1989); 'La variante "soviétique" et le capital politique' (unpublished – East Berlin, 1989); 'Espace social et champ du pouvoir' (unpublished – Madison, 1989), 'Pour une science des oeuvres', English trans., 'Principles of a Sociology of Cultural Works', in S. Kemal, I. Gaskell (eds), *Explanation and Value in the Arts*, [1992]; 'L'illusion biographique' [1986]; 'La double rupture', English trans., '*Animadversiones in Mertonem*', in J. Clark, C. Modgil et S. Modgil (eds), in *Robert K. Merton: Consensus and Controversy* [1990]; 'Esprits d'Etat' [1993]; 'L'esprit de famille'; 'Un acte désintéressé est-il possible?' (unpublished – Lyon, 1988); '*Entretien sur la pratique, le temps et l'histoire*' [1989]; 'L'economie des biens symboliques', (unpublished – Lyon, 1994); 'Le point de vue scolastique' published in English as 'The Scholastic Point of View' [1990]; 'Un fondement paradoxal de la morale', published in English as 'Towards a Policy of Morality in Politics', in W. R. Shea, A. Spadafora (eds), *From the Twilight of Probability. Ethics and Politics* [1992]].

Sur la télévision, Paris, Liber-Raisons d'agir, 1996, 95 pp. Published in English as *On Television*, New York, New Press, 1998.

Méditatons pascaliennes, Paris, Éd. du Seuil, 1997, 316 pp. (Extract: 'La double vérité du don', pp. 229–240), published in English as 'Marginalia – Some Additional Notes on the Gift' (tr. R. Nice), in A. D. Schrift, *The Logic of the Gift*, New York-London, Routledge, 1997, pp. 231–41.

Les usages sociaux de la science. Pour une sociologie clinique du champ scientifique, Paris, INRA, 1997, 79 pp.

Contre-Feux: Propos pour servir à la résistance contre l'invasion néo-liberale, Paris, Liber-Raisons d'agir, 1998; published in English as *Acts of Resistance: Against the Tyranny of the Market*, New York, New Press, 1999.

La domination masculine, Paris, Éd. du Seuil, 1998, 142 pp.

Practical Reason (English translation of *Raisons Pratiques*), Cambridge, Polity Press, 1998.

Articles

'Tartuffe ou le drame de la foi et de la mauvaise foi', *Revue de la Méditerranée*, no. 4–5 (92–93) (July–October 1959), pp. 453–8.

'La logique interne de la civilisation algérienne traditionnelle', in *Le sous-développement en Algérie*, Alger, Secrétariat social, 1959, pp. 40–51.

'Le choc des civilisations', in *Le sous-développement en Algérie*, Alger, Secrétariat social, 1959, pp. 52–64.

'Guerre et mutation sociale en Algérie', *Études méditerranéennes*, 7 (Spring 1960), pp. 25–37.

'Révolution dans la révolution', *Esprit*, 1, January 1961, pp. 27–40.

'De la guerre révolutionnaire à la révolution', in *L'Algérie de demain*, ed. F. Perroux, Paris, PUF, 1962, pp. 5–13.

'Les relations entre les sexes dans la société paysanne', *Les temps modernes*, 195 (August 1962), pp. 307–31.

'Célibat et condition paysanne', *Études rurales*, 5–6 (April–September 1962), pp. 32–136.

'La hantise du chômage chez l'ouvrier algérien. Prolétariat et système colonial', *Sociologie du travail*, 4 (1962), pp. 313–31.

'Les sous-prolétaires algériens', *Les temps modernes*, 199 (December 1962), pp. 1030–51. Published in English as 'The Algerian subprole-tariat', in *Man, State and Society in the Contemporary Maghrib*, I. W. Zartman ed., London, Pall Mall Press, 1973.

'La société traditionnelle. Attitude à l'égard du temps et conduite économique', *Sociologie du travail*, 1 (January–March 1963), pp. 24–44.

'Sociologues des mythologies et mythologies de sociologues', *Les temps modernes*, 211 (December 1963), pp. 998–1021 (with J. C. Passeron).

'The attitude of the Algerian peasant toward time' (tr. G. E. Williams), in *Mediterranean Countrymen*, ed. J. Pitt-Rivers, Paris and The Hague, Mouton, 1964, pp. 55–72.

'Paysans déracinés, bouleversements morphologiques et changements culturels en Algérie', *Études rurales*, 12 (January–March 1964), pp. 56–94 (with A. Sayad).

'Les musées et leurs publics', *L'expansion de la recherche scientifique*, 21 (December 1964), pp. 26–8.

'Le paysan et la photographie', *Revue française de sociologie*, VI, no. 2 (April–June 1965), pp. 164–74 (with M. C. Bourdieu).

'Le musée et son public', *L'information d'histoire de l'art*, 3 (May–June 1965), pp. 120–2.

'The Sentiment of Honour in Kabyle Society' (tr. P. Sherrard), in *Honour and Shame. The Values of Mediterranean Society*, ed. J. G. Peristiany, London, Weidenfeld and Nicholson, 1965, pp. 191–241.

'Langage et rapport au langage dans la situation pédagogique' (with J. C. Passeron), in *Rapport pédagogique et communication*, ed. P. Bourdieu, J. C. Passeron, M. de Saint Martin, Paris and The Hague, Éd. Mouton, Cahiers du Centre de sociologie européenne, 2, 1965, pp. 9–36; also, in *Les temps modernes*, 232 (September 1965), pp. 435–66. Published in English as 'Language and Pedagogical Situation' (tr. R. Teese), *Melbourne Working Papers 1980*, D. McCallum, U. Ozolins (eds), Melbourne, University of Melbourne, Department of Education, 1980, pp. 36–77.

'Les étudiants et la langue d'enseignement' (with J. C. Passeron et M. de Saint Martin), in *Rapport pédagogique et communication*, P. Bourdieu, J. C. Passeron, M. de Saint Martin (eds), Paris and The Hague, Éd. Mouton, Cahiers du Centre de sociologie européenne, 2, 1965, pp. 37–69. Published in English as 'Students and the Language of Teaching' (tr. R. Teese), *Melbourne Working Papers 1980*, ed. D. McCallum, U. Ozolins, Melbourne, University of Melbourne, Department of Education, 1980, pp. 78–124.

'Les utilisateurs de la bibliothèque universitaire de Lille' (with M. de Saint Martin), in *Rapport pédagogique et communication*, ed. P. Bourdieu, J. C. Passeron, M. de Saint Martin, Paris and The Hague, Éd. Mouton, Cahiers du Centre de sociologie européenne, 2, 1965, pp. 109–20.

'Différences et distinctions', in Darras, *Le partage des bénéfices, expansion et inégalités en France*, Paris, Éd. de Minuit, 1966, pp. 117–29.

'La fin d'un malthusianisme?' in Darras, *Le partage des bénéfices, expansion et inégalités en France*, Paris, Éd. de Minuit, 1966, pp. 135–54 (with A. Darbel).

'La transmission de l'héritage culturel', in Darras, *Le partage des bénéfices, expansion et inégalités en France*, Paris, Éd. de Minuit, 1966, pp. 383–420.

'Comment la culture vient aux paysans?', *Paysans*, 62 (October–November 1966), pp. 6–20.

'Une étude sociologique d'actualité: les étudiants en sciences sociales', *Revue de l'enseignement supérieur*, 4 (1966), pp. 199–208 (with L. Boltanski, R. Castel, M. Lemaire, M. de Saint Martin).

'Condition de classe et position de classe', *Archives européennes de sociologie*, VII, no. 2, 1966, pp. 201–23.

'L'école conservatrice, les inégalités devant l'école et devant la culture', *Revue française de sociologie*, VII, no. 3 (July–September 1966), pp. 325–47. Published in English as 'The school as a conservative force: scholastic and cultural inequalities' (tr. J. C. Whitehouse), in *Contemporary Research in the Sociology of Education*, ed. John Eggleston, London, Methuen, 1974, pp. 32–46; also, in *Schooling and Capitalism. A Sociological reader*, ed. R. Dale *et al.*, London, Routledge/The Open University Press, 1976, pp. 192–200.

'Une sociologie de l'action est-elle possible?', *Revue française de sociologie*, VII, no. 4 (October–December 1966), pp. 508–17 (with J. D. Reynaud). Published in English as 'Is a Sociology of Action Possible?', in *Positivism and Sociology*, ed. A. Giddens, London, Heinemann Educational Books Ltd., 1974.

'Champ intellectuel et projet créateur', *Les temps modernes*, Problèmes du structuralisme, 246 (November, 1966), pp. 865–906. Published in English as 'Intellectual field and creative project' (tr. S. France), *Social Science Information*, VIII, no. 2 (April 1969), pp. 89–119; also, in *Knowledge and Control: New Directions for the Sociology of Education*, ed. Michael F. D. Young, London, Collier-Macmillan, 1971, pp. 161–88.

'Les paradoxes et l'automate', *Coopération technique*, 51–52–53 (April 1967), pp. 101–4.

'La communication entre professeurs et étudiants', *Travail social*, Communications humaines, Paris, Fédération française des travailleurs sociaux, 1966–1967, pp. 133–6.

'La comparabilité des systèmes d'enseignement', in *Education, développement et démocratie*, ed. R. Castel and J. C. Passeron, Paris and The Hague, Mouton, Cahiers du Centre de sociologie européenne, 4, 1967, pp. 21–58 (with J. C. Passeron).

'Sociology and Philosophy in France since 1945: Death and Resurrection of a Philosophy without Subject', *Social Research*, XXXIV, no. 1 (Spring 1967), pp. 162–212 (with J. C. Passeron).

'L'image de l'image', *L'année 66*, Catalogue de l'exposition Bernard Rancillac, Paris, Galerie Blumenthal-Mommaton, February 1967.

'L'examen d'une illusion', *Revue française de sociologie*, IX, special number, Sociologie de l'éducation II, 1968, pp. 227–53 (with J. C. Passeron).

'Éléments d'une théorie sociologique de la perception artistique', *Revue internationale des sciences sociales*, Les arts dans la société, XX, no. 4, (1968), pp. 640–64; also, *Noroit*, no. 134 (January 1969), pp. 3–14; 135 (February 1969), pp. 5–14. Published in English as 'Outline of a sociological theory of art perception', *International Social Science Journal*, XX (Winter 1968), pp. 589–612; also, in P. Bourdieu, *The Field of Cultural Production. Essays on Art and Literature*, Cambridge, Polity Press, 1993, pp. 215–37;

'Structuralism and Theory of Sociological Knowledge', (tr. A. Zanotti-Karp), *Social Research*, XXXV, no. 4 (Winter 1968), pp. 681–706.

'Le système des fonctions du système d'enseignement', in *Education in Europe*, ed. M. A. Mattÿssen and C. E. Vervoort, The Hague, Mouton, 1969, pp. 181–9.

'Sociologie de la perception esthétique', in *Les sciences humaines et l'oeuvre d'art*, Bruxelles, La connaissance S. A., 1969, pp. 161–76, 251–4.

'La maison kabyle ou le monde renversé', in *Echanges et communications. Mélanges offerts à Claude Lévi-Strauss à l'occasion de son 60 anniversaire*, ed. J. Pouillion and P. Maranda, Paris and The Hague, Mouton, 1970, pp. 739–58. Published in English as 'The Berber House or the World Reversed', *Social Science Information*, IX, no. 2 (April 1970), pp. 151–70; also, 'The Berber House', in *Rules and Meanings. The Anthropology of Everyday Knowledge. Selected*

Readings. ed. Mary Douglas, Harmondsworth (Middlesex), Penguin, 1973, pp. 98–110.

'L'excellence scolaire et les valeurs du système d'enseignement française', *Annales*, XXV, no. 1, January–February 1970, pp. 147–75 (with M. de Saint Martin). Published in English as 'Scholastic excellence and the values of the educational system' (tr. J. C. Whitehouse), in *Contemporary Research in the Sociology of Education*, ed. John Eggleston, London, Methuen, 1974, pp. 338–71.

'Champ du pouvoir, champ intellectuel et habitus de classe', *Scolies*, Cahier de recherches de l'Ecole normale supérieure, 1 (1971), pp. 7–26.

'Une interprétation de la théorie de la religion selon Max Weber', *Archives européennes de sociologie*, XII, no. 1 (1971), pp. 3–21. Published in English as (modified version), 'Legitimation and Structured Interests in Weber's Sociology of Religion' (tr. Ch. Turner), in *Max Weber. Rationality and Modernity*, ed. S. Whimster and S. Lash, London, Allen & Unwin, 1987, pp. 119–36.

'Genèse et structure du champ religieux', *Revue française de sociologie*, XII, no. 3 (1971), pp. 295–334.

'Disposition esthétique et compétence artistique', *Les temps modernes*, 295 (February 1971), pp. 1345–78.

'Formes et degrés de la conscience du chômage dans l'Algérie coloniale', *Manpower and Unemployment Research in Africa*, vol. 4, no. 1 (April 1971), pp. 36–44.

'Le marché des biens symboliques', *L'année sociologique*, vol. 22 (1971), pp. 49–126. Published in English as 'The Market of Symbolic Goods' (tr. R. Swyer), *Poetics* (Amsterdam), vol. 14, n. 1/2 (April 1985), pp. 13–44; also, in P. Bourdieu, *The Field of Cultural Production. Essays on Art and Literature*, Cambridge, Polity Press, 1993, pp. 112–41.

'La défense du corps', *Information sur les sciences sociales*, X, no. 4 (August 1971), pp. 45–86 (with L. Boltanski, P. Maldidier).

'The Thinkable and the Unthinkable', *Times Literary Supplement*, 15 October 1971, pp. 1255–6.

'Composition sociale de la population étudiante et chances d'accès à l'enseignement supérieur', *Orientations*, 41 (January 1972), pp. 89–102 (with C. Grignon, J. C. Passeron).

'Les doxosophes', *Minuit*, 1 (November 1972), pp. 26–45.

'Les stratégies matrimoniales dans le système de reproduction', *Annales*, 4–5 (July–October 1972), pp. 1105–27. Published in English as 'Marriage Strategies as Strategies of Social Reproduction' (tr. E. Forster), in *Family and Society*, Selections from the Annales, ed. R. Forster and O. Ranum, Baltimore–London, The Johns Hopkins University Press, 1976, pp. 117–44.

'Classes et classement', *Minuit*, 5 (September 1973), pp. 22–4.

'Les stratégies de reconversion. Les classes sociales et le système d'enseignement', *Information sur les sciences sociales*, XII, no. 5 (October 1973), pp. 61–113 (with L. Boltanski, M. de Saint Martin). Published in English as 'Changes in social structure and changes in the demand for education', in *Contemporary Europe. Social Structures and Cultural Patterns*, ed. S. Giner and M. Scotford-Archer, London, Routledge and Kegan Paul, 1977, pp. 197–227 (with L. Boltanski).

'Avenir de classe et causalité du probable', Revue française de sociologie, XV, no. 1 (January–March 1974), pp. 3–42.

'Les fractions de la classe dominante et les modes d'appropriation des oeuvres d'art', *Information sur les sciences sociales*, XIII, no. 3 (June 1974), pp. 7–32.

'Méthode scientifique et hiérarchie sociale des objets', *Actes de la recherche en sciences sociales*, 1 (January 1975), pp. 4–6.

'Le couturier et sa griffe. Contribution à une théorie de la magie', *Actes de la recherche en sciences sociales*, 1 (January 1975), pp. 7–36 (with Y. Delsaut).

'L'invention de la vie d'artiste', *Actes de la recherche en sciences sociales*, 2 (March 1975), pp. 67–94. Published in English as 'The Invention of the Artist's Life' (tr. E. R. Koch), *Yale French Studies*, 73, 1987, pp. 75–103.

'Les catégories de l'entendement professoral', *Actes de la recherche en sciences sociales*, 3 (May 1975), pp. 68–93 (with M. de Saint Martin). Published in English as 'The Categories of Professional Judgement', in P. Bourdieu, *Homo academicus*, London, Polity Press, 1988, pp. 194–225.

'La spécificité du champ scientifique et les conditions sociales du progrès de la raison', *Sociologie et sociétés* (Montréal), VII, no. 1 (May 1975), pp. 91–118; also, Le champ scientifique, *Actes de la recherche en sciences sociales*, 2–3 (June 1976), pp. 88–104. Published in English as 'The specificity of the scientific field and the social conditions of the progress of reason' (tr. R. Nice), *Social Science*

Information, XIV, no. 6 (December 1975), pp. 19–47; also, in *French Sociology. Rupture and Renewal since 1968*, ed. C. C. Lemert, New York, Columbia University Press, 1981, pp. 257–292; also, 'The Peculiar History of Scientific Reason' (tr. C. Newman, L. Wacquant), *Sociological Forum* (6)1 (March 1991), pp. 3–26.

'Le titre et le poste. Rapports entre le système de production et le système de reproduction', *Actes de la recherche en sciences sociales*, 2 (March 1975), pp. 95–107 (with L. Boltanski). Published in English as 'Formal Qualifications and Occupational Hierarchies: the Relationship Between the Production System and the Reproduction System' (tr. R. Nice), in *Reorganizing Education*, Sage Annual Review, Social and Educational Change, vol. 1, 1977, pp. 61–9; also, 'The Educational System and the Economy: Titles and Jobs', in *French Sociology, Rupture and Renewal since 1968*, ed. C. C. Lemert, New York, Columbia University Press, 1981, pp. 141–51.

'Le fétichisme de la langue', *Actes de la recherche en sciences sociales*, 4 (July 1975), pp. 2–32 (with L. Boltanski).

'La critique du discours lettré', *Actes de la recherche en sciences sociales*, 5–6 (November 1975), pp. 4–8.

'L'ontologie politique de Martin Heidegger', *Actes de la recherche en sciences sociales*, 5–6 (November 1975), pp. 109–56; also, *L'ontologie politique de Martin Heidegger*, Paris, Éd. de Minuit, 1988. Published in English as *The Political Ontology of Martin Heidegger* (tr. P. Collier), Cambridge, Polity Press, 1991, 138 pp.

'Le langage autorisé. Note sur les conditions sociales de l'efficacité du discours rituel', *Actes de la recherche en sciences sociales* 5–6 (November 1975), pp. 183–90; also, modified version, 'Le langage autorisé: les conditions sociales de l'efficacité du discours rituel', in *Ce que parler veut dire*, Paris, Fayard, 1982, pp. 103–19.

'La lecture de Marx: quelques remarques critiques à propos de 'Quelques remarques critiques à propos de *Lire le Capital*', *Actes de la recherche en sciences sociales*, 5–6 (November 1975), pp. 65–79; also, modified version, 'Le discours d'importance. Quelques réflexions sociologiques sur "Quelques remarques critiques à propos de *Lire Le Capital*"', in *Ce que parler veut dire*, Paris, Fayard, pp. 207–26.

'Le sens pratique', *Actes de la recherche en sciences sociales*, 1 (February 1976), pp. 43–86.

'Les modes de domination', *Actes de la recherche en sciences sociales*, 2–3 (June 1976), pp. 122–32.

'La production de l'idéologie dominante', *Actes de la recherche en sciences sociales*, 2–3 (June 1976), pp. 3–73 (with L. Boltanski).

'Un jeu chinois. Notes pour une critique sociale du jugement', *Actes de la recherche en sciences sociales*, 4 (August 1976), pp. 91–101.

'Anatomie du goût', *Actes de la recherche en sciences sociales*, 5 (October 1976), pp. 2–112 (with M. de Saint Martin).

'Questions de politique', *Actes de la recherche en sciences sociales*, 16 (September 1977), pp. 55–89.

'Une classe objet', *Actes de la recherche en sciences sociales*, 17–18 (November 1977), pp. 1–5.

'La production de la croyance: contribution à une économie des biens symboliques', *Actes de la recherche en sciences sociales*, 13 (February 1977), pp. 3–43. Published in English as 'The production of belief: contribution to an economy of symbolic goods' (tr. R. Nice), *Media, Culture and Society*, vol 2, no. 3 (July 1980), pp. 261–93; also, in *Media, Culture and Society, A Critical Reader*, London, Sage Publications, 1986, pp. 131–63; also, in P. Bourdieu, *The Field of Cultural Production. Essays on Art and Literature*, Cambridge, Polity Press, 1993, pp. 74–111.

'Remarques provisoires sur la perception sociale du corps', *Actes de la recherche en sciences sociales*, 14 (April 1977), pp. 51–4.

'Capital symbolique et classes sociales', *L'arc*, Georges Duby, 72 (1978), pp. 13–19.

'Le patronat', *Actes de la recherche en sciences sociales*, 20–21 (March–April 1978), pp. 3–82 (with M. de Saint Martin).

'Sur l'objectivation participante. Réponses à quelques objections', *Actes de la recherche en sciences sociales*, 23 (September 1978), pp. 67–9.

'Dialogue sur la poésie orale', *Actes de la recherche en sciences sociales*, 23 (September 1978), pp. 51–66 (with M. Mammeri).

'Titres et quartiers de noblesse culturelle. Eléments d'une critique sociale du jugement esthétique', *Ethnologie française* VIII, no. 2–3 (March–September 1978), pp. 107–44 (with M. de Saint Martin).

'Classement, déclassement, reclassement', *Actes de la recherche en sciences sociales*, 24 (November 1978), pp. 2–22. Published in English as Epilogue, in P. Bourdieu, *The Inheritors. French Students and Their Relation to Culture*, Chicago, London, The University of Chicago Press, 1979, pp. 77–97.

'Les trois états du capital culturel', *Actes de la recherche en sciences sociales*, 30 (November 1979), pp. 3–6.

'Le capital social. Notes provisoires', *Actes de la recherche en sciences sociales*, 31 (January 1980), pp. 2–3.

'Lettre à Paolo Fossati à propos de la *Storia dell'arte italiana*', *Actes de la recherche en sciences sociales*, 31 (January 1980), pp. 90–2.

'Le mort saisit le vif. Les relations entre l'histoire réifiée et l'histoire incorporée', *Actes de la recherche en sciences sociales*, 32–33 (April–June 1980), pp. 3–14.

'Et si on parlait de l'Afghanistan?' (with Pierre and Micheline Cent-livres), *Actes de la recherche en sciences sociales*, 34 (September 1980), pp. 2–16.

'Le Nord et le Midi'. Contribution à une analyse de l'effet Montesquieu, *Actes de la recherche en sciences sociales*, 35 (November 1980), pp. 21–5; also, modified version, 'La rhétorique de la scientificité. Contribution à une analyse de l'effet Montesquieu', in *Ce que parler veut dire*, Paris, Fayard, 1982, pp. 227–39.

'L'identité et la représentation. Eléments pour une réflexion critique sur l'idée de région', *Actes de la recherche en sciences sociales*, 35 (November 1980), pp. 63–72.

'Où sont les terroristes?', *Esprit*, 11–12 (November–December 1980), pp. 253–8.

'Sartre' (tr. R. Nice), *London Review of Books*, vol. 2, no. 22 (20 November–3 December 1980), pp. 11–12.

'La représentation politique. Eléments pour une théorie du champ politique', *Actes de la recherche en sciences sociales*, 36–37 (February–March 1981), pp. 3–24. Published in English as 'Political Representation: Elements for a Theory of the Political Field', in *Language and Symbolic Power*, Cambridge, Polity Press, 1991, pp. 171–202.

'Décrire et prescrire. Note sur les conditions de possibilité et les limites de l'efficacité politique', *Actes de la recherche en sciences sociales*, 38 (May 1981), pp. 69–73; also, modified version in *Ce que parler veut dire*, Paris, Fayard, 1982, pp. 149–61.

'Epreuve scolaire et consécration sociale. Les classes préparatoires aux Grandes écoles', *Actes de la recherche en sciences sociales*, 39 (September 1981), pp. 3–70.

'Pour une sociologie de la perception', *Actes de la recherche en sciences sociales*, 40 (November 1981), pp. 3–9 (with Y. Delsaut).

'Men and Machines', in *Advances in social theory and methodology. Toward an integration of micro- and macro-sociologies*, K. Knorr-Cetina, ed. A. V. Cicourel, Boston, London, Henley, Routledge & Kegan Paul, 1981, pp. 304–17.

'La sainte famille. L'épiscopat français dans le champ du pouvoir', *Actes de la recherche en sciences sociales*, 44–45 (November 1982), pp. 2–53 (with M. de Saint Martin).

'The Philosophical Establishment' (tr. K. McLaughlin), in *Philosophy in France Today*, ed. A. Montefiore, Cambridge, Cambridge University Press, 1983, pp. 1–8.

'Le changement linguistique' (with William Labov and Pierre Encrevé), *Actes de la recherche en sciences sociales*, 46 (March 1983), pp. 67–71.

'Vous avez dit "populaire"?', *Actes de la recherche en sciences sociales*, 46 (March 1983), pp. 98–105. Published in English as 'Did You Say "Popular"?', in P. Bourdieu, *Language and Symbolic Power*, Cambridge, Polity Press, 1991, pp. 90–102.

'Mai 68', *Lire*, 93 (May 1983), p. 22.

'La discipline', *Contact*, special number, 'Exercer l'autorité aujourd'hui', no. 25 (June 1983), pp. 25–6.

'Les sciences sociales et la philosophie', *Actes de la recherche en sciences sociales*, 47–48 (June 1983), pp. 45–52; also, 'L'oubli de l'histoire', in *Méditations pascaliennes*, Paris, Éd. du Seuil, 1997, pp. 54–9.

'The Field of Cultural Production or: the Economic World Reversed' (tr. R. Nice), *Poetics* (Amsterdam), vol. 12, no. 4–5 (November 1983), pp. 311–56; also, in P. Bourdieu, *The Field of Cultural Production. Essays on Art and Literature*, Cambridge, Polity Press, 1993, pp. 29–73; also, in *The Polity Reader in Social Theory*, Cambridge, Polity Press, 1994, pp. 50–65.

'The Forms of Capital' (tr. R. Nice), in *Handbook of Theory and Research for the Sociology of Education*, ed. John G. Richardson, New York, Westport (Connecticut), London, Greenwood Press, 1986, pp. 241–58.

'La perception du monde social: une question de mots?' *Actes de la recherche en sciences sociales*, 52–53 (June 1984), pp. 13–14.

'La représentation de la position sociale', *Actes de la recherche en sciences sociales*, 52–53 (June 1984), pp. 14–15.

'Le hit-parade des intellectuel français, ou qui sera juge de la légitimité des juges?', *Actes de la recherche en sciences sociales*, 52–53 (June 1984), pp. 95–100.

'Le champ littéraire. Préalables critiques et principes de méthode', *Lendemains* (Berlin–Cologne), IX, no. 36 (1984), pp. 5–20.

'Capital et marché linguistiques', *Linguistische Berichte* (Constance), no. 90 (1984), pp. 3–24.

'La dernière instance', in *Le siècle de Kafka*, Paris, Centre Georges Pompidou, 1984, pp. 268–70.

'Consommation culturelle', in *Encyclopaedia Universalis*, new edition, 1984, t. 2, 'Art', pp. 779–82.

'Remarques à propos de la valeur scientifique et des effets politiques des enquêtes d'opinion', *Pouvoirs*, 'Les sondages', 33 (April 1985), pp. 131–9; also, 'Le sondage, une "science" sans savant', in P. Bourdieu, *Choses dites*, Paris, Éd. de Minuit, 1987, pp. 217–24.

'Quand les Canaques prennent la parole', *Actes de la recherche en sciences sociales*, 56 (March 1985), pp. 69–83 (with A. Bensa).

'Effet de champ et effet de corps', *Actes de la recherche en sciences sociales*, 59 (September 1985), p. 73.

'Dialogue à propos de l'histoire culturelle' (with R. Chartier and R. Darnton), *Actes de la recherche en sciences sociales*, 59 (September 1985), pp. 86–93.

'Existe-t-il une littérature belge? Limites d'un champ et frontières politiques', *Etudes de lettres* (Lausanne), 4 (October–December 1985), pp. 3–6.

'The Genesis of the Concepts of Habitus and Field' (tr. Ch. Newman), *Sociocriticism* (Pittsburgh Pa, Montpellier), II, no. 2 (December 1985), pp. 11–24.

'La science et l'actualité', *Actes de la recherche en sciences sociales*, 61 (March 1986), pp. 2–3.

'L'illusion biographique', *Actes de la recherche en sciences sociales*, 63–63 (June 1986), pp. 69–72. Published in English as 'The Biographical Illusion' (tr. Y. Winkin, W. Leeds-Hurwitz), *Working Papers and Proceedings of the Center for Psychosocial Studies* (Chicago), 14 (1987), pp. 1–7.

'Nécessiter', *L'Herne*, Cahier Francis Ponge, Paris, Éditions de l'Herne, June 1986, pp. 434–7.

'La force du droit. Eléments pour une sociologie du champ juridique', *Actes de la recherche en sciences sociales*, 64 (September 1986), pp. 5–19. Published in English as 'The Force of Law: Toward a Sociology of the Juridical Field' (tr. R. Terdiman), *Hastings Law Journal*, vol. 38, no. 5 (July 1987), pp. 814–53.

'Les mésaventures de l'amateur', in *Eclats/Boulez*, ed. R. Samuel, Paris, Éditions du Centre Georges Pompidou, 1986, pp. 74–5.

'An Antinomy in the Notion of Collective Protest', in *Development Democracy, and the Art of Trespassing: Essays in Honor of Albert O. Hirschmann*, ed. A. Foxley, M. S. McPherson, G. O'Donnell, Notre Dame (Indiana), University of Notre Dame Press, 1986, Paperback edition, 1988, pp. 301–2.

'L'institutionalisation de l'anomie', *Les Cahiers du Musée national d'art moderne*, 19–20 (June 1987), pp. 6–19. Published in English as 'Manet and the Institutionalization of Anomie', in P. Bourdieu, *The Field of Cultural Production. Essays on Art and Literature*, Cambridge, Polity Press, 1993, pp. 238–53.

'Agrégation et ségrégation. Le champ des grandes écoles et le champ du pouvoir', *Actes de la recherche en sciences sociales*, 69 (September 1987), pp. 2–50 (with M. de Saint Martin).

'Variations et invariants. Eléments pour une histoire structurale du champ des grandes écoles', *Actes de la recherche en sciences sociales*, 70 (November 1987), pp. 3–30.

'The Historical Genesis of a Pure Aesthetic' (tr. Ch. Newman), *The Journal of Aesthetics and Art Criticism*, vol. XLVI, Special Issue, 1987, pp. 201–10; also, in *Analytic Aesthetics*, ed. R. Shusterman, Oxford and New York, Basil Blackwell, 1989; also, in P. Bourdieu, *The Field of Cultural Production. Essays on Art and Literature*, Cambridge, Polity Press, 1993, pp. 254–66.

'Flaubert's Point of View' (tr. P. Parkhurst Ferguson), *Critical Inquiry*, 14 (Spring 1988), pp. 539–62; also, in P. Bourdieu, *The Field of Cultural Production. Essays on Art and Literature*, Cambridge, Polity Press, 1993, pp. 192–211.

'Penser la politique', *Actes de la recherche en sciences sociales*, 71–72 (March 1988), pp. 2–3.

'La vertu civile', *Le Monde*, 16 September 1988, pp. 1–2.

'Vive la crise! For Heterodoxy in Social Science', *Theory and Society*, 17 (1988), pp. 773–7.

'L'opinion publique', in 50 *Idées qui ébranlent le monde. Dictionnaire de la* Glasnost, Paris, Payot, 1989, pp. 204–6 (with P. Champagne).

'Mouloud Mammeri ou la colline retrouvée', *Le Monde*, 3 (March 1989); also, *Awal*, 5 (November 1989), pp. 1–3.

'Toward a Reflexive Sociology. A Workshop with Pierre Boudieu', *Sociological Theory*, (7)1 (Spring 1989), pp. 1–72 (introd. and tr. L. Wacquant); also, abridged version, in S. P. Turner (ed.), *Social Theory and Sociology*, Oxford-Cambridge, Blackwell, 1996, pp. 213–28; also 'The Purpose of Reflexive Sociology', in *An Invitation to Reflexive Sociology* [1992].

'Reproduction interdite. La dimension symbolique de la domination économique', *Études rurales*, 113–14 (January–June 1989), pp. 15–36; also, in Borut Telban (ed.), 'Multiple Identities', *Anthropological Notebooks* (Slovenia), II(1) (1996).

'Intérêt et désintéressement', *Cahiers de recherche*, Université Lumière-Lyon 2, no. 7 (September 1989), 67 pp.; 2nd edn 1993, 59 pp.; also, in *Methodologica*, Bruxelles-Cordoba, 2 (May 1992), pp. 19–36; also 'Un acte désintéressé est-il possible?' in *Raisons pratiques* [1994].

'Le beau rôle. Une lecture de la *Promenade au phare* de Virginia Woolf', *Liber*, 1 (October 1989), pp. 60–1.

'The Corporatism of the Universal: the Role of Intellectuals in the Modern World', *Telos*, 81 (Fall 1989), pp. 99–110.

'Comment l'innovation est-elle possible?' in Rapport du colloque sur 'Les grandes recontres médicales', Paris, 1989, pp. 35–54.

'Scientific Field and Scientific Thought' (tr. L. Wacquant), in 'Author meets Critics: Reactions to "Theory in Anthropology since the Sixties"', in S. B. Ortner (ed.), *Transformations*, Ann Arbor, University of Michigan, CSST Working Papers, November 1989, pp. 84–94.

'L'histoire se lève à l'Est', *Liber*, 2 (December 1989), p. 3.

'Aspirant philosophe. Un point de vue sur le champ universitaire dans les années 50', *Les enjeux philosophiques des années 50*, Paris, Éd. du Centre Pompidou, 1989, pp. 15–24; also, 'Confessions impersonnelles', in P. Bourdieu, *Méditations pascaliennes*, Paris, Éd. du Seuil, 1997, pp. 44–53.

'Les conditions sociales de la circulation internationale des idées', *Romanistische Zeitschrift für Literaturgeschlichte/Cahiers d'histoire des littératures romanes*, 14th annual, 1–2, 1990, pp. 1–10.

'Animadversiones in Mertonem', in J. Clark, C. Modgil and S. Modgil (ed.), in *Robert K. Merton: Consensus and Controversy*, London-New York, Falmer Press, 1990, pp. 297–301.

'Un signe des temps', *Actes de la recherche en sciences sociales*, (L'économie de la maison), 81–82 (March 1990), pp. 2–5; 'Un placement de père de famille', *ibid.*, pp. 6–33 (with S. Bouhedja, R. Christin, C. Givry); 'Un contrat sous contrainte', *ibid.*, pp. 34–51 (with S. Boujedja, C. Givry); 'Le sens de la propriété', *ibid.*, pp. 52–64 (with M. de Saint Martin); 'La construction du marché', *ibid.*, pp. 65–85 (with R. Christin); 'Droit et passe droit', *ibid.*, pp. 86–96. Published in English (as extract of 'Le sens de la propriété'), 'The Meaning of Property: Real Estate, Class Position, and the Ideology of Home Ownership', in M. Ryan, A. Gordon. *Body Politics. Disease, Desire, and the Family*, Boulder-San Francisco-Oxford, Westview-Press, 1994, pp. 45–71.

'La théorie du champ dans l'espace des possibles théoriques' (Tokyo, October 1989), *Gendaï Shiso*, March 1990, pp. 204–19.

'Le sociologue accoucheur', *Actes*, Caisse des Dépôts, 1 (August 1990), p. 8.

'Academic Order and Social Order. Preface to the 1990 edition' (tr. L. Wacquant), *Reproduction in Education, Society and Culture*, London, Sage Publications, new edition 1990, pp. vii–xiii.

'La domination masculine', *Actes de la recherche en sciences sociales*, 84 (September 1990), pp. 2–31.

'The Scholastic Point of View' (tr. L. Wacquant), *Cultural Anthropology*, no. 5/4 (November 1990), pp. 380–91.

'Contre les divisions scolastiques', followed by 'Questions à Pierre Bourdieu', in *L'Université au défi de la culture*, Toulouse, ADDOCC Midi-Pyrénées, April 1991, pp. 31–57.

'Thinking about Limits' (tr. R. Boyne), *Theory, Culture and Society*, 9 (1992), pp. 37–49; also, in M. Featherstone (ed.), *Cultural Theory and Cultural Change*, London, Sage Publications, 1992, pp. 37–49.

'Le champ littéraire', *Actes de la recherche en sciences sociales*, 89 (1991), pp. 3–46.

'Epilogue: On the Possibility of a Field of World Sociology' (tr. L. Wacquant), in P. Bourdieu, J. S. Coleman (ed.), *Social Theory for a Changing Society*, 1991, pp. 373–87.

'Le démontage impie de la fiction: l'esthétique négative de Stéphane Mallarmé', *Stanford Slavic Studies* (Literature, Culture, and Society in the Modern Age, in honor of Joseph Frank), 1991, pp. 145–50.

'Les juristes, gardiens de l'hypocrisie collective', in F. Chazel and J. Commaille (ed.), *Normes juridiques et régulation sociale*, Paris, LGDJ (1991), pp. 95–9.

'Introduction à la socioanalyse', *Actes de la recherche en sciences sociales*, 90 (December 1991), pp. 3–6.

'Commentary on the Commentaries' (tr. V. Zolberg), *Contemporary Sociology*, (21)2 (March 1992), pp. 158–61.

'L'école et la cité', *Actes de la recherche en sciences sociales*, 91–92 (March 1992), pp. 86–96.

'Les exclus de l'intérieur', *Actes de la recherche en sciences sociales*, 91–92 (March 1992), pp. 71–5 (with Patrick Champagne); also, in *La misère du monde*, Paris, Éd. du Seuil, 1993, pp. 597–603.

'Towards a Policy of Morality in Politics', in W. R. Shea, A. Spadafora (eds), *From the Twilight of Probability. Ethics and Politics*, Canton, Science History Publications, 1992, pp. 146–9.

'L'intraduisible', *Liber*, 10 (June 1992), p. 2.

'Pour une internationale des intellectuels', *Politis*, 1 (1992), pp. 9–15.

'La réappropriaton de la culture reniée: à propos de Mouloud Mammeri', in T. Yacine (ed.), *Amour, phantasmes et sociétés en Afrique du Nord et au Sahara*, Paris, L'Harmattan-Awal, 1992, pp. 17–22.

'Deux impérialismes de l'universel', in C. Fauré and T. Bishop (ed.), *L'Amérique des Français*, Paris, Ed. François Bourin, 1992, pp. 149–55.

'Principles of a Sociology of Cultural Works' (Christian Gauss Seminars in Criticism, Princeton, 1986) (tr. J. Wakelyn, C. Majidi), in S. Kemal, I. Gaskell (eds), *Explanation and Value in the Arts*, Cambridge, Cambridge University Press, 1992, pp. 173–89; also, 'Principles for a Sociology of Cultural Works', in *The Field of Cultural Production. Essays on Art and Literature*, Cambridge, Polity Press, 1993.

'Quelques remarques sur les conditions et les résultats d'une entreprise collective et internationale de recherche comparative', in M. de Saint Martin, M. D. Gheorghiu (eds), *Les institutions de formation des cadres dirigeants*, Maison des sciences de l'homme, 1992, pp. 281–3.

'Les murs mentaux', *Liber*, special number (January 1993), pp. 2–4.

'Esprits d'Etat', *Actes de la recherche en sciences sociales*, 96–97 (March 1993), pp. 49–62; also, 'Esprits d'Etat. Genèse et structure du champ bureaucratique', in P. Bourdieu, *Raisons pratiques*, Paris, Éd. du Seuil, 1994, pp. 99–103. Published in English as 'Rethinking the State: On the Genesis and Structure of the Bureaucratic Field' (tr. L. Wacquant, S. Farage), *Sociological Theory*, 12–1 (March 1994), pp. 1–19.

'Concluding Remarks: For a Sociogenetic Understanding of Intellectual Works', in C. Calhoun, E. LiPuma, M. Postone (eds), *Bourdieu. Critical Perspectives*, Cambridge, Polity Press, 1993, pp. 263–75.

'La responsabilité des intellectuals', *Liber*, 14 (June 1993), p. 2.

'Remarques sur l'"histoire des femmes"', in G. Duby, M. Perrot (eds), *Femmes et histoire*, Plon, 1993, pp. 63–6.

'Table Ronde', in F. Cardi, J. Plantier, P. de Gaudemar (eds.), *Durkheim, Sociologue de l'éducation*, Paris, INRP-L'Harmattan, 1993, pp. 193–216 (with M. Eliard, A. Kadri).

'C'est trop beau', *Art Press*, 184 (October 1993), pp. 5, 7; also, 'Comme aux plus beaux jours des années 30', *Liber*, 16 (December 1993), p. 7. Published in English as 'Really too beautiful', *Art-Press*, 184 (October 1993); also, 'Too Good to be True', in P. Bourdieu, H. Haacke, *Free Exchange* (trans. of *Libre-Echange* [1994]), pp. 113–16.

'L'Impromptu de Bruxelles', *Cahiers de l'Ecole des sciences philosophiques et religieuses*, 14 (1993), pp. 33–48.

'Strategies de reproduction et modes de domination', *Bulletin d'information de la Mission historique française en Allemagne*, 26–27 (June–December 1993), pp. 125–41.

'A propos de Sartre...', *French Cultural Studies*, (4)3, no. 12 (October 1993), pp. 209–11.

'A propos de la famille comme catégorie réalisée', *Actes de la recherche en sciences sociales*, 100 (December 1993), pp. 32–6. Published in English as 'On the Family as a Realised Category' (tr. R. Nice), *Theory, Culture and Society*, 1996, 13(3), pp. 19–26.

'L'emprise du journalisme', *Actes de la recherche en sciences sociales*, 101–102 (March 1994), pp. 3–9.

'Comment sortir du cercle de la peur', *Liber*, 17 (March 1994), pp. 22–3. Published in English as 'The Politics of Fear' (tr. K. Brown), *Méditerranéennes*, 6 (Summer–Autumn 1994), pp. 267–9.

'*Libé* vingt ans après', *Actes de la recherche en sciences sociales*, 101–102 (March 1994), p. 39.

'Les jeux olympiques' (abridged version), *Actes de la recherche en sciences sociales*, 103 (June 1994), pp. 102–3.

'A Reflecting Story' (tr. R. Nice), in M. S. Roth (ed.), *Rediscovering History. Culture, Politics, and the Psyche* (Essays in honor of Carl E. Schorske), Stanford, Stanford University Press, 1994, pp. 371–7; also, in *The Rules of Art*, Cambridge, Polity Press, 1996, pp. 324–6.

'Le corps et le sacré', *Actes de la recherche en sciences sociales*, 104 (September 1994), p. 2.

'Un Parlement pour quoi faire? (What purpose a Parliament?), *Littératures*, revue du Parlement International des Ecrivains (October–November 1994), pp. 3–4; also, 'Un Parlement des écrivains pour quoi faire?, *Libération*, 3 November 1994.

'Stratégies de reproduction et modes de domination', *Actes de la recherche en sciences sociales*, 105 (December 1994), pp. 3–12.

'Piété religieuse et dévotion artistique. Fidèles et amateurs d'art à Santa Maria Novella', *Actes de la recherche en sciences sociales*, 105 (December 1994), pp. 71–4.

'L'oeil du XVIIᵉ siècle' (review of Marc Fumaroli, *La Diplomatie de l'esprit. De Montaigne à La Fontaine*), *Liber*, 20 (December 1994), p. 32.

'L'Etat et la concentration du capital symbolique', in B. Théret, *L'Etat, la finance et le social*, Paris, La Découverte, 1995, pp. 73–105.

'La cause de la science. Comment l'histoire sociale des sciences sociales peut servir le progrès de ces sciences', *Actes de la recherche en sciences sociales*, 106–107 (March 1995), pp. 3–10.

'Sollers tel quel', *Liber*, 21–22 (March 1995), p. 40.

'Le sort des étrangers comme schibboleth', *Libération*, 3 May 1995, p. 9 (with J. P. Alaux).

'La violence symbolique', in M. de Manassein(ed.), *De l'égalité des sexes*, Paris, CNDP, 1995, pp. 83–7.

'Une double cosmogonie nationale', *Liber*, 24 (October 1995), p. 2 (with K. Dixon).

'La parole du cheminot', *Alternatives algériennes*, 1 (7–21 November 1995), p. 3.

'Sciences sociales et démocratie' (modified version), in P. Combenale, J.-P. Piriou (eds), *Nouveau manuel de sciences économiques et sociales*, Paris, Éd. La Découverte, 1995, pp. 673–4; also 'Les sciences sociales et la démocratie' (Paris-HEC, November 1995), in *Conférences des professeurs Honoris Causa du Groupe HEC*, Chambre de Commerce et d'Industrie de Paris, 1997, pp. 9–23.

'Le parti de la paix civile', *Alternatives algériennes*, 2 (22 November–7 December 1995), p. 4 (with M. Virolle).

'Et pourtant…', *Liber*, 25 (December 1995), pp. 1–2.

'Je suis ici pour dire notre soutien…', *Libération*, Thursday 14 December 1995, p. 7; also, 'En finir avec la tyrannie des experts', *Futurs*, 91 special issue, March 1996, p. 91.

'Apollinaire, Automne malade', *Cahiers d'Histoire des Littératures Romanes (Romanistische Zeitschrift für Literaturgeschichte)*, 3–4(19) (1995), pp. 330–3.

'Champ politique, champ des sciences sociales, champ journalistique' (Lyon, 14 November 1995), *Cahiers de recherche* du Groupe de Recherche sur la Socialisation, 15 (1996), 42 pp.

'La télévision peut-elle critiquer la télévision. Analyse d'un passage à l'antenne', *Le Monde diplomatique*, April 1996, p. 25.

'Des familles sans nom', *Actes de la recherche en sciences sociales*, 113 (June 1996), pp. 3–5.

'Juin 1991. Ahmed X', *Revue de littérature générale* (POL), 96/2 digest, 1996.

'Sociologie et histoire', in *Aux Frontières du savoir*, Paris, presses de l'Ecole Nationale des Ponts et Chaussées, 1996, pp. 111–31.

'La double vérité du travail', *Actes de la recherche en sciences sociales*, 114 (September 1996), pp. 89–90; also, in *Méditations pascaliennes*, Paris, Éd. du Seuil, 1997, pp. 241–4; also, in *Res publica* (revue de l'Association de philosophie de l'Université Paris XII-Créteil), 15 (1997), pp. 13–16.

'In memoriam Gilles Deleuze', *Liber*, 28 (September 1996), p. 16.

'Contre la "pensée" Tietmeyer, un Welfare state européen', *Libération*, 25 October 1996; also, 'Le nouvel opium des intellectuels', *Liber*, 29 (December 1996), p. 16; also, abridged version, in *Le Soir* (Bruxelles), 28–29 December 1996, p. 2.

'Qu'est-ce que faire parler un auteur? A propos de Michel Foucault', *Sociétés et Représentations*, 3 (November 1996), pp. 13–18.

'Passport to Duke' (Durham, 21–23 April 1995), in M. Sabour, 'Pierre Bourdieu's Thought in Contemporary Social Sciences', *International Journal of Contemporary Sociology*, 33(2) (October 1996), pp. 145–50; 'Intellectuels and the Internationalization of Ideas: An Interview with M'hammed Sabour' (Paris, July 1993), *ibid.*, pp. 237–53; also, 'Passport to Duke', *Metaphilosophy*, 28(4) (October 1997), pp. 449–55.

'Je suis ici pour dire notre soutien...' *Les Cahiers de l'IRSA* (Mouvements Sociaux et Exclusions), 1 (March 1997), pp. 23–6.

'De la maison du roi à la raison d'Etat. Un modèle de la genèse du champ bureaucratique', *Actes de la recherche en sciences sociales*, 118 (June 1997), pp. 55–68.

'Historiciser la différence', *Liber* (Destins nordique), 31 (June 1997), p. 1.

'Dévoiler et divulguer le refoulé' (Freiburg, 1995), in J. Jurt (ed.), *Algérie-France-Islam*, Paris, L'Harmattan, 1997, pp. 21–7.

'L'architecte de l'euro passe aux aveux' (Freiburg, October 1996), *Le Monde diplomatique*, 522 (September 1997), p. 19.

'Nous en avons assez du racisme d'Etat', *Les Inrockuptibles*, 121 (8–14 October 1997), pp. 4–5.

'Pour une historicisme rationaliste' (tr. N. Chmatko) (unpublished – Montréal, 29 March 1996), *Socio-Logos*, 1997.

'Quelques questions sur la question gay et lesbienne' (Beaubourg, 23 June 1997), *Liber*, 33 (December 1997), pp. 7–8.

'Les actions des chômeurs flambent', *Le Monde*, 17 January 1998, p. 13 (with G. Mauger, F. Lebaron).

'Questions sur un quiproquo', *Le Monde diplomatique*, 527 (February 1998), p. 26.

Oral Presentations

'L'idéologie jacobine, Communication à la Semaine de la pensée marxiste' (9–15 March 1966), *Démocratie et liberté*, Paris, Editions sociales, 1966, pp. 167–73.

'Systèmes d'enseignement et systèmes de pensée', Communication au VIe Congrès mondial de la sociologie (Evian, September 1966), *Revue internationale des sciences sociales*, Fonctions sociales de l'éducation,

XIX, no. 3 (1967), pp. 357 88. Published in English as 'Systems of Education and Systems of Thought', *International Social Science Journal*, XIX, no. 3 (1967), pp. 338–58; also, in *Readings in the Theory of Education System*, ed. Earl Hopper, London, Hutchinson & Co. 1971, pp. 159–83; also, in *Knowledge and Control: New Directions for the Sociology of Education*, ed. Michael F. D. Young, London, Collier-Macmillan, 1971, pp. 189–207; also, in *Schooling and Capitalism. A sociological reader*, ed. Roger Dale *et al.*, London, Routledge and Kegan Paul/The Open University Press, 1976, pp. 192–200.

Emissions de philosophie 1966–1967, consacrées au langage, Paris, Institut pédagogique national, Dossiers pédagogiques de la radiotélévision scolaire, 1967.

'Introduction à la sociologie', *Emissions de philosophie 1967–1968*, Paris, Ministère de l'Education nationale, 1968 (with J. C. Passeron).

'Système et innovation', Communication au Colloque national d'Amiens (1968), in *Pour une école nouvelle. Formation des maîtres et recherches en éducation*, Paris, Dunod, 1969, pp. 347–50.

'Reproduction culturelle et reproduction sociale' (Presentation at the Colloquium at Durham, April 1970), *Information sur les sciences sociales*, X, no. 2 (April 1971), pp. 45–99. Published in English as 'Cultural Reproduction and Social Reproduction', in *Knowledge, Education, and Cultural Change*, ed. Richard Brown, London, Tavistock, 1973, pp. 71–112; also, in *Power and Ideology in Education*, ed. J. Karabel and A. H. Halsey, New York, Oxford University Press, 1977, pp. 487–511.

'L'opinion publique n'existe pas', Conference (Arras, Noroit, 155, January 1971), *Noroit*, 155 (February 1971); debate, *Noroit*, 156 (March 1971); also, *Les temps modernes*, 318 (January 1973), pp. 1292–1309; also, in P. Bourdieu *Questions de sociologie*, Paris, Éd. de Minuit, 1980, pp. 222–35. Published in English as 'Public Opinion Does Not Exist' (tr. M. C. Axtmann), in *Communication and Class Struggle*, ed. A. Mattelart and S. Siegelaub, New York/Bagnolet, International General/IMMRC, 1979, vol. 1 'Capitalism, Imperialism', pp. 124–30.

Compte-rendu of Group I, in *Vie active et formation universitaire*, Actes du Colloque d'Orléans (November 1970), Paris, Dunod, 1972, pp. 109–13.

'Haute couture et haute culture', *Noroit*, 192 (November 1974), pp. 1–2, 7–17; debate, *Noroit*, 193–194 (December 1974–January 1975), pp. 2–11; also, in P. Bourdieu, *Questions de sociologie*, Paris, Éd. de Minuit, 1980, pp. 196–206.

'Les conditions sociales de la production sociologique: sociologie coloniale et décolonisation de la sociologie', Intervention au Colloque sur 'Ethnologie et politique au Maghreb' (Paris, June 1975), in *Le mal de voir*, Paris, Union générale d'éditions (UGE), coll. 10/18, Cahiers Jussieu 2, 1976, pp. 416–27; also, 'Pour une sociologie des sociologues, in P. Bourdieu, *Questions de sociologie*, Paris, Éd. de Minuit, 1980, pp. 79–85.

'Sur le pouvoir symbolique', conference (Harvard University, 1973), *Annales*, 3 (May–June 1977), pp. 405–11. Published in English as 'Symbolic Power' (tr. C. Wringe), in *Identity and Structure: Issues in the Sociology of Education*, ed. D. Gleeson, Driffield, Nafferton Books, 1977, pp. 112–19; also, *Critique of Anthropology* (tr. R. Nice), vol. 4, no. 13/14 (Summer 1979), pp. 77–85; also, in P. Bourdieu, *Language and Symbolic Power*, Cambridge, Polity Press, 1991, pp. 163–70.

'L'économie des échanges linguistiques', 'Seminar (Paris, EHESS, 25 November 1976), *Language française*, 34 (May 1977), pp. 17–34. Published in English as 'The economics of linguistic exchanges' (tr. R. Nice) *Social Science Information*, XVI, no. 6 (December 1977), pp. 645–68.

Participation à la Table ronde, 'Linguistique et sociologie du langage' (Paris, Maison des sciences de l'homme, October 1976), *Langue française*, 34 (May 1977), pp. 35–51 (with J. C. Chevalier, S. Delesalle, P. Encrevé, G. Fauconnier, J. C. Milner, A. Rey).

'Le censure', Intervention au Colloque sur la science des œuvres (Lille, May 1974), *Information sur les sciences sociales*, XVI, no. 3/4 (1977), pp. 385–8; also, in P. Bourdieu, *Questions de sociologie*, Paris, Éd. de Minuit, 1980, pp. 138–42.

'Le paradoxe du sociologue', Conference (Arras, Noroit, October 1977), *Noroit*, 222 (November 1977); debate, *Noroit*, 223 (December 1977); also, *Sociologie et sociétés* (Montréal), XI, no. 1 (April 1979), pp. 85–94; also, in P. Bourdieu, *Questions de sociologie*, Paris, Éd. de Minuit, 1980, pp. 86–94.

'Pratiques sportives et pratiques sociales', Conférence inaugurale au Congès international de l'HISPA (Paris, INSEP, 28 March–2 April 1978), *Actes du VIIe Congrès international*, Paris, INSEP, 1978, tome 1, pp. 17–37; also, 'Comment peut-on être sportif?' in P. Bourdieu, *Questions de sociologie*, Paris, Éd. de Minuit, 1980, pp.

173 95; also 'Comment peut on être sportif?' *Revue française du marketing*, 138(3) (1992), pp. 7–16. Published in English as 'Sport and social class' (tr. R. Nice), *Social Science Information*, XVII, no. 6 (1978), pp. 819–40.

'Savoir ce que parler veut dire', Intervention au Congès de l'AFEF (Limoges, 30 October 1977), *Le français aujourd'hui*, 41 (March 1978), pp. 4–20 (debate, 'Questions à Pierre. Bourdieu, *Le français aujourd'hui*, Supplement to no. 41, March 1978, pp. 51–7); also, in P. Bourdieu, *Questions de sociologie*, Paris, Éd. de Minuit, 1980, pp. 95–112.

'Le racisme de l'intelligence', *Cahiers Droit et liberté* (Races, sociétés et aptitudes: apports et limites de la science, Colloque de l'UNESCO, 27 May 1978), Supplement to no. 382, 1978, pp. 67–71; also, *Réforme*, 1 December 1979, pp. 6–7; also, in P. Bourdieu, *Questions de sociologie*, Paris, Éd. de Minuit, 1980, pp. 264–8; also, in Jean Belkhir, *L'intellectuel: l'intelligentsia et les manuels*, Paris, Éd. Anthropos, 1983, pp. 187–94; also, 'Tout racisme est un essential-isme', *Différences*, 24–25 (June–July 1983), p. 44.

'Numerus clausus', Intervention aux Assises de l'enseignement de l'architecture (May 1978), *Pré-livre blanc*, 1979; also, 'Débat: numerus clausus ou débouchés?' *BIP*, 94 (29 October 1980), p. 3.

'La fin des intellectuels?' Conference (Arras, Noroit, October 1980), *Noroit*, 253 (November 1980), pp. 2–8, 17–23; debate, *Noroit*, 254 (December 1980).

'Mais qui a créé les "créateurs"?' Conference (Paris, ENSAD, 1980), in *Art: Sur 10 ans, aujourd'hui, 1981*, Paris, Ministère de la culture, 1981, pp. 71–84; also, in P. Bourdieu, *Questions de sociologie*, Paris, Éd. de Minuit, 1980, pp. 207–21.

'Lecture, lecteurs, lettrés, littérature', in *Recherches sur la philo-sopie et le langage*, Grenoble, Université des sciences sociales, 1981, pp. 5–16; also in *Choses Dites*, Paris, Éd Minuit, 1987, pp. 132–43.

'Les rites d'institution' (Neuchâtel, October 1981), *Actes de la recherche en sciences sociales*, 43 (June 1982), pp. 58–63; also, 'Les rites comme actes d'institution', in *Les rites de passage aujourd'hui*, ed. P. Centlivres and J. Hainard, Actes du Colloque de Neuchâtel 1981, Lausanne, Éditions L'Age d'Homme, 1986, pp. 206–15; also, modified version in *Ce que parler veut dire*, Paris, Fayard, 1982, pp. 121–33. Published in English as 'Rites as Acts of Institution' (tr. R. Just), in J. G. Peristiany, J. Pitt-Rivers (eds), *Honor and Grace in*

Anthropology, Cambridge, Cambridge University Press, 1992, pp. 79–89.

Résumé des cours et travaux, *Annuaire du Collège de France 1981–1982*, Paris, Collège de France, 1982, pp. 473–6.

Résumé des cours et travaux, *Annuaire du Collège de France 1982–1983*, Paris, Collège de France, 1983, pp. 519–24.

'Espace social et genèse des "classes"' (University of Frankfurt, February 1984), *Actes de la recherche en sciences sociales*, 52–53 (June 1984), pp. 3–12. Published in English as 'The Social Space and the Genesis of Groups' (tr. R. Nice), *Social Science Information*, vol. 24, no. 2 (1985), pp. 195–220; also, *Theory and Society* (tr. R. Nice), no. 14 (1985), pp. 723–44; also, 'Social Space and the Genesis of "Classes"', in P. Bourdieu, *Language and Symbolic Power*, Cambridge, Polity Press, 1991, pp. 229–51.

'Pour une critique de la lecture' (Strasbourg, Centre de documentation en histoire de la philosophie, 1984), *La lecture II*, Cahiers du Séminaire de philosophie, 2, 1984, pp. 13–17.

'La délégation et le fétichisme politique' (Paris, Association des étudiants protestants, June 1983), *Actes de la recherche en sciences sociales*, 52–53 (June 1984), pp. 49–55; also, in P. Bourdieu, *Chose dites*, Paris, Éd. de Minuit, 1987, pp. 185–202. Published in English as 'Delegation and Political Fetishism' (tr. K. Robinson), *Thesis Eleven*, no. 10–11 (November 1984–March 1985), pp. 56–70; also, in P. Bourdieu, *Language and Symbolic Power*, Cambridge, Polity Press, 1991, pp. 203–19.

'Réponse aux économistes' (Paris Colloquium on 'Le modèle économique dans les sciences sociales', Université de Paris-I, April 1981), *Economies et sociétés*, XVIII, no. 10 (October 1984), pp. 23–32; also, 'L'intérêt du sociologue', in P. Bourdieu, *Choses dites*, Paris, Éd. de Minuit, 1987, pp. 124–31.

Conference introductive (VIIIe Symposium de l'ICSS, Paris, July 1983), in *Sports et sociétés contemporaines*, Paris, Société française de sociologie du sport, 1984, pp. 323–31.

Résumé des cours et travaux, *Annuaire du Collège de France 1983–1984*, Paris, Collège de France, 1984, pp. 551–3.

'Le champ religieux dans le champ de production symbolique' (Strasbourg, October 1982), Afterword, in *Les nouveaux clercs*, Geneva, Labor et fides, 1985, pp. 255–61; also, 'La dissolution du religieux', in P. Bourdieu, *Choses dites*, Paris, Éd. de Minuit, 1987, pp. 117–23.

'Les professeurs de l'Université de Paris à la veille de Mai 68' (Paris, Colloque organisé par l'Institut d'histoire moderne et contemporaine et l'EHESS, June 1984), in *Le personnel de l'enseignement supérieur en France au XIXe et XXe siècles*, Paris, Ed. du CNRS, 1985, pp. 177–84.

Résumé des cours et des travaux, *Annuaire du Collège de France 1984–1985*, Paris, Collège de France, 1985, pp. 559–62.

'Habitus, code et codification', Conference (Neuchâtel, May 1983), *Actes de la recherche en sciences sociales*, 64 (September 1986), pp. 40–4; also, 'La codification', in P. Bourdieu, *Choses dites*, Paris, Éd. de Minuit, 1987, pp. 94–105.

'De quoi parle-t-on quand on parle du "problème de la jeunesse"?' (Paris, Colloque organisé par le Programme mobilisateur Technologie, Emploi, Travail, du Ministère de la recherche et de la technologie, December 1985), in *Les jeunes et les autres. Contributions des sciences de l'homme à la question des jeunes*, Vaucresson, CRIV (Centre de recherche interdisciplinaire de Vaucresson), 1986, volume II, pp. 229–34.

Résumé des cours et travaux, *Annuaire du Collège de France 1985–1986*, Paris, Collège de France, 1986, pp. 555–60.

'Intervention devant les étudiants en sociologie de l'Université Lumière-Lyon II', 14 January 1987, *Sociofil* (Brochure de l'association d'étudiants *Sociofil*), 1987.

'Sociologues de la croyance et croyances de sociologues' (Paris, Congrès de l'Association française de sociologie religieuse, December 1982), *Archives de sciences sociales des religions*, 63, no. 1 (January–March 1987), pp. 155–61; also, in P. Bourdieu, *Choses dites*, Paris, Éd. de Minuit, 1987, pp. 106–11.

'La révolution impressioniste' (Arras, Noroit, January 1987), *Noroit*, 303 (September–October 1987), pp. 3–18.

'What Makes a Social Class? On The Theoretical and Practical Existence of Groups' (Chicago, The University of Chicago, Symposium 'Gender, Race, Class and Age', April 1987; tr. L. Wacquant, D. Young), *Berkeley Journal of Sociology*, vol. XXXII (1987), pp. 1–17.

'L'évolution des rapports entre le champ universitaire et le champ du journalisme', Intervention aux entretiens de Bordeaux (Sigma, 16–21 November 1987), duplicated.

'On Interest and the Relative Autonomy of Symbolic Power: A Rejoinder to Some Objections' (Düsseldorf, February 1987; tr.

L. Wacquant, M. Lawson), *Working Papers and Proceeding of the Centre for Psychosocial Studies* (Chicago), 20, 1988, pp. 1–11.

'Une leçon de journalisme de Pierre Bourdieu' (Bordeaux, November 1987), Supplément du journal école Imprimatur, IUT de Bordeaux, 1988.

Résumé des cours et travaux, *Annuaire du Collège de France 1987–1988*, Paris, Collège de France, 1988, pp. 483–92.

'Gens à histoires, gens sans histoires' (dialogue between Pierre Bourdieu and Roger Chartier), *Politix*, no. 6 (spring 1989), pp. 53–60.

Résumé des cours et travaux, *Annuaire du Collège de France 1988–1989*, Paris, Collège de France, 1989, pp. 431–6.

Résumé des cours et travaux, *Annuaire du Collège de France 1989–1990*, Paris, Collège de France, 1990, pp. 519–23.

Résumé des cours et travaux, *Annuaire du Collège de France 1990–1991*, Paris, Collège de France, 1991, pp. 591–95.

Résumé des cours et travaux, *Annuaire du Collège de France 1991–1992*, Paris, Collège de France, 1992, pp. 577–81.

Résumé des cours et travaux, *Annuaire du Collège de France 1992–1993*, Paris, Collège de France, 1993, pp. 611–15.

'Nouvelles réflexions sur la domination masculine' (séminaire du GEDISST, 14 June 1995), *Cahiers du GEDISST*, 11, 1994, pp. 91–104.

Résumé des cours et travaux, *Annuaire du Collège de France 1993–1994*, Paris, Collège de France, 1994, pp. 627–32.

'Extra-ordinaire Baudelaire' (Communication au Colloque 'Baudelaire, nouveaux chantiers', Lille, 15 May 1993), in J. Delabroy, Y. Charnet (eds), *Baudelaire: nouveaux chantiers*, Lille, Presses universitaires du Septentrion, 1995, pp. 279–88; also, in H. Krauss (ed.), *Cahiers d'Histoire des Littératures Romanes* (20 ans), 1–2 (1996), pp. 134–41; also, 'Comment lire un auteur?', in *Méditations pascaliennes*, Paris, Éd. du Seuil, 1997, pp. 101–9.

Résumé des cours et travaux, *Annuaire du Collège de France 1994–1995*, Paris, Collège de France, 1995, pp. 589–91.

'Journalisme et éthique' (communication au colloque fondateur du Centre de recherche sur le journalisme à l'ESJ Lille, 3 June 1994), *Les Cahiers du journalisme*, 1 (June 1996), pp. 10–17.

Résumé des cours et travaux, *Annuaire du Collège de France 1995–1996*, Paris, Collège de France, 1996, pp. 675–84.

'Organiser les résistances' (Séances inaugurale des Etats généraux du mouvement social, 23 November 1996), *Avancées* (Bruxelles), 53 (March 1997), p. 13.

'Conformismes et résistance' (debate with J. Bouveresse) (Oxford, 1996), in *La Lettre de la Maison française d'Oxford*, 7 (1997), pp. 177–89.

Résumé des cours et travaux, *Annuaire du Collège de France 1996–1997*, Paris, Collège de France, 1997, pp. 651–7.

Interviews

'Pour une pédagogie rationelle', *Lambda* (November 1966), pp. 3–5.

'La théorie' (with O. Hahn), *VH 101*, 2 (Summer 1970), pp. 12–21.

'Les intellectuels dans le champ de la lutte des classes' (with A. Casanova and M. Simon), *La nouvelle critique*, 87 (October 1975), pp. 20–6.

'Le droit à la parole' (with P. Viansson-Ponté), *Le Monde*, Les grilles du temps (11 October 1977), pp. 1–2; sequel, 'La culture, pour qui et pourquoi?', *Le Monde*, Les grilles du temps (12 October 1977), p. 2.

'Les intellectuels sont-ils hors jeu?' (with F. Hincker), *La nouvelle critique*, 111–112 (February–March 1978), pp. 56–61; also, in P. Bourdieu, *Questions de sociologie*, Paris, Éd. de Minuit, 1980, pp. 61–6.

'Deux doigts de Ravel sec' (with C. Huvé), *Le Monde de la musique*, 6 (December 1978), pp. 30–1; also, 'L'origine et l'évolution des espèces de mélomanes', in P. Bourdieu, *Questions de sociologie*, Paris, Éd. de Minuit, 1980, pp. 155–60.

Interview (with A. M. Métailié), in *Les jeunes et le premier emploi*, Paris, Association des âges, 1978, pp. 520–30; also, 'La "jeunesse" n'est qu'un mot', in P. Bourdieu, *Questions de sociologie*, Paris, Éd. de Minuit, 1980, pp. 143–54.

'Des goûts artistiques et des classes sociales' (with D. Eribon), *Libération*, 3–4 November 1979, pp. 12–13; also, 'L'art de résister aux paroles', in P. Bourdieu, *Questions de sociologie*, Paris, Éd. de Minuit, 1980, pp. 10–18.

'Des contradictions linguistiques léguées par le colonisateur' (with D. Eribon), *Libération*, 19–20 (April 1980), p. 13.

'La grande illusion des intellectuels' (with D. Eribon), *Le Monde Dimanche* (4 May 1980), p. i and xvii; also, 'Comment libérer les intellectuels libres?' in P. Bourdieu, *Questions de sociologie*, Paris, Éd. de Minuit, 1980, pp. 67–78.

'La sociologie est-elle une science?' (with P. Thuillier), *La recherche*, 112 (June 1980), pp. 738–43; also, 'Une science qui dérange', in P. Bourdieu, *Questions de sociologie*, Paris, Éd. de Minuit, 1980, pp. 19–36.

'Retrouver la tradition libertaire de la gauche' (with R. Pierre and D. Eribon, concerning Poland), *Libération*, 23 December 1981, pp. 8–9; also, *Libération*, special issue, Pologne, 500 jours de libertés qui ébranlèrent le communisme, January–February 1982, pp. 209–10.

'Dévoiler les ressorts du pouvoir' (with D. Eribon), *Libération*, 19 October 1982, p. 28.

'Université: les rois sont nus' (with D. Eribon), *Le nouvel observateur*, 2–8 (November 1984), pp. 86–90.

'La lecture: une pratique culturelle' (with R. Chartier), in *Pratiques de la lecture*, Paris, Rivages, 1985, pp. 218–39.

'De la règle aux stratégies' (with P. Lamaison), *Terrains*, 4 (March 1985), pp. 93–100; also, in P. Bourdieu, *Chose dites*, Paris, Éd. de Minuit, 1987, pp. 75–93. Published in English as 'From Rules to Strategies' (tr. R. Hurley), *Cultural Anthropology*, vol. 1, no. 1 (February 1986), pp. 110–20.

'Du bon usage de l'ethnologie' (with M. Mammerie), *Awal*, Cahiers d'études berbères, no. 1, 1985, pp. 7–29.

'Le rapport du Collège de France: Pierre Bourdieu s'explique' (with J. P. Salgas), *La Quinzaine Littéraire*, 445 (1–31 August 1985), pp. 8–10.

'The Struggle for Symbolic Order' (tr. J. Bleicher), *Theory, Culture & Society*, vol. 3, no. 3 (1986), pp. 35–51.

'D'abord défendre les intellectuels' (with D. Eribon), *Le nouvel observateur*, 12–18 September 1986, p. 82.

'A quand un lycée Bernard Tapie?' (with A. de Gaudemar), *Libération*, 4 December 1986, p. 4; also, *Libération*, special issue, La nouvelle vague, January 1987, pp. 106–7. Published in English as

'Revolt of the Spirit' (tr Ch. Turner), *New Socialist*, 46 (February 1987), pp. 9–11.

'Equisse d'un projet intellectuel: un interview with Pierre Bourdieu' (with C. Duverlie), *The French Review*, vol. 61, no. 2 (December 1987), pp. 194–205.

'Heidegger par Pierre Bourdieu: le krach de la philosophie' (with R. Maggiori), *Libération*, 10 March 1988, Supplément Livres, pp. vi–vii.

'Le paradoxe du sociologue' (interview with A. Renyi), *Doxa. Etudes philosophiques* (Budapest), 16 (1989), pp. 95–107.

'For a Socio-Analysis of Intellectuals: on "*Homo Academicus*"' (interview in English with L. Wacquant), *Berkeley Journal of Sociology*, XXXIX (1989), pp. 1–29.

'Academicus Unchained' (interview in English with J. Turner), *City Limits*, 4–11 (January 1990).

'Profession scientifique: Pierre Bourdieu' (interview with P. Boulanger), *Pour la Science*, 149 (March 1990), pp. 4–6.

'Que faire de la sociologie?' (interview with J. Bass), *CFDT Aujourd'hui*, 100 (March 1991), pp. 111–24.

'Meanwhile, I have come to know all the diseases of sociological understanding' (interview with B. Krais), in *The Craft of Sociology*, 1991, pp. 247–59.

'L'ordre des choses' (interview with two young adults from north of France), *Actes de la recherche en sciences sociales*, 90 (December 1991), pp. 7–19; also, in *La misère du monde*, Paris, Éd. du Seuil, 1993, pp. 81–99.

'Une vie perdue' (interview with two Béarnais farmers), *Actes de la recherche en sciences sociales*, 90 (December 1991), pp. 29–36; also, in *La misère du monde*, Paris, Éd. du Seuil, 1993, pp. 519–31.

'Une mission impossible' (interview with Pascale Raymond, director of a project in the north of France), *Actes de la recherche en sciences sociales*, 90 (December 1991), pp. 84–94; also, in *La misère du monde*, Paris, Éd. du Seuil, 1993, pp. 229–44.

'Le sens de l'Etat' (interview with R. P. Droit and T. Ferenczi), *Le Monde*, 14 January 1992, p. 2; also, *Lignes*, 15 (1992); also 'Il n'y a pas de démocratie effective sans vrai contre-pouvoir critique', *Dossiers et Documents du Monde*, v. I (June 1993), pp. 87–9.

'Doxa and Common Life' (in conversation with Terry Eagleton), *New Left Review*, 191 (January–February 1992), pp. 111–21.

'La saine colère d'un sociologue' (interview with L. Roméo), *Politis*, 19 March 1992, pp. 68–70.

'Tout est social' (interview with P. M. de Baisi), *Magazine littéraire*, 303 (October 1992), pp. 104–11.

'Pour une science des oeuvres' (interview with I. Champey), *Art Press*, November 1992, pp. 124–9.

'From Ruling Class to Field of Power: an Interview with Pierre Bourdieu on *La noblesse d'Etat*' (Interview with L. Wacquant). *Theory, Culture and Society*, 10–1 August [1993], p. 19–44.

'Notre Etat de misère (interview with S. Pasquier), *L'Express*, 18 March 1993, pp. 112–15.

'La souffrance sociale dans l'oeil du sociologue' (interview with P. Aeby), *Actualités sociales hebdomadaires*, 1837 (18 June 1993), pp. 1–2.

'Résistance' (on Patrick Saytour) (interview with I. Champey), *Art Press*, 181 (June 1993), pp. 58–60.

'L'intellectuel dans la cité', (interview with F. Dutheil), *Le Monde*, 5 November 1993, p. 29.

Interview with Franck Nouchi, *Le Monde*, 7 December 1993, p. 2; also, 'Réinventer une sorte d'intellectuel collectif', *Prétentaine*, 2–3 (December 1994), pp. 37–41.

'L'intelligence qu'on assassine' (interview with E. Sarner), *La Chronique d'Amnesty International*, 86 (January 1994), pp. 24–5.

'Avant-Propos dialogué avec P. Bourdieu', in J. Maître, *L'autobiographie d'un paranoïaque*. L'abbé Berry (1878–1947) *et le roman de Billy* Introïbo, Paris, Anthropos, 1994, pp. 5–22.

'Questions à Pierre Bourdieu' (concerning *Réponses. Pour une anthropologie réflexive*), in G. Mauger et L. Pinto, *Lire les sciences sociales*, Paris, Bélin, 1994.

'Il dit ce que nous cachons' (interview with J. Cordy), *Le Soir de Bruxelles*, 21 April 1994, p. 2.

'A propos de *La misère du monde*' (interview with Yan Ciret), *Revue du Théâtre de la Bastille*, 6 (January 1995), pp. 28–9.

'La misère des médias' (interview with François Granon), *Télérama*, 2353, 15 February 1995, pp. 8–12.

'Sur les rapports entre la sociologie et l'histoire en Allemagne et en France' (interview with L. Raphael), *Actes de la recherche en sciences sociales*, 106–107 (March 1995), pp. 108–22.

'Le refus de la complaisance' (interview with L. Klejman), *Page*, June 1995.

Interview, *Littératures*, Autumn 1995, p. 6. Published in English as (tr. D. Crowe), *ibid.*

'Défataliser le monde' (interview with S. Bourmeau), *Les Inrockuptibles*, 99 (9–15 April 1997), pp. 22–9.

'Pierre Bourdieu éditeur' (interview with F. Piault), *Livres-Hebdo*, 244 (11 April 1997), pp. 40–1.

Miscellaneous Writings (Reviews, Prefaces, Postscripts, and Tributes)

Compte-rendu (concerning de P. Levêque, P. Vidal-Naquet, *Clisthène l'Athénien*), *L'homme*, IV, no. 3 (September–December 1964), pp. 143–4.

Afterword in E. Panofsky, *Architecture gothique et pensée scolastique*, trans. P. Bourdieu, Paris, Éd. de Minuit, 1967, new augm. edn, 1970, pp. 133–67.

Preface, in *Le français chassé des sciences*, Actes du Colloque d'Orsay, Paris, CIREEL (Centre d'Information et de Recherche pour l'Enseignement et l'Emploi des Langues), 1981, pp. 9–10.

Preface, in P. Lazarsfeld, M. Jahoda, H. Zeisel, *Les chômeurs de Marienthal*, Paris, Éd. de Minuit, 1981, pp. 7–12.

Introduction, in *Le grande livre du rugby français 1981–1982*, Bellville (Rhône), F. M. T. Editions SA., 1981, p. 7.

'Erving Goffman est mort', *Libération*, 2 December 1982, p. 23.

'Goffman, le découvreur de l'infiniment petit', *Le Monde*, 4 December 1982. Published in English as 'Erving Goffman, Discoverer of the Infinitely Small' (tr. R. Nice), *Theory, Culture and Society*, vol. 2, no. 1 (1983), pp. 112–13.

'Zaslawsky, contre la magie des mots', *Libération*, 7 December 1982, p. 21.

'Le plaisir de savoir' (on Michel Foucault), *Le Monde*, 27 June 1984, pp. 1 and 10.

'Les intellectuels et les pouvoirs', in *Michel Foucault, une histoire de la vérité*, Paris, Syros, 1985, pp. 93–4.

'A Free Thinker: "Do not ask me who I am"' (tr. R. Nice), *Paragraph* (London), vol. 5. (March 1985), pp. 80–7.

'L'assassinat de Maurice Halbwachs', *La liberté de l'esprit*, Visages de la Résistance, 16 (Autumn 1987), pp. 161–8.

Preface, in P. Rabinow, *Un ethnologue au Maroc*, Paris, Hachette, 1988, pp. 11–14.

Preface, in B. Mazon, *Aux origines de l'Ecole des hautes études en sciences sociales. Le rôle du mécénat américain*, Paris, Ed. du cerf, 1988, pp. i–v.

Preface, in T. Yacine Titouh, *L'Izli ou l'amour chanté en kabyle*, Paris, Ed. de la Maison des sciences de l'homme, 1988, pp. 11–12.

'A long trend of change' (concerning M. Lewin, *The Gorbachev Phenomenon: A historical interpretation*), *The Times Literary Supplement*, August 12–18, 1988, pp. 875–6.

Preface, in *Cahiers de l'Université de Pau et des Pays de l'Adour*, 13 (July 1989); also, 'Ce que parler veut dire', *Atlantica*, no. 2 (April 1994), pp. 6–7.

'Un analyseur de l'inconscient' (preface), in A. Sayad, *L'immigration ou les paradoxes de l'altérité*, Bruxelles, De Boeck-Wesmael, 1991, pp. 7–9.

'Un progrès de la réflexivité', preface, in W. Doise, A. Clemence, F. Lorenzi-Cioldi (ed.), *Représentations sociales et analyses de données*, Grenoble, Presses Universitaires de Grenoble, 1992, pp. 7–8.

'Pour une "généthique"', (preface), in T. Duster, *Retour à l'eugénisme*, Paris, Kimé, 1992, pp. 7–9.

'Lettre à Jean-Daniel Reynaud', in *Variations autour de la régulation sociale* (Tribute to Jean-Daniel Reynaud), Paris, Presses de l'Ecole Normale Supérieure, 1994, pp. 35–6.

'Agrippine et le moderne', Catalogue de l'exposition Claire Bretécher 'Portraits privés' (10 March-15 April 1995, Bibliothèque Elsa Triolet, Pantin), pp. 20–1; also, in *Lecture Jeune*, 77 (1996), p. 22.

'Il ne faisait jamais le philosophe' (On Georges Canguilhem), *Les Inrockuptibles*, 25 (27 September-3 October 1995), p. 12.

'Foreword', in Y. Dezalay, D. Sugarman, *Professional Competition and Professional Power. Lawyers, Accountants and the Social*

Construction of Markets, London-New York, Routledge, 1995, pp. xi–xiii.

'Foreword', in Y. Dezaley, B. G. Garth, *Dealing in Virtue*, Chicago–London, The University of Chicago Press, 1995, pp. vii–viii.

'Apologie pour une femme rangée' (Preface), in T. Moi, *Simone de Beauvoir. Conflits d'une intellectuelle*, Paris, Diderot Editeur, 1995, pp. vi–x; also, in *Liber*, 33 (December 1997), p. 8.

Index

Aboulafia, M., 7
academia, 11, 101, 104, 109
action(s), 7, 17, 20, 34–7, 60, 93;
  dialogical, 35–7; "free" vs.
  "constrained," 48–9; and *habitus*,
  136; intelligent, 34, 60;
  monological, 35; rational, 159,
  172–3 n23; theory about, 159;
  see also agency; agent(s); the
  subject
activity(-ies): nonreflective, 156,
  162; practical, 119; reflective,
  156; theoretical, 22
adaptation: ideal of, 117–18
Adorno, T., 3
aesthetics, 18; in Anglo-American
  philosophy, 9; in nineteenth-
  century America, 203–10; in
  nineteenth-century France, 215; as
  philosophical field, 3, 9; pure, 18;
  see also art
agency, 5, 7; aggregated, 80; in
  Bourdieu's theory of practice,
  129–52; as embodied, 32;
  generative, 10; reflexive, 142,
  145–8
agent(s): autonomous, 149;
  cognitive competence of, 80; as
  engaged in practices, 33, 53; as
  free and responsible, 50; and
  "norms," 35; as not mere subjects
  following rules, 65; and self-
  consciousness, 165;
  understanding in practice, 33;

see also action(s); agency; the
  subject
Alexander, J., 188 n19
Algeria, 104; Bourdieu's personal
  experience in, 2, 111 n19;
  ethnology/anthropology of, 2, 65
alterity, 102, 206, 210
Althusser, L., 70, 118, 120, 126 n2,
  127 n15, 185
analogical operator, 74, 75
anthropology: authorities in, 97;
  Bourdieu's impact on, 1, 107; and
  notion of rule, 38; structuralist,
  101
Apel, O., 226
apriorism, 179
aptitude(s): as encultured, 76–7
architecture: in America, 203–10
Aristotle, 48, 78; and *phronesis*, 41,
  78, 129
art: analytic philosophy of, 9; and
  art world, 9; and autonomous
  experiences, 9, 217; Bourdieu on,
  214–19; Dewey on, 20–1, 23;
  Institutional Theory of, 9, 216
arts, the: fine, 180–1; in
  nineteenth-century America,
  203–10
askesis: Bourdieu's reflexive, 12
ataraxia, Stoic, 169, 183
atoms, 198–9
Attali, J., 175
attitude(s): and *habitus*, 163–4
Aufklärung, 226

injustice: social, 92–3
instinct: animal, 79
intellectualism: and accounts of
agency, 5, 29–43, 129–30, 185;
anti-intellectualism, 12;
Bourdieu's critique of theory's, 6,
107; philosophical, 1, 10, 12, 102,
106, 153
interestedness, 170
internationalism: scientific, 220; see
also idea(s)
interpretation: transgressive textual,
10
intersubjectivity, 11
intuition: and rules, 46, 57;
linguistic, 54
intuitionists, 57
irrationality, 226

James, W., 155–6, 162, 170;
Psychology, 162
Jefferson, T., 206
judgement(s): in application of rules,
55; in cultural domains, 19;
predicates and aesthetic, 18
Jünger, E., 221
jurisprudence, 140
justice, 123

Kabyle, the, 40, 41, 66, 69, 71, 72,
97, 110n12, 131, 202
kairos, 40
Kant, I., 186, 218
Katz, J., 54
Kauffman, S., 212n5
Kelvin, W. T. (Lord), 60
Kestenbaum, V., 171n1
Kitsch, 215
knowledge: of human beings, 33;
practical, 78; scholarly, 94–112;
theoretical, 10
Koyré, A., 95
Kripke, S., 4, 15, 191n51; and
rule-following, 29, 31–2, 46

Laclau, E., 127n18

language, 6, 18, 24, 74; Bourdieu's
theory of, 124; as calculus, 45,
54–5; and common action, 37;
game of, 22, 176; Habermasian
theory of, 7; and individual
agents, 80; learning a, 52, 58;
official, 131; ordinary, 16, 22–3,
176; and political change, 6, 24,
123; and rules, 59; and social
practice, 4, 17; see also rules;
speech act(s)
law(s): as expression of regularity,
50; and instances, 192–3; inverse
square, 40; in natural science, 40;
of nature, 50; social, 211; in social
science, 50
learning: as transformation of self
and world, 212
Lebensform(-en), 17, 67, 72, 74–5,
78, 80, 87, 176; and habitus, 74,
80, 146
Leibniz, 2, 4, 47–8, 49, 105, 218
Lévi-Strauss, C., 6, 39, 40, 50–1, 70,
88, 98, 185, 224; his vision of
human science, 69
liberation and Bourdieu's theory, 7,
12, 92
liberty: intellectual, 106; limits of
Bourdieu's, 12
life: cultural, 72, 78–9; existence of,
199; the good, 156; intellectual,
220; ordinary, 68, 71
linguistics: generative, 54;
structuralist, 121
literary semiology: 121; and
intellectualism, 113–14
Locke, J., 33, 208, 218
Louis XIV, 183
Lukes, S., 149n2
Lyotard, J.-F., 10

McDowell, J., 56
McGinn, C., 191n51
Machiavelli, N., 213n10
Manet, E., 215
Marcuse, H., 3